MAKE
YOUR
OWN
FURNITURE

MAKE YOUR OWN FURNITURE

A Working Handbook

Edited by
Ron Bloomfield

Consultants
David Day and Albert Jackson

Techniques section consultant
Nick Frewing

**Additional help and
furniture making**
Charles Gardner

British Broadcasting Corporation

This book accompanies the BBC Continuing Education
television programmes **Make Your Own Furniture**
First broadcast in Autumn 1979

Series produced by Ron Bloomfield

The book contains complete building instructions.
You do not need to have seen the television
programmes to make the furniture.

Published to accompany a series of
programmes in consultation with the
BBC Continuing Education Advisory Council

Acknowledgment is due to the following
Bateson Graphics for the diagrams
Baker Design Associates for the title drawings
Photographs by Mike Martin
Cover photograph by Mike Busselle
Extract from BS 4471 on page 108 by permission
of the British Standards Institution,
2 Park Street, London W1A 2BS, from whom
complete copies may be obtained.

This book is set in 9d/10pt Univers Light

Printed in England by Sir Joseph Causton and Sons, Ltd., Eastleigh.

CONTENTS

Note: Every effort has been made to ensure that the measurements given in this book are correct. However, readers are advised to guard against possible error by making frequent checks of all measurements as work on the furniture progresses.

INTRODUCTION

David Day and Albert Jackson

There is little doubt that making your own furniture can be a rewarding experience. Seeing a finished piece in its correct place in your home and knowing that it is 'all your own work' is a real pleasure. But there is one important proviso. It has to look good. Most of us have seen pieces of furniture, usually designed with the home maker in mind, which lack all grace and delight and which, however well constructed, have that tell-tale amateur look. We have tried to put together a range of furniture which has that touch of class which lifts it above the common-place, and which is, nevertheless, within the range of the home furniture maker.

Most of the designs in this book are intended for someone who has done a few DIY jobs already and has collected some hand tools on the way. The projects also require an electric power drill, some of the attachments for it, and the occasional specialised tool, like a sash cramp, which you can hire over the weekend rather than buying it. But if you are a complete beginner, don't despair. The projects progress from the very simple to the more demanding, and the first few projects, for example Alf Martensson's wall storage range and bunk beds, are well within the capabilities of a beginner. If you make something like this to gain experience, there is no reason why you shouldn't move on to something more intricate, like the elm dining table and chairs.

All the furniture in this book has been designed by professional furniture designers, who have provided detailed step-by-step making instructions for each of the projects, together with tips and ideas which they have picked up from years of making furniture by hand. In addition, Nick Frewing's section 'Timber, Tools and Techniques' gives you all the background information you need on skills such as sawing, drilling, joint making and so on, which are common to all the projects. From all this, you can see that we have tried to make the book comprehensive and if there is one message we want to leave with you loud and clear it is:

You do not need to have seen the television programmes to make the furniture.

The book is complete in itself, and it is not essential to have watched us putting the furniture together on television.

One of the things the television programmes did emphasise was the large number of *variations* available from one design. In the colour photographs and in the instructions, we are forced to go for one set of options, but you can vary the type of timber, fabric, paint colour, choice of laminate and so on, to suit your particular requirements. A good example of this is Brian Davey's dining table, originally built in solid elm with a cork top, but easily varied to a solid teak

David Day

Albert Jackson

underframe with a teak veneered board on the top, or to a pine kitchen table with a white plastic laminate top.

In some of the designs, it is possible not only to vary the finish, but to make small structural alterations so that the piece of furniture has a totally new purpose. Thus the boxes in Alf Martensson's wall storage range can easily be modified to record storage cabinets, bathroom cabinets and toy cupboards, whilst two of Bill Brooker's elegant stationery cabinets can be brought together to make a desk.

Some of our furniture can be made from materials readily available from your local DIY stores, but some of it requires hardwoods or fabrics which are available only from specialist suppliers. The exact material suggested by our designers may not be obtainable in some parts of the country, in which case have a chat with your supplier and substitute another material of similar quality. It's worth keeping an eye on the craft and DIY magazines, as specialist firms supplying by mail order usually advertise in them.

You will notice that all the dimensions given in this book are metric. Although most of us still think in Imperial measure, the move to metric is inevitable and the timber trade has sold wood in metric sizes since 1970. The change-over is not yet complete, however, and certain items, for example woodbits, screws and nails, are still sold in Imperial sizes and are given as such in the parts lists. Whatever you do, don't attempt to convert the metric dimensions in our projects back to Imperial. The conversion is never exact and if you try it, you will end up with some very nasty fitting problems.

The cost of materials varies considerably both nation-wide and locally, and shopping around usually pays dividends. Making your own furniture can never be cheap, but if you compare the cost of any of the projects in this book with an item of similar quality in your local store, you will see that you are saving quite a lot. Another way of keeping costs down is to buy old furniture, which looks superb when renovated. We spent some time in the television series renovating an old dining table and a set of chairs, and the process is described in this book.

Making your own furniture can become a life-long hobby. You start by making one or two things that are absolutely vital for the house, then you make something just for fun and after that you are hooked. We've been hooked for years and as you turn the pages of this book, we hope that you will find something that attracts you and that you will join us in the pleasure of making furniture that is really your own.

David Day

Albert Jackson

WALL STORAGE SYSTEM

Alf Martensson

The demand today is for storage systems which are versatile, simple and attractive. These modular units should fulfil that demand very well. Depending on the material and finish they will serve equally well as elegant sitting room wall units, as cheerful kitchen or bathroom cabinets, or even as bright and inexpensive storage boxes in the children's room.

The construction is really very simple. The boxes and shelves are just screwed and nailed together using almost any sheet materials such as chipboard, block-board or plywood.

For the main unit we used birch plywood, which is extremely strong and produces a nice smooth finish. But don't be afraid to use whatever material you have at hand. Even basic chipboard will make very beautiful furniture if you finish it well. The children's storage boxes, for example, are made from 18mm standard chipboard and painted a bright green colour to match the roller blind, which keeps the toys out of view.

But the best part of this system is the way it hangs on the wall. The uprights have holes drilled at regular spacings to take short lengths of dowel which support the boxes and shelves. This way you can move them around to suit your own need.

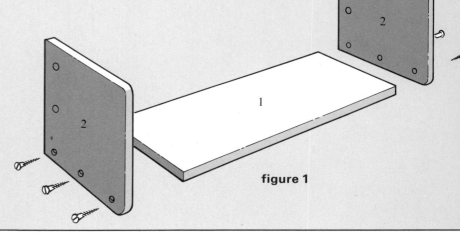

figure 1

Cutting List. See figure 1

No.	Part	Material	Qty	Length	Width	Thickness
1	Shelf	Birch Plywood	1	720	220	15
2	Upright	Birch Plywood	2	225	225	15

Other Materials

6 × 1½" No. 8 brass countersunk screws	Clear matt polyurethane varnish
6 × No. 8 brass screw cup washers	Matt brown paint for edges
6 × 1" No. 8 fibre wall plugs	Woodworking glue

Making Instructions
Shelf Unit

Cut the shelf and two uprights to size. Make sure that they are accurate and square, because the units must be all the same size to be interchangeable.

The shelf is located 4mm up from the bottom edges of the uprights, **figure 4**. You will find it much easier to construct this rebate if you first make yourself a special jig, **figure 2**. This has the added advantage of making the repetitive work much quicker. Since there are seven shelf units in the completed wall storage system, this is quite a consideration!

Take a 15mm plywood base 850×350mm and nail and glue flush with one end, a piece of 15mm plywood 100×350mm. Then nail and glue a piece of 4mm plywood 720×350mm to the base, leaving a space exactly the thickness of the 15mm plywood between them.

To assemble the shelf unit, first mark, centre punch and drill the three holes marked A at the bottom of each upright, 11mm up from the bottom edge, using a 4·5mm drill bit, **figure 3**. Drill the holes straight through the plywood, then place the shelf on the jig with an upright at either end, **figure 4**. The jig will now hold the pieces accurately together while you drill through the holes you have already made into the end of the shelf. Drill about 25mm into the end of the shelf, then take away the upright and insert a fibre wall plug into each hole. Replace the upright and screw a brass screw with a cup washer into each hole. Screwing into the end grain of plywood is not usually very strong, but by using wall plugs in this way, you will obtain a very strong and durable joint.

Now simply turn the shelf around and attach the other end in the same way.

The final step before finishing the shelves is to drill the holes B on **figure 3** for the

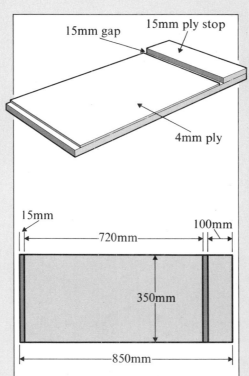

figure 2 *a simple jig which ensures that the 4mm rebate is the same on all the shelf units.*

figure 4

dowel peg supports. These must be drilled accurately at the same spacing as on the uprights. Use the drilling jig made for drilling the uprights (see later page) to make sure that the holes will match up. Hold the jig so that the end lines up with the top edge, **figure 5**, then drill two holes through the sides. To avoid the plywood breaking out on the other side, mount the work on a softwood block, **figure 5**.

Finally sand the shelf unit well, making sure the edges are smooth. Also round the front corners to about 8mm radius with a file or rasp. Finish with clear polyurethane and paint the edges matt brown.

Box Unit

Take the two sides — part 3 — and the bottom — part 4 — and screw them together on the spacer jig in exactly the same way as you did for the shelf unit. Note that the sides are larger than the uprights of the shelf unit and have different screw positions, **figure 7**.

To attach the top, turn the unit upside down and drill the holes as before on the jig, but instead of removing the side to insert the plugs, just use another plug to push the plugs straight through the hole in the side into the hole in the end of the shelf. Then insert the screws as before.

figure 3

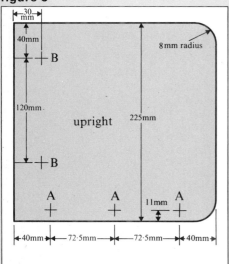

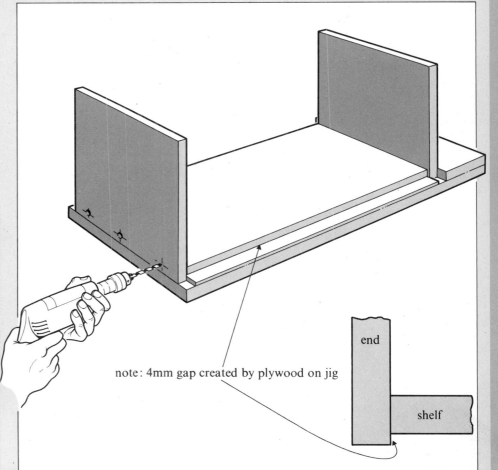

note: 4mm gap created by plywood on jig

Wall Storage System

The frame of the box will still be 'wobbly' at this stage, so to make it stronger and more stable nail the 4mm plywood back, part 5, to the back of the frame. Start by nailing two or three pins along the bottom with the edges lining up neatly. Then push the box into shape so that the edges line up with the back and fix with a pin at each corner. Then pin the other three sides. If the back is cut squarely and accurately, the box will then be square, as in **figure 8**, which has been exaggerated to explain the method.

Now drill the holes for the dowel peg supports, sand down and round the front corners and finish as for the shelf unit.

Box with Shelves

Adding shelves and dividers to the boxes is very easy. Their positions are shown in **figure 9**. Cut the dividers out of 15mm plywood exactly 300×332mm, and the shelves out of 6·5mm plywood. The shelves are also 300mm deep, but it's best to leave cutting them to size until after the dividers and plastic channels are attached. That way it's easier to measure the exact width to fit between the channels.

Slide the dividers into the box to make sure they fit snugly as in **figure 10**. If not,

figure 5

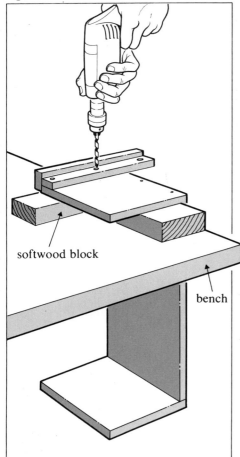

softwood block

bench

Cutting List. See figure 6						
No.	Part	Material	Qty	Length	Width	Thickness
3	Sides	Birch Plywood	2	370	325	15
4	Top and bottom	Birch Plywood	2	720	320	15
5	Back	Birch Plywood	1	750	362	4

Other Materials

Apx. 15 × ¾″ panel pins
12 × 1½″ No. 8 brass screws
12 × No. 8 brass screw cup washers

12 × 1″ No. 8 fibre wall plugs
Clear matt polyurethane varnish
Matt brown paint for edges

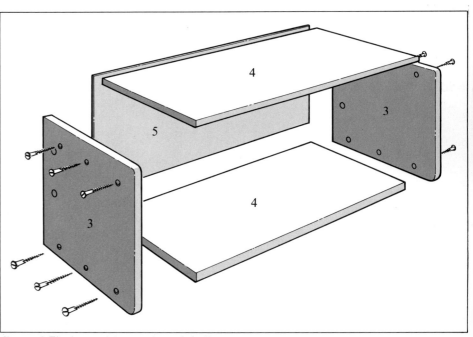

figure 6 *The box unit is an enlarged shelf unit with an extra top and 4mm ply back.*

plane the edge off until they do. To fix them in position, first mark out their locations as shown in **figure 9**. The shelving will be held in place with plastic channels, so before attaching the dividers, mark out the locations of the channels on the dividers and on the sides. Next nail and glue the dividers in place using 25mm panel pins, three along each edge. Make sure the nails line up with the centre of the divider by marking a light pencil line on the outside of the box as a guide for the nails. Also make sure that the dividers are pushed all the way against the back before nailing them in.

Next cut off lengths of black plastic channel for the 6·5mm plywood shelves. Cut them off 295mm long at a slight angle, then sand off the cut end before gluing them in place.

Use contact adhesive for gluing. Spread a smooth even layer on both surfaces, on the back of the plastic channel and on the plywood, between the lines marked out earlier. Allow the glue to set for about 10 minutes

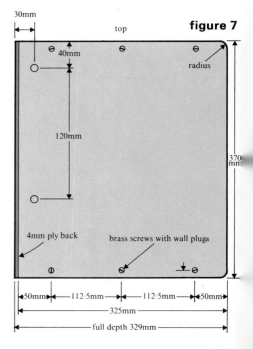

figure 7

30mm
top
40mm
radius
120mm
370 mm
4mm ply back
brass screws with wall plugs
50mm — 112·5mm — 112·5mm — 50mm
325mm
full depth 329mm

until it is touch-dry, then simply bring the two glued surfaces together with firm pressure to make a good bond. Remember that you can't adjust the pieces once contact between the glued surfaces has been made, so be precise when bringing them together.

If the shelves will have to take very heavy objects, reinforce the glued connection with a couple of 12mm panel pins nailed through the plastic into the plywood with the pin head set flush with a nail punch.

The 6·5mm thick shelves look better with the front corners slightly rounded, so before sliding them into the channels, use a coping saw or a file to round them to a radius drawn with any small round object such as a jar lid or a spool of thread.

Notice that the shelves and dividers are set back about 20mm from the front edge to allow space to add sliding doors.

Adding Sliding Doors

The box with sliding doors has two shelves, as shown in **figure 11**. The shelves are constructed in the same way as before. The doors are made of two sheets of 6·5mm birch plywood, each 324×370mm. They slide in a two-track plastic runner, which is shown in **figure 12**. This runner is sold in pairs, one of which has deeper grooves than the other and goes at the top. The doors are fitted by simply pushing up into the deeper groove, swinging the bottom of the door over the shallower groove and dropping into place.

Stick the plastic runner to the inside front edges of the top and bottom of the box, setting them back 2mm from the edge, **figure 12**. Cut the doors to size and drill 25mm diameter holes in them to serve as handles, as shown in **figure 11**. Instead of making holes you can buy wooden knobs from a Do-It-Yourself shop. It will add to the appearance of the doors if you round their corners, as in the rest of the design.

The sliding doors can alternatively be made of smoked glass, or of mirror, if the box is destined to be a bathroom cabinet. In either case, order the glass or mirror to the exact dimensions from a glass merchant, who will cut it accurately and also smooth the edges for you. For handles, use small rectangular pieces of clear perspex stuck on with epoxy adhesive.

Record Dividers

The dividers for the record cabinet are attached exactly like the shelves using 10 lengths of plastic channel 295mm long to hold them in place, **figure 13**. Cut five dividers out of 6·5mm plywood. Make them 300mm deep and measure the height after installing the plastic channel. Then round the corners, sand and finish them before sliding them in place. You can add doors to this cabinet too, to keep the records dust free.

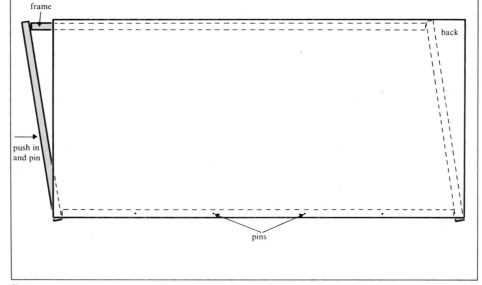

figure 8

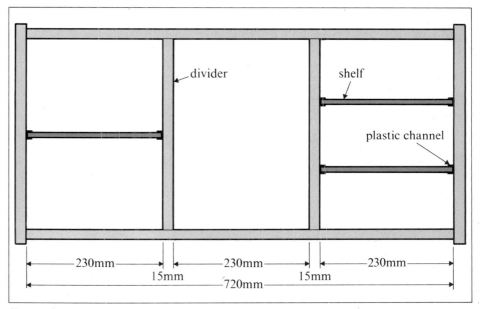

figure 9

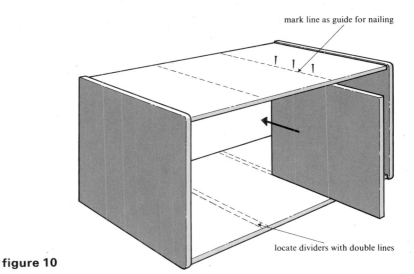

figure 10

Wall Storage System

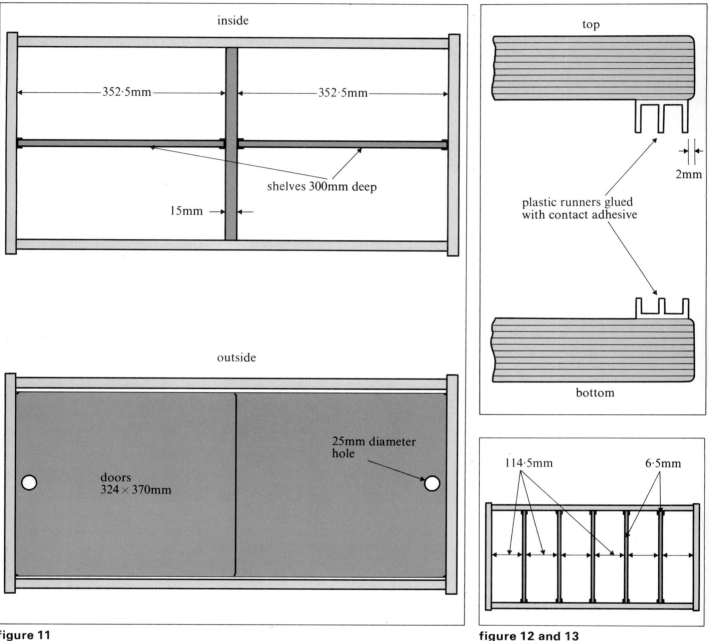

inside

352·5mm   352·5mm

shelves 300mm deep

15mm

top

2mm

plastic runners glued
with contact adhesive

bottom

outside

doors
324 × 370mm

25mm diameter
hole

figure 11

114·5mm   6·5mm

figure 12 and 13

Wall Supports

To make the full wall storage system you will
need four wall supports made of planed
softwood—see the illustration at the start of
the chapter. Remember when buying softwood that the cutting list gives *planed
finished* sizes and that you should ask for
nominal sizes 4—5mm thicker and wider.
See Buying Timber, page 109.

Before starting work on the wall supports,
you will need to make the drilling jig illustrated in **figure 15**.

Start by cutting two pieces of softwood
A and B, each 320×45×21mm. It is very
important to cut these pieces accurately.
Mark the three hole centres on piece A first,

30mm in from the edge and spaced 120mm
apart, starting 40mm in from either end as in
figure 15. Make sure to measure and mark
accurately and then to mark the hole centres
with a centre punch as a guide for the drill
bit. If possible drill the holes using a drill
press to keep the holes exactly vertical. If
you don't have access to a drill press or to a
drill-stand attachment for the electric drill,
drill the holes carefully with a try square
standing on the bench as a guide.

After drilling the holes nail and glue piece
B to piece A keeping the ends exactly
together, then use this jig to drill the holes
not only in the uprights but also in the box
and shelf units. That way you will be sure
all the holes will match up.

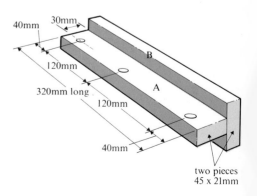

40mm   30mm

B

120mm

320mm long

120mm

A

40mm

two pieces
45 x 21mm

figure 15

Make the wall supports by first temporarily nailing pairs of 21 × 45mm uprights together with three or four panel pins, leaving the nail heads exposed for easy removal later. Line them up exactly before pinning them together. Then place the drilling jig flush with the end and sides and drill the first hole through the jig and the two sides, **figure 16**. Lay a piece of scrap wood under the sides to avoid damaging the work bench and also to keep the wood from breaking out around the hole as the drill goes through.

After drilling the first hole place a short length of dowel through that hole to keep the jig in place. Then drill the other two holes, **figure 17**. Drill all the other holes two at a time positioning the jig by placing the dowel through the last hole until you reach the end of the sides, **figure 18**.

Next take the centre posts, part 7, and drill four 5mm diameter countersunk holes for the No. 10 screws as in **figure 19**. (Countersinking, page 126). Then assemble the four wall supports by nailing and gluing each pair of uprights to a centre post as shown in **figures 20** and **21**. Line up the ends carefully and place a dowel through

figure 16

figure 17

figure 18

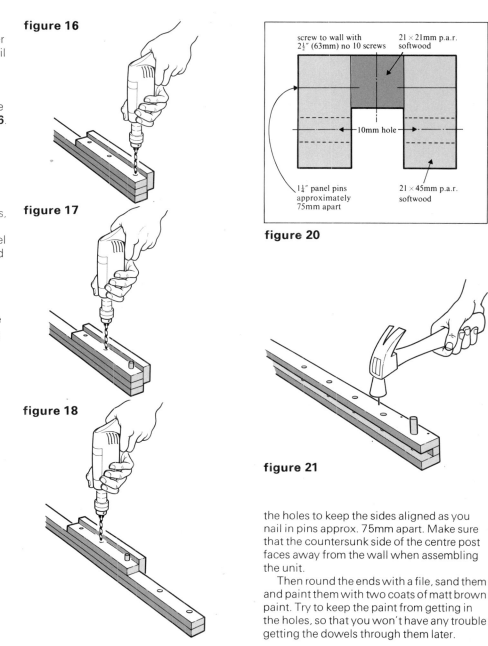

figure 20

figure 21

the holes to keep the sides aligned as you nail in pins approx. 75mm apart. Make sure that the countersunk side of the centre post faces away from the wall when assembling the unit.

Then round the ends with a file, sand them and paint them with two coats of matt brown paint. Try to keep the paint from getting in the holes, so that you won't have any trouble getting the dowels through them later.

figure 19

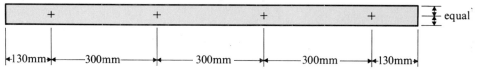

centre post

|←130mm→|←—300mm—→|←—300mm—→|←—300mm—→|←130mm→|

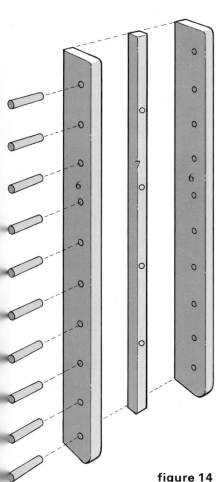

figure 14

Cutting List. See figure 14

No.	Part	Material	Qty	Length	Width	Thickness
6	Upright	Softwood	8	1160	45	21
7	Centre post	Softwood	4	1160	21	21

Other Materials

40 pieces of 9·5mm dowelling 80mm long for attaching the shelves and boxes to the wall supports (you will probably need a few dowels 95mm long where a box or shelf occurs on either side of the support at the same level)

Apx. 100 × 1¼" panel pins
16 × 2½" No. 10 countersunk screws
16 × 1½" No. 10 fibre wall plugs
Woodworking glue
Matt brown paint

Wall Storage System

Installing the Wall Storage System

It is very important that you position the wall supports accurately when screwing them to the wall. It's rather a cumbersome job and you'll find it easier if you have someone to help you.

Start by deciding on the height and position of the whole unit. Do a rough drawing on paper, if necessary to get an idea of how the unit will look. Then place the last wall support on the right against the wall and use a spirit level to get it exactly vertical. Hold it in position while you draw a light line along one edge and a line along the top, **figure 22**. Put the support aside for a moment while you use the spirit level to extend a light line from the top mark straight across the wall, **figure 23**. This will ensure that all the uprights are at the same level, so that the units will hang horizontally.

Go back to the first wall support. Put the 2½" No. 10 screws in their holes, then, holding the vertical exactly against the marks, mark the screw locations on the wall by tapping the screws lightly with a hammer. Remove the support, then drill the holes with a No. 10 masonry drill bit, insert the wall plugs, then finally screw the support in position. If you have a bad wall, you may need to use plastic plugs or filler.

Having located the first support vertically it's then easy to get the others right by using a shelf as a spacer, **figure 24**. Get someone to help you hold a shelf against the first support while you mark the location of the next one. Remember to locate the top exactly against the horizontal line, and also to allow about 1—2mm clearance to make it easier to get the units in and out.

Continue to attach all four wall supports, then simply hang the units in place with the 9·5mm diameter dowel pegs, **figure 25**.

Variations

The wonderful thing about a modular storage design such as this one is that you can use it almost anywhere. It will make elegant kitchen storage units, bathroom cabinets, toy cupboards for the children's rooms and almost any other kind of storage cabinets you can think of. And they can be finished to match their function.

Kitchen Units

Figure 26 and colour photograph, page 17. These kitchen units were stained bright red to give a little sparkle to the kitchen. You make the boxes exactly as for the wall storage system, but instead of supporting them on the special uprights, screw them to the wall with metal brackets as shown in **figure 27**. Either of the designs shown are available from hardware shops.

To make kitchen units easier to hang, first screw to the wall a pine 21 × 120mm batten cut to the length you require,

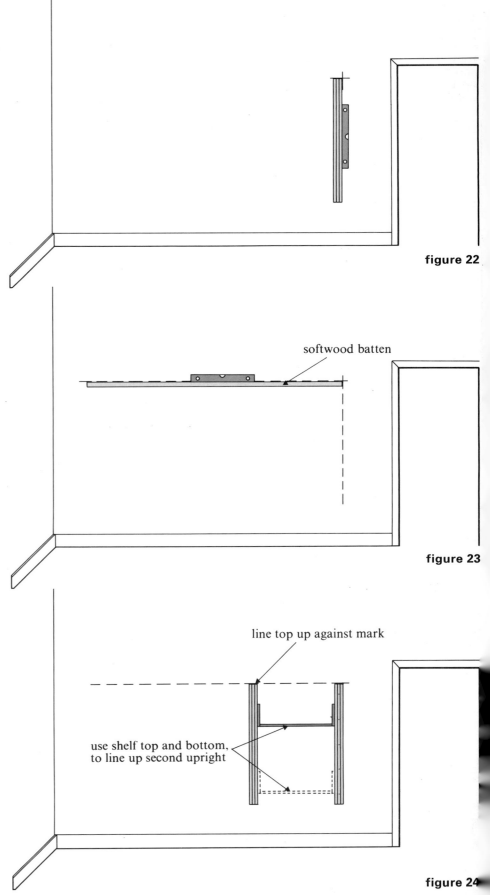

figure 22

softwood batten

figure 23

line top up against mark

use shelf top and bottom, to line up second upright

figure 24

checking it with a spirit level to make sure it is horizontal. Then use the batten as a ledge to place the units on while you screw them to the wall. Since the screws on both the batten and the units will carry a great deal of weight, make very sure that they are securely fixed to the wall— the alternative is an almighty crash and considerable loss of china! Use 1½" No.10 screws with a

fibre or plastic wall plug and ensure that the screw will not turn in the hole when tightened. If it does, use a longer screw, say 2", and asbestos filling compound in the hole. If you screw hooks into the batten, you also have somewhere to hang cups, mugs, and kitchen tools. You can add as many units as you like, with solid or glass doors to keep the dust away from the food and plates.

Bathroom Cabinet

See **figure 28** and photograph, page 17. This bathroom cabinet is made to exactly the same dimensions as the box units in the wall storage system, except that it is only 150mm deep. Use 15mm white melamine coated chipboard, which is available in boards 150mm wide and 2400mm long, with the long edge already lipped. Just saw off the lengths you want and assemble in the usual way, using matching iron-on lipping (page 146) to cover any bare edges. The back is made of 4mm melamine covered hardboard and the shelves of the 15mm board with white plastic runner at the ends. Use sliding doors made of mirror as described on page 11, to give a really professional looking cabinet. The cabinet is fixed to the wall with metal brackets and wall plugs as for the kitchen cabinet. Note that because you are working in chipboard, which does not take curves well, the corners of the cabinet are left square.

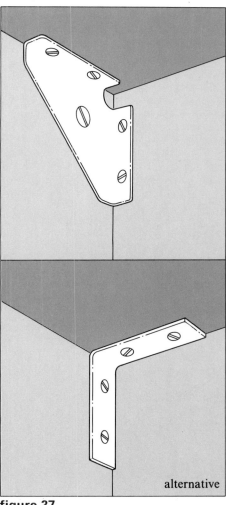

alternative

figure 27

hang shelf and box unit with two dowel pegs into holes in uprights

figure 25

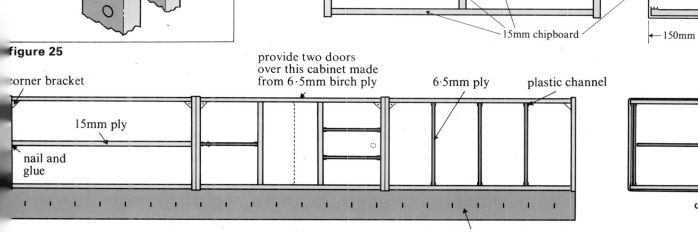

figure 28

note: do not round corners

corner bracket

brackets

4mm hardboard

15mm chipboard

150mm

provide two doors over this cabinet made from 6·5mm birch ply

6·5mm ply

plastic channel

corner bracket

15mm ply

nail and glue

21 × 120mm p.a.r. pine board screwed to wall

figure 26

Wall Storage System

Children's Toy Cupboard

See **figure 29** and colour photograph, page 17.

This is simply a series of the basic boxes stacked on top of each other. A suggested shelf pattern is given in **figure 29**. The boxes are held together with short rounded connectors of 21 × 70mm pine which fit on to the boxes with 35mm long dowel pegs, see **figure 30**.

We used the cheapest building material of all, plain chipboard, for this cupboard and made it look beautiful with a few coats of bright green gloss paint. For contrast we painted the connectors in bright red.

A clever alternative to sliding doors is to use a matching roller blind to keep the toys and clothes out of sight. If you want the edges of the blind to fall flush with the edges of the box, you will have to attach a softwood batten to the side of the cupboard to bear the bracket for the blind as in **figure 31**. Alternatively, you can fit the bracket to the edge of the box, in which case the blind will be slightly narrower than the cupboard, as in **figure 32**.

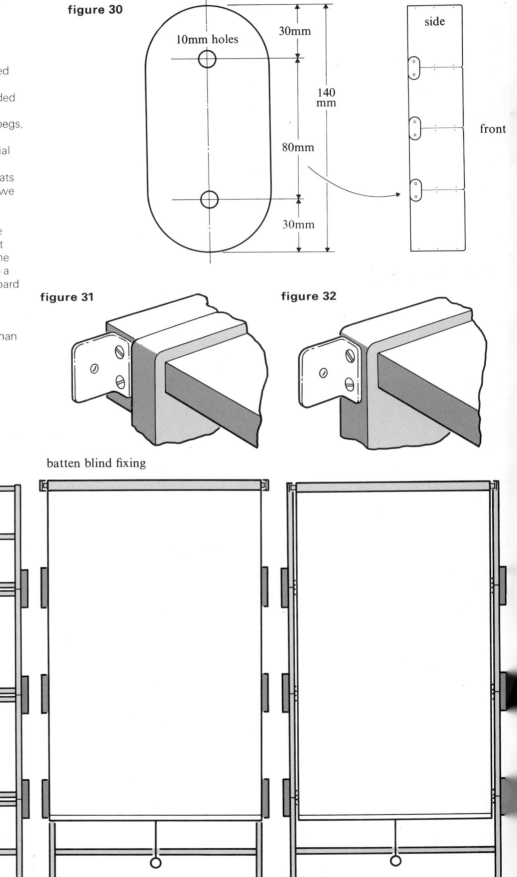

figure 30

10mm holes

30mm

140 mm

80mm

30mm

side

front

figure 31

figure 32

batten blind fixing

figure 29

Above *Alf Martensson's wall storage system makes a distinctive addition to any living room. Change the colours to suit your own requirements.*
Left *The same design modified to a cheerful row of kitchen cabinets. The wooden doors can be replaced by glass, or the shelves can be left open.*

Far Left *Pile three or four of the basic boxes on top of one another and you have an easily-made toy cupboard.*
Left *Make a box in white melamine-covered chipboard and add mirror glass doors for an economical bathroom cabinet.*

Occasional Tables

Above Left *Coffee table by Nick Frewing with a solid mahogany underframe and a mahogany veneered chipboard top.*
Above *The same underframe with a top made of solid marble. Not the cheapest variation, but very beautiful!*
Left *The table can be extended lengthwise, as in this version made of oak, but you should not exceed 950×600mm without strengthening the underframe. (see chapter 2)*

Far Left *This elegant easy-make table with a smoked glass top takes only 15 minutes to assemble.*
Left *The easy-make table with its folding top. Here it is laid out for chess, but it can be painted to suit any game you like.*

OCCASIONAL TABLES

Nick Frewing

This occasional table can be made in a variety of hardwoods, such as teak, mahogany or oak. Softwoods, and hardwoods with a coarse, wild or uneven grain pattern are not suitable, as they will not take the scratch moulding which decorates the piece.

The basic design is for a square table with an underframe 600×600×350mm. The top is 610×610mm, giving an overhang of 5mm all round, but you can make the overhang deeper if you wish. Similarly, there is no need to make a square table if you prefer an oblong, but if you exceed 600×950mm, the width of the rails will have to be increased to give extra strength.

The finish of the wooden top is critical, as any inaccurate work is bound to show, so beginners, or those with a limited amount of time available, may prefer to build the underframe only and to use a ready-made top in glass or marble. Obviously this will increase the cost, but the finished table will still be cheaper than anything of comparable quality in a shop.

Buying Timber

The best way to buy the hardwood is in a single board, then to cut all the pieces from it. This ensures consistency of colour and grain. Hardwood boards are sold in a standard thickness of 32mm, so you will need to plane your board down to the finished thickness of 25mm. If this looks too difficult, most hardwood timber merchants will saw and plane to size within a few days of receiving the order. It is a good idea to ask for each piece about 25mm overlength, to allow for squaring off and end finishing as the job progresses. See Buying Timber, page 109.

Keep the prepared timber in the house for as long as possible before you use it. The Timber Section explains the reasons for this and shows the correct way to stack the wood whilst it is drying out.

Making Instructions

The Underframe

Assemble the four legs first. Each is made from a leg flat and a leg return – parts 1 and 2 in **figure 1**. Cut each of these pieces overlength by about 25mm, to allow for squaring off at either end later. Pair off one part 1 and one part 2. With each of these pairs, select the face of part 2 which most closely matches one edge of part 1 and mark them for easy identification as in **figure 2**. Clean up the surfaces which will become the inner faces of the legs – it is far easier to do it now than after gluing.

Apply adhesive to the appropriate surfaces and cramp the parts together. Use pieces of softwood (softening) between the leg and the cramp to prevent marking and to distribute the effect of cramping along the whole length of the legs. Use at

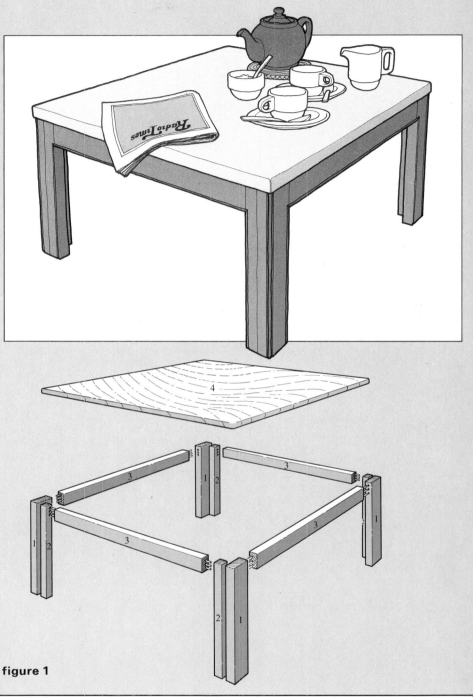

figure 1

No.	Part	Material	Qty	Length	Width	Thickness
1	Leg Flat	Hardwood	4	350	50	25
2	Leg Return	Hardwood	4	350	25	25
3	Side Rails	Hardwood	4	500	50	25
4	Top	Veneered Chipboard	1	610*	610*	18 or 15
		Or Marble P.A.R.	1	610	610	22
		Or Glass P.A.R.	1	610	610	12

Cutting List. See figure 1

Note: Remember that the cutting list gives *finished* sizes only, see Buying Timber, page 109.

*If using 3mm thick lippings for the top, reduce size to 604 × 604mm.

Other Materials

For the wooden top:	2·4 metres self-adhesive edge veneer ('iron-on lipping')
For the wooden or marble top:	8 × 2″ No. 10 steel countersunk woodscrews
For the glass top:	4 × 15mm diameter black rubber washers 2·5mm thick or pieces of cork 5mm thick
6 or 9mm dowelling for joints	

Occasional Tables

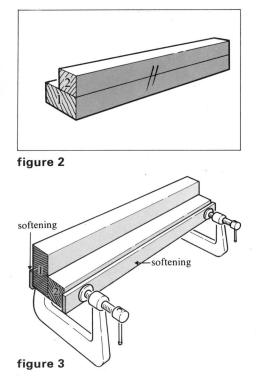

figure 2

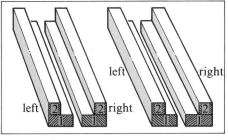

figure 3

least 2 cramps, as in **figure 3**. Check that the marked faces are together and flush. Check that the ends are in line. Wipe away all traces of excess adhesive with a damp cloth and allow the joint to set.

Cut the side rails — part 3 — to length and square off their ends accurately. Mark each with a face side and face edge. Clean up the unmarked face and edge. If you intend to use either a wood or marble top, two counterbored holes are required in the undersurface of each side rail to take the 2" No. 10 woodscrews. For the technique of counterboring, see page 126. The holes should be counterbored to a depth equal to the

figure 4

thickness of the top less 5mm. Bore the holes centrally in the thickness of the rails and 75mm in from each end.

When the four legs are dry, remove them from the cramps. Two of them are to become left-handed and two right-handed, and to achieve this, lay the legs out as in **figure 4** with the glued square section uppermost. Turn them around until two have the glued upstands on the left and two on the right. The ends facing you will become

the bottoms and must now be cut square and chamfered at 45° all round, **figure 5**.

Measure up 350mm from each leg bottom and mark with a knife cut all round the L section. This is the line to which the top edge of the adjoining side rails must butt. Do not cut, **figure 5**.

You are now ready to start joining the frame together. This design uses a dowel joint, details of which are given on page 150. Arrange the legs and rails on a flat surface in the order in which they are to go together, as in **figure 6**. Note that the side rails are lining up with the foot, rather than the top, of the leg, but this does not matter for the time being. Making sure you have the legs the right way round, number each component of each joint as shown in **figure 6**. This will allow easy identification when you come to drilling and assembly. Now drill the dowel holes in the legs and side rails, using one of the drilling methods on page 151. The joint can be made with either three 6mm dowels or two 9mm dowels and remember when drilling that the tops of the side rails line up with the cut marked on the legs — not the top, which is to be cut off later.

Assemble and cramp up the entire frame with the dowels in place but without glue. Check that all joints fit correctly and that the parts are flush with one another on the faces. Make any necessary adjustments before

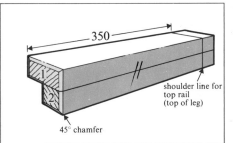

figure 5

continuing. Take the frame apart and remove all dowels. See Cramps etc., page 127.

Place all the parts in their numbered order and glue each joint carefully. Pay particular attention to gluing the inside of each hole and all around each dowel. Assemble each joint as it is glued.

If you have only two sash cramps, assemble two opposite side frames, each comprising a rail with a leg at each end. When they are set, use the same cramps to join the two completed side frames to the remaining rails. Use softening blocks at either end of the cramps.

Check the frame for squareness as described in the section Keeping Square on page 145, first between the leg and the rail, using a try square, then between the top corners using a measuring rod and finally by sighting across the opposite side rails. When the frame is true, allow the adhesive to harden, then remove the cramps.

Cleaning up and scratch moulding

If you have used the dowelling jig carefully and made sure the frame is square, there should not be too much cleaning up to do. Begin by cutting off the waste at the top of each leg with a tenon saw, following the cut line previously made.

With a freshly sharpened smoothing plane, plane all the outside faces of the legs and rails, ensuring that all the joint edges are flushed off. Plane along the tops of the legs and rails with a block plane, then finish all the surfaces with a fine grade of abrasive paper wrapped on a flat cork block. If you haven't got a cork block, a piece of softwood will do. Follow the line of the grain, taking particular care where the grain of the legs crosses that of the rails—do not cut across the grain at this point in the final strokes or it

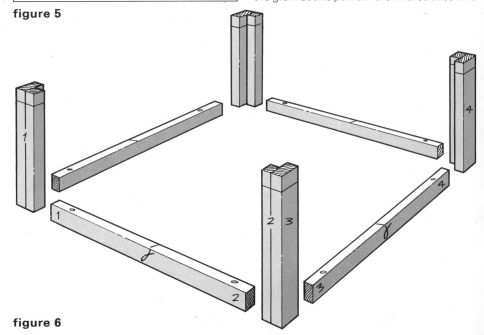

figure 6

will show through the finish. The smoother the surface achieved at this point, the better the polished frame will look.

The next job is to cut the scratch moulding on all the outer edges of the legs and the lower edges of the rails, as shown in **figure 7**. If you are fitting the frame with a see-through glass top, you may wish to scratch mould the inside surfaces as well.

Make the scratch tool from a piece of thin sheet steel. An ordinary cabinet scraper is ideal. **Figure 8** shows the shape of the cut-out corner, which can be cut out with a hack saw, then finished with a 6" medium-cut flat file and a round needle file. Keep the half-round area square and sharp, but round off the straight side, so that it does not cut the edge of the leg.

Try the scratch tool out on a spare piece of timber first, to get the feel of it. Hold it firmly into the edge of the wood and at a slight angle into the cutting direction, **figure 9**. You will find that it is best to make a series of shallow and short cuts rather than a few long strokes. The grain will dictate the direction of cut required. If the tool tends to tear the wood, you are working the wrong way.

The scratch tool will not cut right into the corners. The last 5mm will have to be removed with a chisel and a file. Line up a straight edge with each cut and pencil a line into the corner. Using a narrow bevelled-edge chisel, cut the waste from the inside of the moulding into the corner. Remove the waste from the outside with a file. Finally clean up all the moulded edges with fine abrasive paper, taking care at the corners.

The completed frame is now ready for staining (if required) and polishing or varnishing. See page 160. Note that the same type of underframe is used for the sideboards on page 105. The sections and construction remain the same, but the lengths of all the components are different.

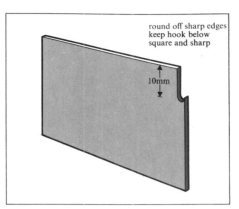

figure 8

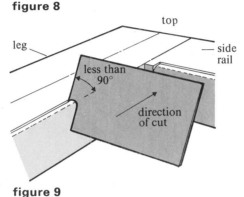

figure 9

Making the Top

The wooden top is made of chipboard veneered in the same wood as the underframe. The common makes of veneered chipboard are available only in teak, mahogany or oak, so if you choose some other hardwood, you will need to find a specialist supplier of veneered boards and these exist only in large towns. When buying the chipboard, take some of the underframe wood with you to ensure a decent match between the two, as wood colours can vary considerably.

It is probably best to ask your timber merchant to cut the top accurately to size, rather than attempt to saw the edges yourself. All you need to do then is to apply the iron-on lipping—for technique see page 146.

. Alternatively, the edges can be lipped with 3×15 or 18mm hardwood strips mitred at the corners and glued in position, as in **figure 11**. For mitreing see page 148. Finish the top in the same way as the underframe.

To finally assemble the table, place the top upside down on a firm surface covered with a soft cloth to protect the finish. Place the frame upside down on top of it and square up, then mark the position of the countersunk screw holes with a pencil. Remove the frame. Drill pilot holes with a bradawl or hand drill, then screw the frame to the top.

The marble top is also fixed by screwing up from below, and your supplier will cut the screw holes for you if you supply him with a template. To do this, cut a 610×610mm piece of hardboard. Place the completed frame upside down on it as before and drill through the counterbored holes into the hardboard. Mark the template and frame so that you know exactly which way round the top has to be fixed to the base

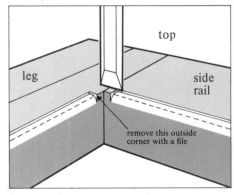

figure 10

figure 11

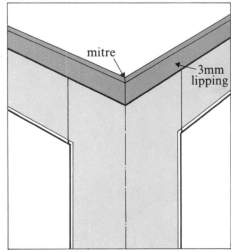

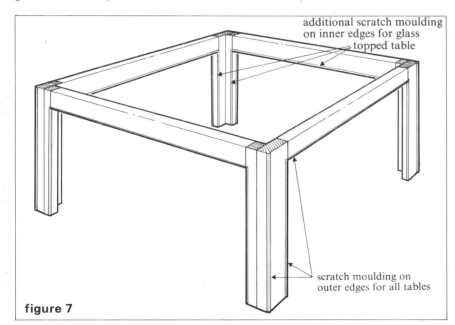

figure 7

Occasional Tables

when it arrives. The supplier will also fit plugs to the screw holes in the marble if you ask him. This will ensure that the screws will bite properly when you assemble the table.

For glass tops it is advisable to let cork or rubber rests into the tops of the legs. These allow a certain amount of levelling and also help to keep the glass in place. Drill 16mm diameter holes to a depth of 3mm for cork or 1½mm for rubber (ball valve washers are ideal) centrally in each corner of each leg top. Bond in place after polishing is completed.

Easy Make Tables

All these tables are made from the satin-finished metal tube used by shopfitters for window displays and shelving, colour photograph, page 18. The tables in the television programmes were made of silver tube 25×25mm with black plastic drive-in corner joints supplied by Abstracta Construction Ltd., Eldon Wall Trading Estate, Staples Corner, Edgware Road, London, NW2 who will sell this material to the general public. Other systems are available from other manufacturers differing in design and colour, and if you live a long way from London, you may want to see what is available locally. You could start by looking in the 'Yellow Pages' telephone directory under 'Shop Fitting Manufacturers'.

Making a Glass Topped Table

Set out four of the long metal sections and four corner joints on a flat surface as in **figure 12**. Some brands of tubing tend to scratch and mark easily, so cover the surface with a soft cloth.

Push fit the parts together, then drive home each corner joint with a rubber mallet. Repeat this with the second frame. Join the two frames together, using the four short sections, as shown in **figure 13**. Check that all the joints are tight, with the tube ends firmly up against the shoulders of the plastic corner joints.

Fix one self-adhesive rubber pad to each end of each top rail, as shown in **figure 13**, 50mm from the end. Place the smoked glass top on the frame, flush with the edges, and you have a beautiful and very rapidly constructed table.

figure 12

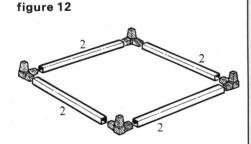

No.	Part	Material	Qty	Length	Width	Thickness
1	Top	Smoked glass, edges polished and ground	1	750	750	9
2	Long rails	Satin finished square metal tube	8	700	25	25
3	Short rails	Satin finished square metal tube	4	325	25	25

Cutting List. See figure 13.

Other Materials

8 black plastic corner joints 25×25×25mm ⎤
8 self-adhesive rubber pads ⎦ From same supplier as tube

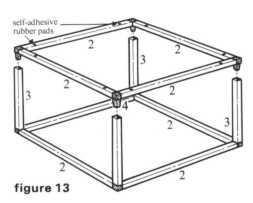

figure 13

Making a Games Table

This table uses exactly the same metal frame as the glass topped table. The only difference is that the glass top is replaced by a folding wooden games board. I have laid this out as a chess board, but it is a comparatively simple matter to change it to backgammon or whatever game you fancy.

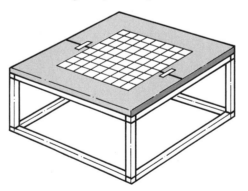

figure 14 Left *the games table ready for use.* Right *the games table in the storage position.*

No.	Part	Material	Qty	Length	Width	Thickness
1	Top panel	Oak veneer chipboard	2	750	375	12
2	Long rails	Satin finished square metal tube	8	700	25	25
3	Short rails	Satin finished square metal tube	4	325	25	25

Cutting List. See figure 14.

Other Materials

8 black plastic corner joints 25×25×25mm
4½m oak iron-on edge strip
2 brass card table hinges 12×75mm (Woodfit HW400)
8×⅜" brass countersunk woodscrews to fit

1 piece self-adhesive plastic film 420mm square
Black and clear cellulose aerosol spray paint
4 pieces of 6mm dowel, 52mm long
4 pieces of 6mm dowel, 14mm long
PVA glue

The table can be used at two levels. A high table is provided when the metal frame stands upright and the top is folded. In this position the games board is closed. A double sized low table is produced by laying the underframe flat with the board unfolded to reveal the chess top. See **figure 14**.

The top is made from two pieces of oak veneered chipboard 375 × 750mm which are 'ebonised' with black cellulose. The chess board is marked out by masking off alternate squares before spraying. The top can of course be made from other timber veneered panels which can be given a clear cellulose finish.

Make the metal frame as instructed for the glass topped table.

Now turn your attention to the two oak-veneered chipboard panels. The grain on each side will vary, so select the faces for the best match between the pairs. For easy identification, pencil a face side mark on each chess board side. The butting edges will be hinged together and should be marked as face edges, see **figure 15**.

figure 15

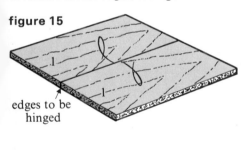

edges to be hinged

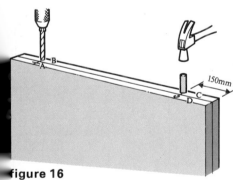

figure 16

Fold the two panels together, face sides and face edges together, with all edges as flush as possible. Hold them together in a vice and plane each pair of edges in turn until they are flat and square. By planing them together in this way, both pieces will become exactly the same size as one another.

Re-mark the face edges. Close the panels together again, face sides inside and face edges uppermost. Grip them in a vice. Check that the ends and tops are flush.

Mark a line across the two face edges 150mm in from either end. Mark another line across each of these, in the centre of each board edge thickness as in **figure 16** (A).

Extend the lines across the edges down the outer faces of the panels so that you know, later, the exact positions of those centres.

Drill a 6mm diameter hole at each centre mark to a depth of 50mm (B). Glue each hole and four 52mm lengths of 6mm dowel and drive them into position (C). Wipe off all surplus glue. Flush off the dowel ends with a plane (D). These dowels provide local reinforcement for the hinge screws.

Iron on edge veneer all around the edges of both panels. Trim off overhanging veneer as you go. See page 146.

Place the two panels together again in a vice with the two face sides inside and the two face edges uppermost. Check that they are flush at the ends and along their length. Mark a line on the edge lipping across the top edges of both boards, 6mm either side of the centre lines of the dowel positions (marked on the outer faces). Check that the gap between each pair of lines is exactly the width of the hinges — adjust the lines if necessary.

Place the panels on a flat surface, face sides down. Using a try square, extend the hinge lines on the face edges on to the upper faces of each panel, **figure 17**. Follow the hinge fitting instructions on page 140.

When the fitting is complete, remove the hinges and clean up all the faces and edges with fine abrasive paper. Support the abrasive paper on a cork or softwood sanding block and use in the direction of the grain

figure 19

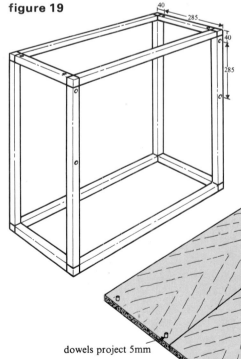

dowels project 5mm

figure 17

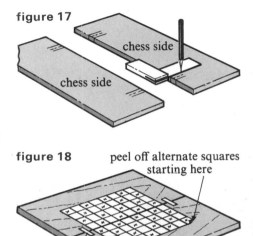

chess side

chess side

figure 18

peel off alternate squares starting here

plastic mask over hinge

only. Re-fit the hinges. Spray with two coats of clear cellulose lacquer over the chess board side.

Take the 420mm square piece of plastic film and peel off the paper backing. Stick the film accurately in the centre of the playing surface. Pencil mark on it a 400mm square chess board with 50mm squares.

With a straightedge and knife score through the 50mm lines. Peel off the surplus film from the edges then alternate squares starting with the front right-hand square (as you stand with one of the long unhinged edges facing you) **figure 18**. Cut two small pieces of plastic to cover over the hinges exactly. In order to locate the top on to the frame in either the upright or flat positions, a series of four 6mm dowels are let into the face side of the top (underneath the chess board side). Corresponding holes are drilled into the frame as shown in **figure 19**.

Mark the holes accurately 12·5mm in from both the edges of the tubes and chipboard top. Centre punch the hole centres before drilling to prevent the drill from wandering. See page 126.

Drill the holes in the table top 6mm diameter and 9mm deep. Glue 6mm dowels which are 14mm long and rounded on their top ends into the holes.

Spray paint both sides and all the edges of the table top with black cellulose. Allow to dry thoroughly before rubbing down and re-spraying. Apply at least two coats. Peel off the plastic film carefully from the chess board and the hinges. Ensure when spraying that you do so in a dust free, well ventilated area. Extinguish all naked flames or glowing heating elements. The room must, however, be warm for good drying results.

BEDS and BUNKS
Alf Martensson

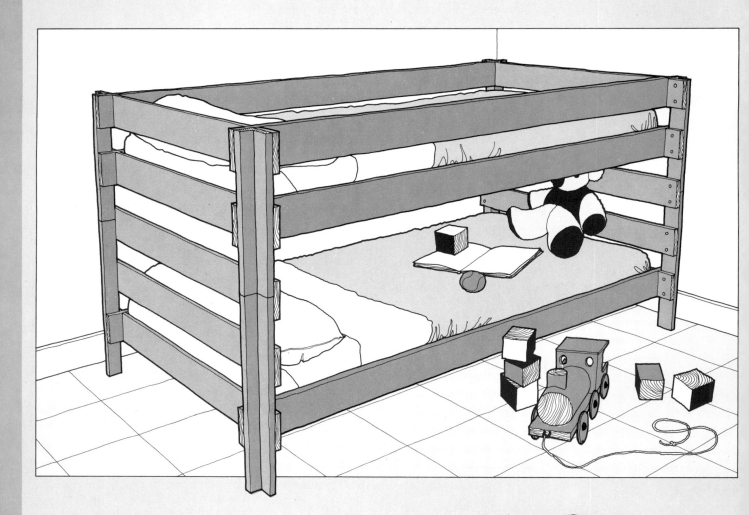

Children's Bunk Bed

A bunk bed is an ideal project to make yourself because it is so difficult to find simple well-built ones in the shops. These beds have been designed to separate into two full-sized single beds when they outlive their life as bunk beds.

The construction is especially simple. The whole bed is screwed together without complicated woodworking joints. The rails at either end serve as a built-in ladder to reach the top bunk, and the removable guard rail at the top not only stops children falling, but also lifts out to allow easy access for making the top bed.

So for a fraction of the shop price you can build a sturdy, elegant bunk bed which converts into two single beds. And if you organize the work carefully, having the timber merchant cut the pieces accurately to length for you, it shouldn't take longer than a weekend or two. The use of softwood throughout keeps the cost down and this has the added advantage that softwood takes coloured wood stain well, opening out a whole range of decorative possibilities.

Then when you have finished the bunk bed, use exactly the same techniques to make the single bed or the beautiful double bed with cane headboards.

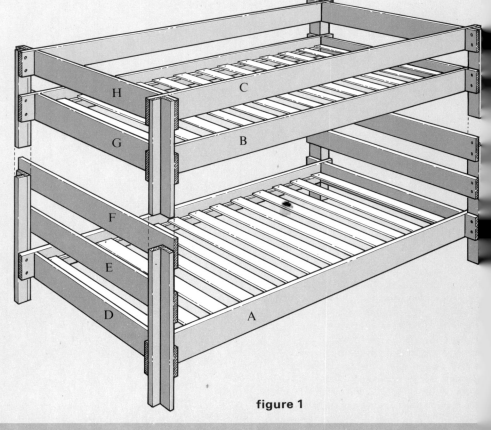

figure 1

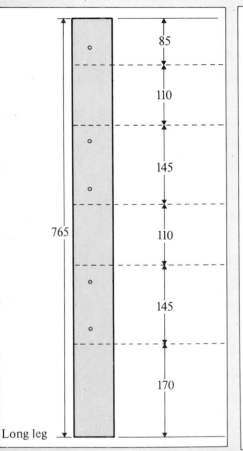

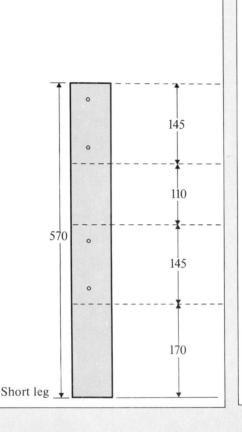

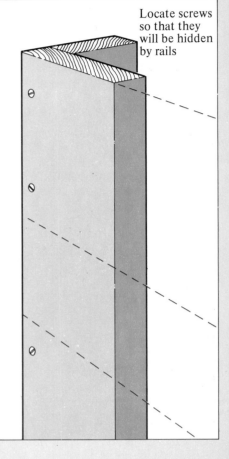

Locate screws so that they will be hidden by rails

figure 2

Making Instructions

There is really nothing difficult about making the bunk beds. The only hard work is in marking and cutting all the pieces accurately and squarely. If possible, take the cutting list to a local timber merchant and have him cut the pieces for you. But be sure to bring a tape measure to check the length of the pieces. If you plan to saw the pieces yourself it's a good idea to organize the work carefully. Study the cutting list and be sure

to buy timber in lengths which leave the minimum waste. When cutting off the lengths mark each piece A, B, C, etc., and cross it off the list, so that you will keep track of all the pieces.

After cutting all the rails, legs, slats and battens to length, start work on the legs. There are four long legs 765mm long for the bottom bunk and four short legs 570mm long for the top, and each leg is an L-section made up of a leg flat 21×70mm and a leg

return 21×45mm. The L-section is screwed and glued together, so it is a good idea to mark the position of the end rails on the leg flat as in **figure 2**, so that the rails will hide the screw heads after assembly.

The first stage in assembling the legs is to glue together a matching pair of leg flats and leg returns and to set them up in cramps as in **figure 3**. When the glue has set, take them out of cramps and mark the positions for the screws as shown in **figure 2**. Drill

Cutting List. See figure 1. All softwood P.A.R.

No.	Part	Qty	Length	Width	Thickness
A,B,C	Side rails	6	2100	145	21
D,E,F,G,H	End rails	10	1100	145	21
I	Long leg flat	4	765	70	21
J	Long leg return	4	765	45	21
K	Short leg flat	4	570	70	21
L	Short leg return	4	570	45	21
M	Side batten	4	1920	21	21
N	Bed slats	28	917	70	16

Note: Remember that the cutting list gives *finished* sizes only, see Buying Timber, page 109.

Other Materials

Apx. 80×1½″ No. 10 round headed screws, black Japanned

Apx. 10×1½″ No. 10 countersunk steel screws

Apx. 60×1¼″ No. 8 countersunk steel screws

Apx. 60×1¼″ panel pins

PVA woodworking glue

Apx. 2 litres blue polyurethane stain

Red gloss paint

Masking tape

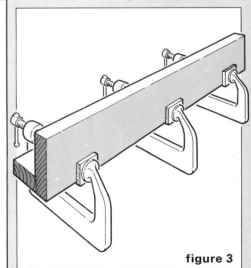

figure 3

Beds and Bunks

pilot holes and countersink, see page 126, then put in the 1½" No. 10 countersunk screws. Repeat for each leg until you have four short ones and four long ones. Plane and sand the joints flush.

Next, carefully mark and cut the halving joints between the side rails and end rails. Instructions for making halving joints are given on page 149. Reference to **figure 1** will show that side rails A fit into end rails D. B to G, and C to H, so check the fit between these components as you go. Dimensions for the joints are given in **figure 4**.

Now screw and glue the side battens M to the four side rails, as shown in **figure 5**. These battens will support the slats, and thus the whole weight of the mattress and child, so make sure to glue along the entire length and then use four 1½" No. 10 countersunk screws per batten to make the connection even stronger. See Right-Angled Butt Joint, page 147.

Owing to the grain direction in the rails, there is a point of potential weakness beyond the halving joint where a piece of wood may snap off, **figure 6**. It is therefore a wise precaution to strengthen it with a piece of dowel or a long screw both in the side and end rails. See **figure 7**.

Cramp the side rail in a vice and drill a hole about 125mm deep, using a 9·5mm drill bit. Make sure you hold the drill vertically as you do this, if necessary getting a helper to 'sight' the drill as you go. If you can get hold of a vertical drill stand, this will make the job much easier. Cut a piece of 9·5mm dowel a little longer than 125mm and cut a groove down one side of it to act as a glue channel, see Dowel Joint, page 150. Coat the dowel and hole liberally with glue and push the dowel into the hole leaving a bit sticking out. Clean off excess glue with a damp rag and leave till glue has set. Then cut off the excess dowel and plane flush with top edge of rail.

Now you are ready to assemble the bed. Start by making the four end frames, using the long and short legs in pairs.

Lay out the first pair of long legs on the bench or floor, so that the rail locations marked earlier face upward. Place 50mm softwood blocks under the free edges so that they do not fall over, see **figure 8**. Mark and drill the clearance and pilot holes at both ends of the rails, then screw the rails to the legs with the black round-headed screws. Notice that these screws should all line up 40mm in from the edge so that they become a decorative feature of the bed, **figure 9**. If possible, use the right size screwdriver so that you don't damage the screw head. If the screwdriver should slip remember to remove any metal splinters with a file so that children can't hurt themselves.

Make two large and two small ends in the same way. Notice that the rail F on the long leg ends extends 60mm above the leg so that it can be screwed to the top leg to form

a rigid connection between the bottom and top bunk, **figure 10**.

This is a good stage to apply the blue polyurethane finish and the bright red accents on the ends of the boards. The pieces are much easier to manage and to lay flat now than they are after the bed is completely assembled.

First, sand the pieces well with medium,

then fine, glasspaper. Round all the edges so they feel nice and smooth to touch. Remember that the children will climb up the end rails so there should be no sharp edges for them to hurt themselves on. Wipe off any dust and apply at least three coats of the coloured polyurethane varnish. This is available in various other colours as well, so you may want to choose another colour

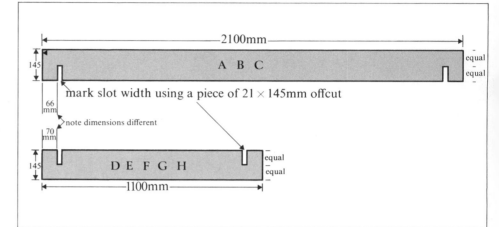

figure 4

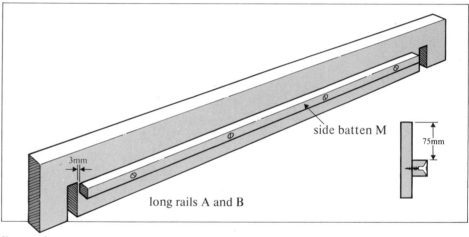

figure 5

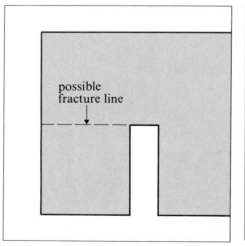

figure 6

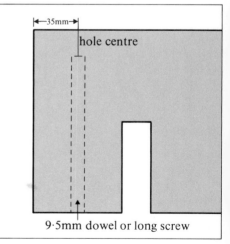

figure 7

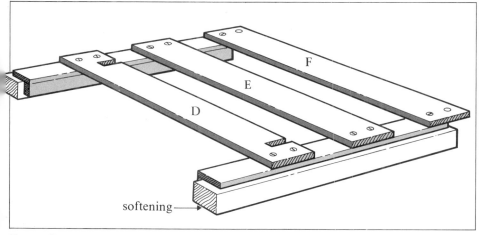

softening

figure 8

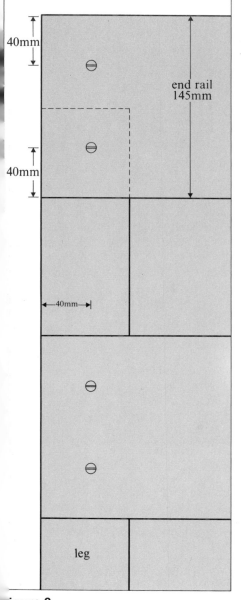

40mm

40mm

end rail
145mm

←40mm→

leg

figure 9

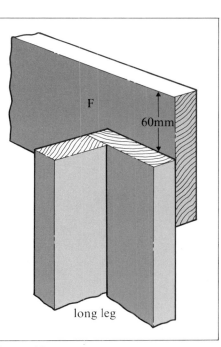

F

60mm

long leg

figure 10

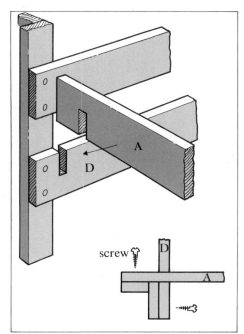

A

D

screw D

A

figure 11

bottom half, then the shorter top half. As mentioned earlier, the two guard rails for the top bunk are not screwed to the legs.

Before lifting the top bed in place, attach the bed slats N to the side battens M, 14 slats per bed, **figure 12**. Place the first slat near the end, nail it in place with the 1¼" panel pins, one pin per end. Then use another slat as a spacer between successive slats, leaving a space between the slats to allow the mattresses to 'breathe'. After nailing in the fourteen slats, go back and reinforce them with the 1¼" screws, drilling clearance holes and countersinking before driving the screws in.

Finally place the top bunk carefully on top of the bottom bunk, and make sure the legs

which best matches the colour scheme in the children's room.

Between coats rub down with fine glasspaper to make the next coat nice and smooth. After the third coat the finish should be a luxurious deep blue.

Then apply masking tape over the ends of the boards, and paint the ends with two coats of bright red gloss paint. After it is dry, carefully peel off the tape and if any paint has run down under the tape, remove it with fine glasspaper, then touch up with the blue stain. There is no need to stain the bed slats N. These can be left unfinished.

To assemble the bed, get another person to help hold the ends while you slot the side rails A in place, **figure 11**. Screw them to the legs with two round-headed screws exactly as for the end rails. Make the two beds separately. First make the longer

line up exactly before screwing through the end rail F, to make the whole bed rigid, **figure 13**.

Taking the bunk bed apart to make two full-sized single beds is very easy. Simply unscrew the four screws on rails F, which connect the two beds. This leaves you with two beds, one with short ends and one with long ends. To make the beds identical, with a tall headboard and a short footboard, just interchange two ends. Undo the four screws which hold the long rails to one end frame, then switch the ends, securing them again with the same screws. It may be necessary to re-drill one or two of the holes, to make the screws fit in the legs.

It's also a good idea to either turn the end rails H over so that the slot is underneath or perhaps to replace it altogether with a new one, **figure 14**.

Beds and Bunks

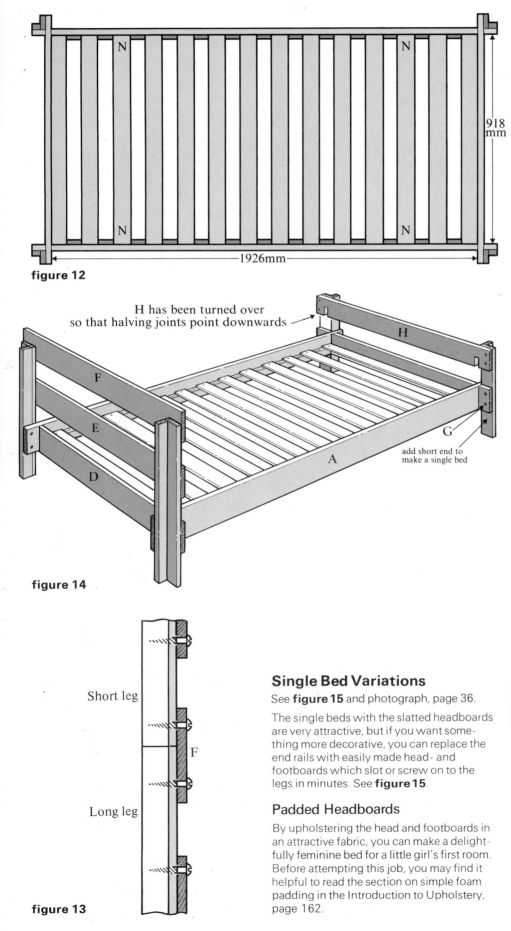

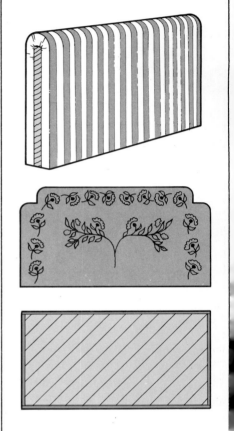

N

N

N

N

918 mm

1926mm

figure 12

H has been turned over
so that halving joints point downwards

H

F

E

D

A

G

add short end to
make a single bed

figure 14

Short leg

F

Long leg

figure 13

figure 15

Single Bed Variations

See **figure 15** and photograph, page 36.

The single beds with the slatted headboards
are very attractive, but if you want something more decorative, you can replace the
end rails with easily made head- and
footboards which slot or screw on to the
legs in minutes. See **figure 15**.

Padded Headboards

By upholstering the head and footboards in
an attractive fabric, you can make a delight-
fully feminine bed for a little girl's first room.
Before attempting this job, you may find it
helpful to read the section on simple foam
padding in the Introduction to Upholstery,
page 162.

To make the padded boards, you will need:
1 piece 12mm plywood 1100×450mm
for the headboard
1 piece 12mm plywood 1100×255mm
for the footboard
Apx. 1·5m of fabric, at least 1·2m wide
Apx. 1·5m of medium density polyether foam,
at least 1·2m wide
Apx. 40 upholstery tacks
(or use staples in staple gun)
4m × 18mm wide ribbon
Contact adhesive
Fabric adhesive
Either 4 flush mount brackets or 10 × 1¼"
No. 10 screws, to attach the boards to the bed

Cut the foam into two pieces with a sharp
breadknife, one 1120×940mm for the
headboard and one 1120×550mm for the
footboard. If you happen to own an electric
carving knife, this will make the job even
easier. Cover both sides of the plywood
headboard with contact adhesive, also one
side of the appropriate piece of foam. When
the adhesive has gone off (see manufacturer's instructions), carefully wrap
the foam over the board, using a sheet of
brown paper between the foam and the
board to allow you to position the foam
properly, **figure 16**, see Adhesives, page 131

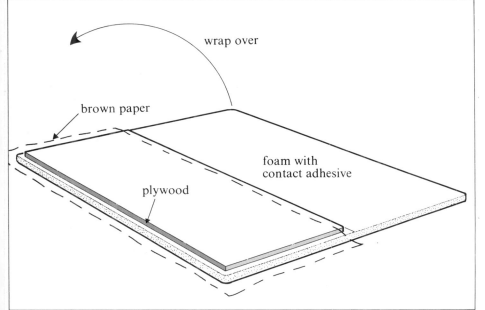

figure 16

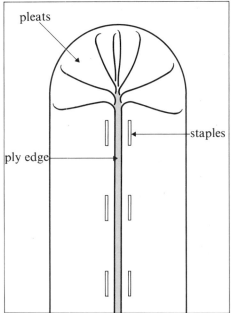

figure 19

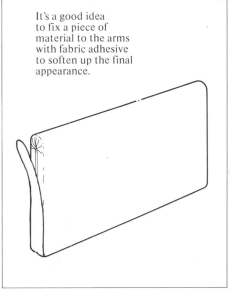

> It's a good idea to fix a piece of material to the arms with fabric adhesive to soften up the final appearance.

figure 20

Do not tension the foam—let it stretch over the headboard naturally. When the foam is stuck in place, trim off the edges flush with the board using a breadknife, **figure 17**.

Take a piece of 1120 × 940mm fabric and make two small marks on the inside at the midpoint, i.e. 470mm from the end. Line this up with the top edge of the headboard so that equal amounts of fabric hang down on each side. Staple or tack in position at the top edge of the headboard, **figure 18**A. Now pull the fabric firmly downwards and attach it to the bottom edge of the board, **figure 18**B. When this is secure, work steadily down the side edge of the board, carefully pulling out any creases and stapling as you go, **figure 18**C. Take particular care to pleat the top edge carefully, **figure 19**. Repeat this operation on the other side of the board and finally tidy up any loose ends on the bottom edge. If the bed is to stand permanently against a wall, you can economise on materials by

covering only one side of the headboard.

Whether you have covered one or both sides of the board, the fabric edges and staples will still show on the edges. See **figure 20**. These are unsightly, so cover them with the 18mm ribbon, using fabric adhesive. This can be a messy business, so follow the manufacturer's instructions.

To make the footboard, repeat all the stages exactly as above.

The simplest way to attach the boards to the legs is to screw them on, using the screw holes left by the removal of the end rails F, E and H. Use black japanned round-headed screws to make a decorative feature of them **figure 21a**. The alternative is to use flush mount brackets, available from larger hardware shops, **figure 21b**, but you will then have to plug the screw holes, preferably with small pieces of dowel. See page 140.

figure 17

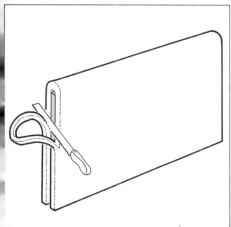

figure 18

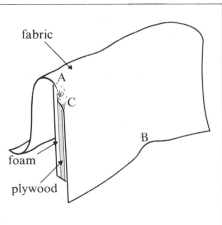

Beds and Bunks

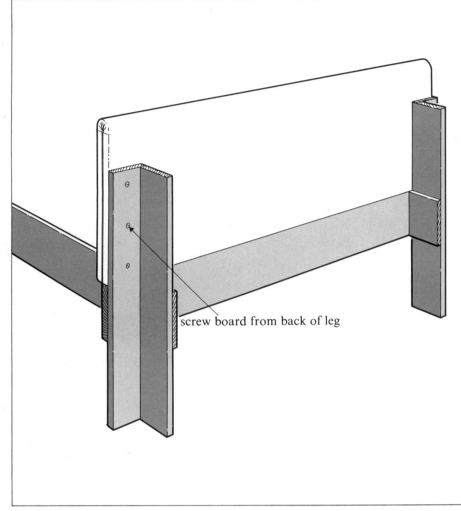

screw board from back of leg

above figure 21a, below figure 21b

To make the stencilled head- and
footboards you will need:
1 piece 12mm plywood 600 × 1100mm
for the headboard
1 piece 12mm plywood 400 × 1100mm
for the footboard
Stencil designs (available from art shops)
Teak wood stain
Red and green acrylic paint for the stencils
Clear polyurethane varnish

Stencilled Headboard

This is the easiest of all the headboards to
make. It's just two pieces of plywood cut to
shape, which then have stain and a stencil
design applied to them to give an interesting
Austrian effect.

The shape and dimensions of the boards
are given in **figure 22**. Mark up the 100×
150mm corner inset on each board and mark
the curves at the angles using any convenient round object, such as the lid of
a coffee jar, then cut out the shape with a
power jig saw or coping saw. Sand the
plywood, making the edges smooth, before
applying a light coat of teak wood stain.
After the stain has dried, paint on the stencil
design, using a pleasing symmetrical
pattern. It is best to stipple the paint on
carefully with a small stiff brush or a sponge,
so as to stop it running under the cardboard
stencil. Obviously the choice of red and
green paint and teak wood stain is arbitrary
and should be adjusted to suit the particular
bed frame you are using.

When the paint is dry, seal the two boards

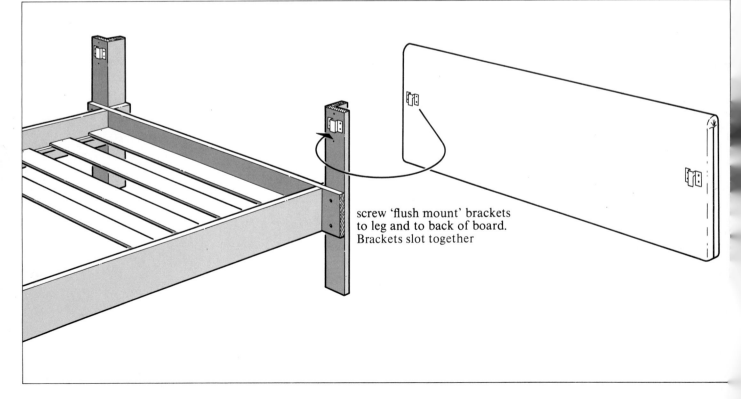

screw 'flush mount' brackets
to leg and to back of board.
Brackets slot together

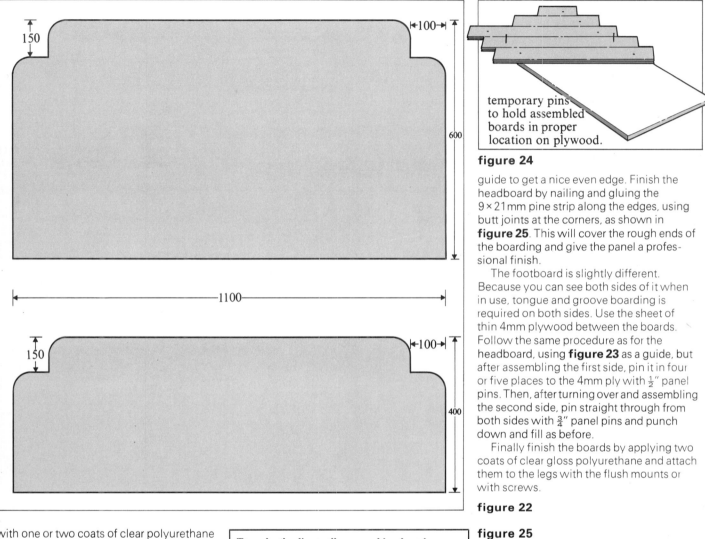

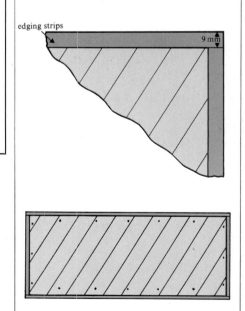

temporary pins to hold assembled boards in proper location on plywood.

figure 24

guide to get a nice even edge. Finish the headboard by nailing and gluing the 9 × 21mm pine strip along the edges, using butt joints at the corners, as shown in **figure 25**. This will cover the rough ends of the boarding and give the panel a professional finish.

The footboard is slightly different. Because you can see both sides of it when in use, tongue and groove boarding is required on both sides. Use the sheet of thin 4mm plywood between the boards. Follow the same procedure as for the headboard, using **figure 23** as a guide, but after assembling the first side, pin it in four or five places to the 4mm ply with ½" panel pins. Then, after turning over and assembling the second side, pin straight through from both sides with ¾" panel pins and punch down and fill as before.

Finally finish the boards by applying two coats of clear gloss polyurethane and attach them to the legs with the flush mounts or with screws.

figure 22

figure 25

with one or two coats of clear polyurethane varnish. Then attach them to the legs with screws or flush mount brackets as before.

Tongue and Groove Boarding

You can give your bed an attractive Scandinavian look by using pine tongue and groove boarding, which can be bought ready jointed at Do-It-Yourself shops. I show how to fix this boarding diagonally, but it looks good vertically too and uses rather less material.

The only complicated step in making this headboard is cutting and fixing the tongue and groove boarding. It is best to cut each piece as you go along, following **figure 23**, then to trim all the boards at once when they are attached to the plywood base.

Start with the 9mm ply headboard. Cut and join the boards one by one, using the plywood underneath as a guide in positioning each board. Lay the first board in place, then add a thin line of glue to the tongue of the next board and simply push it into the groove. To get the tongue all the way in, tap it home with a mallet or hammer, protecting the boards with a block of softwood. After making three or four joints,

To make the diagonally grooved head- and footboards you will need:

1 piece of 9mm plywood 450 × 1100mm for the headboard
1 piece of 4mm plywood 250 × 1100mm for the footboard
Apx. 20 metres of 100 × 9mm pine tongue and groove boards

6m of 9 × 21mm pine strip
½" and ¾" panel pins
PVA woodworking glue
Clear gloss polyurethane varnish

put in a couple of temporary panel pins to position the boards on the plywood, **figure 24**. Then continue marking, cutting and joining each board until all are in place.

Fix the assembled boards to the plywood with ¾" panel pins, using about 5 pins along each edge. Sink the pins below the surface with a nail punch, then fill the holes with plastic wood filler. At all stages be careful to wipe away excess adhesive with a damp rag, as this will spoil the eventual finish.

Finally trim the edges, preferably with a circular saw, using a metal straight edge as a

Beds and Bunks

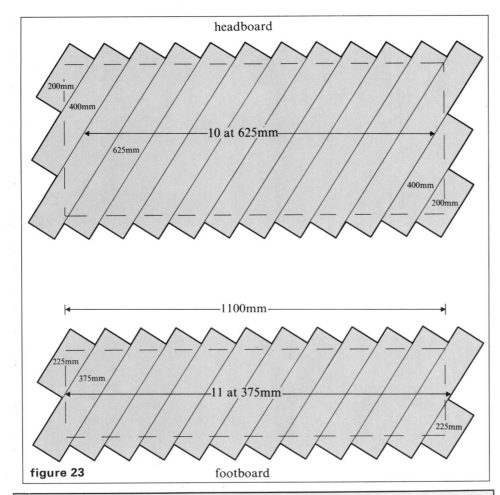

headboard

200mm

400mm

625mm

10 at 625mm

400mm

200mm

1100mm

225mm

375mm

11 at 375mm

225mm

figure 23

footboard

Double Bed

The same design can very easily be used to make a very elegant double bed with caned headboards. The only difference is in the length of the pieces and also in the slat structure which supports the mattress.

Making Instructions

The first job is to measure the mattress which you intend to use for the bed. The dimensions given are for a standard mattress 1500×2000mm and if yours is different, you should change the dimensions as indicated in the cutting list. Before starting work, read carefully through the making instructions for the children's bunk bed (page 25) as the double bed is made in exactly the same way.

Cut and label all the pieces, then join parts A to B and C to D to give four L-shaped legs, two 800mm long and two 600mm long. As before, glue and cramp them together before drilling the holes and adding the No. 10 countersunk steel screws.

Cut halving joints in the side rails E and the end rails F, following the dimensions in **figure 27**. Then screw and glue the 21×21mm battens to the insides of the rails. The end battens I should be positioned 17mm down from the top edge of the end rails F, while the side battens H are 45mm below the top edges of the side rails E.

To assemble the main frame screw first the end rails F and then the side rails E to the legs, with halving joints at the corners.

Before adding the bed slats, screw the two cross struts G to the side battens H, using two 1½" No. 10 countersunk screws per end, as shown in **figure 28**. Then screw down the 13 slats J with the No. 8 screws, spacing them out evenly and allowing approx. 50mm space between them, **figure 29**.

When making the headboards, it is important that the ends of the frame components K, L, M and N are square. Make two rectangular frames by dowel jointing the corners with two dowel pegs per joint, **figure 30**. Dowel joint details, page 150. Round the corners of the frames and nail and glue the 9mm beading to the inside edges to take the plywood panels, **figure 31**.

Before attaching the plywood panels, stain or paint them a dark colour, then staple the cane to them along the edges, trimming off any excess with a sharp knife. Make sure to stretch the canework fairly tightly to stop it sagging later, if necessary adding a bit of contact cement underneath, to hold it against the plywood.

Cutting List. Double bed to suit standard 1500 × 2000mm mattress. See figure 26.

No.	Part	Material	Qty	Length	Width	Thickness
A	Long leg flat	Softwood (pine)	2	800	70	21
B	Long leg return	Softwood (pine)	2	800	45	21
C	Short leg flat	Softwood (pine)	2	600	70	21
D	Short leg return	Softwood (pine)	2	600	45	21
E	Side rails	Softwood (pine)	2	2200*	145	21
F	End rails	Softwood (pine)	2	1700†	145	21
G	Cross struts	Softwood (pine)	2	1517	95	28
H	Side battens	Softwood (pine)	2	1500	21	21
I	End battens	Softwood (pine)	2	1500	21	21
J	Bed slats	Softwood (pine)	13	2023	70	16
K	Headboard cross members	Softwood (pine)	2	1700	95	21
L	Headboard verticals	Softwood (pine)	2	310	95	21
M	Footboard cross members	Softwood (pine)	2	1700	70	21
N	Footboard verticals	Softwood (pine)	2	160	70	21
O	Headboard panel	Plywood	1	1510	310	9
P	Footboard panel	Plywood	1	1510	160	9

Note: Remember that the cutting list gives *finished* sizes only, see Buying Timber, page 109.

Other Materials

Apx. 7m quadrant or rectangular beading, 9mm×9mm

Apx. 40×¾" panel pins

16×1½" No. 10 round head screws, black Japanned

40×1½" No. 10 countersunk steel screws

50×1¼" No. 8 countersunk steel screws

Apx. 50×1¼" panel pins

16×9mm dowel plugs 50mm long for joining headboard frame

3m of woven split cane 600mm wide (available in rolls from craft shops or by mail order in craft magazines)

PVA woodworking glue

Clear gloss polyurethane varnish

Dark stain or paint

*To suit other size mattresses, measure mattress length and add 200mm. Change parts E and J to suit

†To suit other size mattresses, measure width and add 200mm, then change parts F, G, I, K, M, O, P to suit

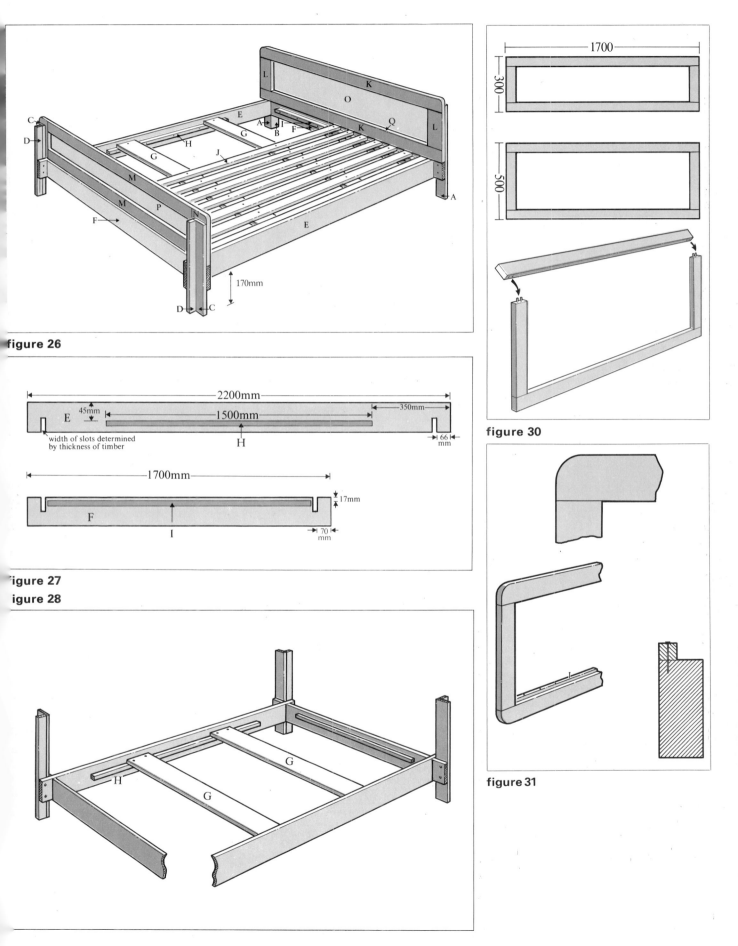

figure 26

figure 27

figure 28

figure 30

figure 31

Beds and Bunks

For the footboard, apply the woven cane to both sides of the plywood.

Run a thin line of glue around the beading you have already nailed into the frame. Push the ply and cane panel into position, **figure 32**. Now apply the second lot of beading, gluing its inside faces first, then fixing with panel pins, **figure 33**. When the glue is dry, punch down nails and fill. Sand down and apply polyurethane to the entire bed, using at least two coats to give a smooth protective finish.

As an alternative to the cane headboards, you can use any of the headboard variations described earlier for single beds.

figure 32

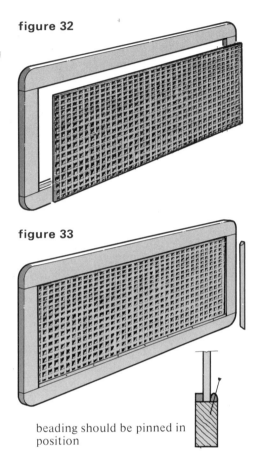

figure 33

beading should be pinned in position

figure 29

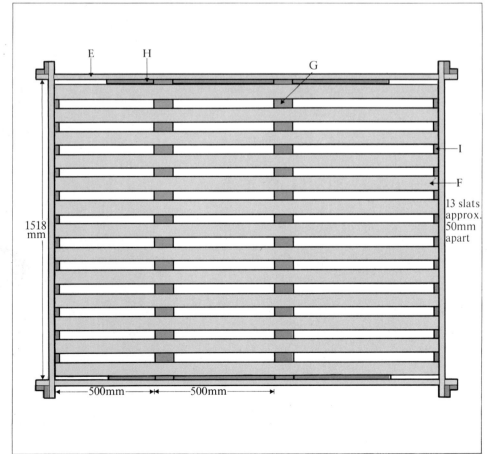

Above *Children's bunk bed designed by Alf Martensson. With a few small adjustments it can be modified to two single beds.*

Left *Give your bed the professional touch, by picking out the end grain in a contrasting colour.*

Beds and Bunks

Above *Our magnificent double bed, made in pine with caned head and footboards.*

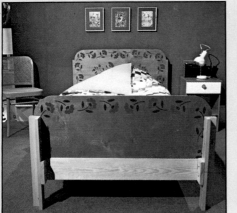

Above left *The head and footboards of our single bed give plenty of scope for the aspiring artist. Here they are decorated with stencilled designs in red and green acrylic paint.*
Above Right *Another version in diagonally set tongue-and-groove pine boarding.*
Left *Padding the boards with fabric and foam rubber gives them a more feminine look.*

Above *In Bill Brooker's bedroom storage range, you can build as many units as you need to fit your wall. This array uses two double wardrobes, a single cupboard with drawers and a dressing table.*

Left *The double wardrobe gives plenty of space for hanging clothes, plus extra storage on the shelf above.*

Bedroom Storage Range

Left *The dressing table consists of no more than a shelf, a mirror and a light box above. Adjust its length to make sure the range fits your wall exactly.*

Left *The drawers are of very straight-forward construction and only simple butt joints are used. Note that the door jambs have been stained a darker shade of brown to give the range some colour variation.*

Bill Brooker

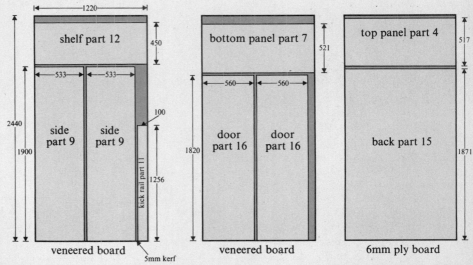

At first sight, this imposing range of bedroom furniture looks rather daunting for the home maker, but it is in fact surprisingly simple. All it consists of is a series of large boxes, or modules, joined together.

There are three basic modules — the double wardrobe, the small cupboard with drawers and the dressing table, whose width is adjustable to make the range fit your wall. The units are free-standing and the joints between them are covered by vertical door jambs, which means that you won't have to leave them behind, irrevocably screwed to the wall, when you move house. For the same reason all the joints have been left dry, so that you can simply unscrew each unit and take it apart. On the other hand, if you have a liking for built-in storage, there is a section later which shows how to adapt the design to this purpose, and which includes an extra range of top cupboards for even greater storage capacity.

The main material used is 18mm veneered blockboard or chipboard, plus a small amount of solid hardwood to give the range a touch of quality. From the home maker's point of view, economy of materials is an absolute necessity, so the cupboards have been designed to give a minimum of waste from standard 2440×1220mm boards and all pieces which do not show are made of softwood or 6mm plywood.

The commonly available veneered boards are supplied only in oak, teak or mahogany. We chose oak and stained the door jambs a slightly darker contrast, but boards covered in more exotic veneers are available from specialist suppliers. Whatever you choose, try to buy the veneered boards and the hardwood from the same supplier at the same time, to ensure a good colour match between the two.

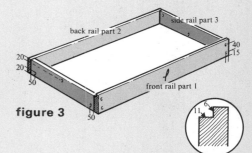

back rail part 2   side rail part 3

20
20
50

front rail part 1

figure 3   50

40
15

11 6

figure 2

	1220	

shelf part 12   450

533   533

2440

1900

side part 9   side part 9

100

kick rail part 11

1256

veneered board

5mm kerf

bottom panel part 7   521

560   560

1820

door part 16   door part 16

veneered board

top panel part 4   517

back part 15   1871

6mm ply board

39

Bedroom Storage Range

figure 1

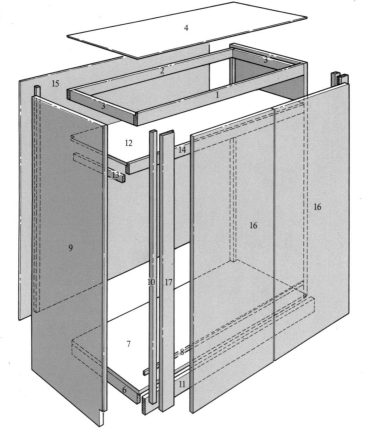

Cutting List. See figure 1

No.	Part	Material	Qty	Length	Width	Thickness
1	Top frame front rail	Hardwood	1	1220	77	21
2	Top frame back rail	Softwood	1	1220	71	21
3	Top frame side rails	Softwood	2	485	71	21
4	Top panel	Plywood	1	1220	517	6
5	Bottom frame front/back rails	Softwood	2	1220	71	21
6	Bottom frame side rails	Softwood	2	467	71	21
7	Bottom panel	Veneered board	1	1220	521	18
8	Bottom panel lipping	Hardwood	1	1220	19	6
9	Wardrobe side panels	Veneered board	2	1900	533	18
10	Corner fillets	Softwood	4	1705	21	21
11	Kick rail	Veneered board	1	1256	100	18
12	Shelf	Veneered board	1	1220	450	18
13	Shelf supports	Softwood	2	410	21	21
14	Shelf lipping	Hardwood	1	1220	71	21
15	Back panel	Plywood	1	1871	1220	6
16	Doors	Veneered board	2	1820	560	18
17	Door jambs	Hardwood	2	1800	71	21

Note: Remember the cutting list gives *finished* sizes only, see Buying Timber, page 109.

Other Materials

1220mm of 25mm dia. chrome plated tube
for the hanging rail
2 thimble ends and 1 centre support for above,
complete with screws
2 door knobs
2 pairs flush hinges, 65mm long,
and ¾″ screws to match
2 adjustable magnetic catches and plates,
complete with screws
2 pieces of iron-on veneer edging, 1900mm long

1½″ No. 8 countersunk steel woodscrews
for side panels, door jambs, etc.
2½″ No. 12 countersunk steel woodscrews
for the top and bottom frames
¾″ No. 6 countersunk steel woodscrews
for the back panel
1″ and 2″ panel pins
PVA glue
Contact adhesive
Finishing materials

Both the double wardrobe and the single cupboard with drawers can be built as free-standing units, or joined side-by-side to make one large piece of storage furniture, but for simplicity's sake we will start by describing the double wardrobe as a free-standing unit.

The Double Wardrobe
Making Instructions

Read carefully through all these instructions and make sure you understand them before starting work.

The wardrobe consists basically of two strong rectangular frames, to which are added two side panels, a top and bottom, and a back. The doors are hung last of all. All the parts for the wardrobe, apart from the solid timber, can be cut from three standard 2440×1220mm boards, two of veneered chipboard or block board and one of 6mm plywood, as shown in **figure 2**.

Managing boards of this size in a home workshop can be awkward and you may be able to persuade your supplier to cut them for you at a little extra cost. If you decide to cut them up at home, remember to mark out the boards with a marking knife, which will cut the veneer and stop it splitting off. Cut as near to the line as possible and finish off with a sharp plane on a fine setting.

Begin by making up the rectangular top frame from parts 1, 2 and 3. Cut each part to length and mark it with face side and edge, see page 142. Make sure that the ends are square. Note that the front rail (1) is 6mm deeper than the other two rails and is made of hardwood because it will show in the complete wardrobe. Cut a rebate 6mm deep and 11mm wide in its top inner face as shown in **figure 3**. This rebate will receive the 6mm ply top. For details of cutting rebates, see page 155.

Drill three holes 4·5mm in diameter in each side rail (3) in the positions shown in **figure 3**. Note that the holes are drilled one upper and two lower on the left side, and two upper and one lower on the right side. The reason for drilling the holes in a different fashion is to prevent the fixing screws of mating units from striking one another.

Countersink these holes to take No. 8 screws on the back—not the face—of each side rail. Using a 7mm bit, drill and countersink a pair of holes at each end of the front and back rails to the dimensions shown in **figure 3**.

Lay the front, back and sides on the bench in the positions they will occupy in the completed frame, with the face edges down on the front, back and left side and the face edge up on the right. Hold each corner firmly together and drill 3·5mm pilot holes into the end grain of each side rail through the holes in the front and back rails. Screw the frame together with 2″ No. 10 countersunk woodscrews.

Cut the 6mm plywood top panel – part 4 to size and make sure that it is square. Lay it tightly into the rebate on the front rail and fix the front corners with 1" panel pins. Pull the top frame square under the top panel and pin the back corners, then infill with more pins along the rails at 100mm intervals.

The bottom frame is made in exactly the same way as the top, except that the front rail is made of softwood and does not have a rebate. The bottom panel (7) has a hardwood lipping (8) on its front, to hide the cut edge of the veneered board. Glue the lipping to the bottom panel and leave in cramps till dry–for technique see page 127.

When the lipping is dry, flush off the top and bottom edges with a very sharp plane, being careful not to damage the veneer. Make sure the bottom panel is square, then fix it to the bottom frame with 2" panel pins. Again, use the bottom panel to square up the frame, but start at the back corners this time. Note that the lipped edge of the bottom panel should overhang the front rail of the frame by 18mm. If necessary, plane off any slight overhang elsewhere on either frame.

Next cut the wardrobe shelf (12) and its front lipping (14) to size. They must both be exactly the same size as the frame fronts and backs. Note that two small notches 21 × 21mm are cut out of the back edge of the shelf to leave room for the back pair of corner fillets (10). Mark these out with a knife to prevent veneer splitting and cut out with a tenon saw.

Rebate the inside top edge of the lipping 18mm deep and 12mm wide, **figure 4**.

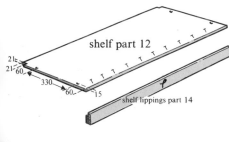

figure 4

Drill two 4·5mm dia. holes in either end of the shelf to the dimensions shown and countersink them to take the heads of 1½" No. 8 woodscrews. Place a thin line of glue along the rebate, then pin the shelf to its lipping, using 2" panel pins 100mm apart.

Now turn your attention to the side panels (9), which should be cut to size with the edges planed flat and square. Mark the face side of each panel. Mark and cut out the 100×18mm notch at the lower front corner of each side panel, **figure 5**, which houses the plinth. Mark both sides of the board, using a try square and marking knife, to prevent any splitting of the face veneers when sawing. Cut out with either a panel or

large tenon saw, keeping as close to the cut line as possible. Finally clean down to the line with a sharp chisel. Note that the corners must be 'handed' to produce one left and one right side. This is particularly important on board which is face veneered on only one side.

The design includes an optional shallow rebate detail on the outer front edge of the side panels. This is purely decorative and provides a shadow line to disguise any unintentional gaps or misalignment between the side panels and the door jambs. Cut this about 2·5×2·5mm with a power drill rebating attachment. Do not attempt it with a hand tool if you are using veneered blockboard, because immediately beneath the surface veneer the grain runs in the opposite direction and it will tear. If you don't have a rebating attachment, leave the detail out. It makes no structural difference whatsoever.

Square a pencil line across the inside face of each side panel 118mm up from the bottom as shown in **figure 5**. This marks the position of the top edge of the bottom frame. Mark another line 77mm down from the top to show the position of the bottom edge of the top frame. Another line 375mm below this line marks the top edge of the shelf support (13). If everything is accurately to size and marked out correctly, the gap between the lines at the top and bottom will be 1705mm – the length of the corner fillets (10).

The front pair of corner fillets (fillets A in **figure 6**) are important because they attach the door jambs (17) to the side panels, as shown in **figure 7** and therefore carry a lot of screws. The back pair of fillets B have only one set of screw holes to attach them to the side panels. Drill 4·5mm dia. holes in the fillets at the centres, **figure 6**. Countersink to give matched pairs, left and right.

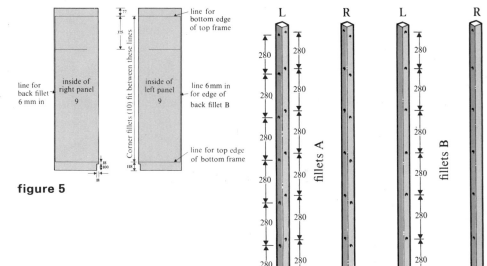

figure 5

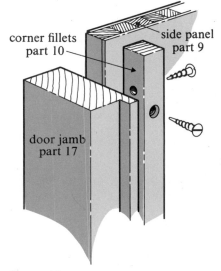

figure 7

Screw and glue the fillets in place so that the ends butt exactly against the lines at the top and bottom of the side panels. Fillets A are fitted flush with the front edge of the side panel, whereas fillets B are fitted 6mm in from the back edge, **figure 5**. Screw the shelf supports to the side panels with three screws spaced at centre and 30mm in from either end, butting up their back ends to the back corner fillets. Use 1¼" No. 8 countersunk woodscrews throughout. Wipe off all surplus glue with a damp rag.

Cut the hardwood door jambs (17) to length and square off their ends with a sharp plane. These jambs are rebated along one edge to house the flush hinges on the doors, **figure 8**. You should therefore inspect the edges for the best grain direction for rebate cutting, see page 155, then pencil in face

Bedroom Storage Range

edge and face side marks, selecting at the same time the best faces for the front.

Set your plough plane or shaper craft tool to a depth cut equal to the thickness of the closed hinge A in **figure 8** and a width cut equal to B. Cut the rebate along the entire length of the face edge of each jamb, working with the width fence pressing against the face side.

It is possible to make the wardrobe without rebating the jambs. In this case the hinge is screwed directly on to the face edges and a compensating amount is cut from the width of each door.

If you are making the parts in a workshop or other convenient space, now is the time completely to finish each component made so far. Rub down with fine abrasive paper supported on a cork block all those surfaces which will be visible when the wardrobe is in its final position. Apply stains, polish or varnish as you choose. See Finishing Techniques, page 158.

You are now ready to start assembling the wardrobe. You will need a large clear area and someone to give you a hand. If you are making the wardrobe some distance away from its eventual location, it is as well to assemble the whole thing where you are, so that you don't have the job of carrying it back again if something doesn't fit. When you know it goes together, dismantle it and take it to the room it is to live in.

Choose the largest area of floor you can and clean it thoroughly. Be sure there is nothing on the floor which will scratch or dent the surfaces of the wardrobe as you assemble it. Cover the area with a clean old sheet or brown paper to give more protection—avoid newsprint because some of it comes off and may mark the polish.

Begin assembly by screwing the door jambs to the side panels. Lay the jamb on the floor with its outside face downwards. With the aid of your helper, take the appropriate side panel and hold it upright with its front edge on the back of the door jamb, **figure 9**. Keep the outside edge of the jamb flush with the outer surface of the side panel —this will need a little care if you have cut the 2·5 × 2·5mm rebate on the front edge

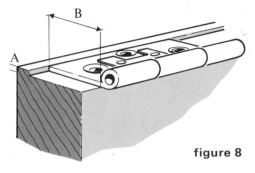

figure 8

of the side panel. Check that the top of the jamb is flush with the top of the side panel. Pass a bradawl through the holes in the front corner fillet and mark the centres for the screws in the jambs. Take the side panel off the jamb temporarily and drill 3mm pilot holes to a depth of 15mm. Replace the side panel on the jamb, check again that it is flush all round, then screw the jamb in place with 1¼″ No. 8 countersunk woodscrews. Repeat this procedure to screw the other door jamb to its side panel.

Now take one of the side panels and lay it on the floor with its outer surface downwards and the door jamb projecting upwards. Put the top and bottom frames in position on the side panel, butted up to the lines marked previously and against the jambs at the front. Mark the screw positions through the holes in the side rails of the frames, drill 3mm pilot holes and screw firmly into place, again using 1¼″ No. 10 screws, **figure 10**.

Place the second side panel face downwards on the floor and turn the whole assembly over on to it. Locate the positions of the top and bottom frames as before, drill pilot holes and screw the frames to the second side panel. Screw the shelf on to the top of the shelf supports with the notches on its back edge fitting snugly round the back corner fillets.

Turn the assembly over on to its front and check that the back panel (15) fits. Measure its diagonals to make sure that it is square. Drill and countersink a series of holes to take ¾″ No. 6 countersunk woodscrews. Place one at each corner and space the others at about 300mm intervals along each

edge. Keep the holes 12mm in from the sides and about 40mm in from the top and bottom edges. Screw the back in position, **figure 11**. Mark on the back panel the position of the centre of the thickness of the shelf, drill three more holes and screw into the back edge of the shelf. This will prevent articles of clothing getting caught between the shelf and the back.

Turn the whole wardrobe over on to its back. Measure from outside edge to outside edge of the wardrobe sides inside the notch cut at the bottom and cut the kick rail (11) to fit exactly. Do not fix it yet.

Lift the wardrobe into the place where it is to stand permanently and you will see that now it is really beginning to take shape. Offer up the kick rail into the notches at the bottom of the wardrobe. If the floor is level, it should slip in without difficulty. If it does not, mark and cut away the parts of its bottom edge which need to be removed. Repeat this operation until a good fit is achieved. Finally fix it into place with contact adhesive (page 131 for technique) or alternatively pin through the front rail of the bottom frame from behind into the kick rail.

Fit the thimble ends and centre support to the hanging rail and slide it into position. Fix the centre support in the middle of the length of the shelf 245mm from the back. Screw the end fittings to either side in line with the central fitting.

The carcase is now complete and the final stage is to fit the doors. If everything has gone together perfectly and is exactly square, you will have performed a wood-working miracle. Just in case you haven't, the door sizes in the cutting list are oversize, to allow for correction at this late stage.

Before doing anything else, measure between the door jambs at the centre of their height and divide the total by two. Compare that with the 560mm given for the door width. If your measurement is less than 560mm, all is well. If not, one or both the top or bottom frames is too large.

Arrange the pair of door panels to give the best combined grain effect. Mark them left and right and at the top and the hinge side, so that you can keep them the right

figure 9

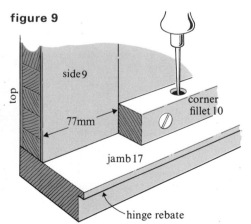

side 9

corner fillet 10

77mm

jamb 17

hinge rebate

top

figure 10

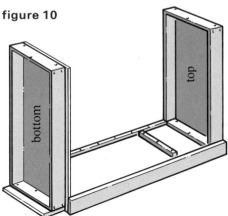

top

bottom

figure 11

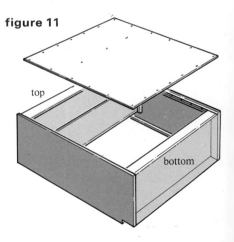

top

bottom

way round. Plane the hinge edge of each door so that it is square to the face and straight along its length. Mark an exact centre line down the face of the top frame front rail and the front edge of the lipping on the bottom panel.

The fitting of the door hinge is shown in **figure 12**; there are two hinges per door, each 200mm from the end. Screw the inner hinge leaf to the edge of the door so that the hinge knuckle fits tightly to the face side of the door and the outer leaf hangs loose.

Lift the door into place against the jamb with its top about 10mm above the top of the jamb. This is heavy work and you will certainly need someone to take the weight of the door for you while you screw both the outer hinge leaves into the rebate (or where no rebate has been cut, straight on to the edge of the jamb). Fix temporarily with two screws in each hinge and check that the hinges swing freely. Slight adjustment may be necessary.

Close the door and transfer the centre line marks on the front of the bottom panel and the top frame on to the door back. Remove the door, transfer the lines on to the front and draw a straight line between these marks. Draw a second line 2mm inside that as in **figure 13**, then saw and/or plane the edge of the door down to that line. Rehang the door with its two screws and rub out the centre marks on the top frame and bottom panel.

Temporarily hang the second door as you did the first and close it, then close the first door on top of it. Mark a pencil line down the whole length of the edge of the first door on to the door beneath it. Remove the second door and mark a second line 2mm inside it as you did for the first door. Trim down to the line as before. Rehang the second door, fit the remaining screws to the hinges of both doors and check that they are firmly driven in. Close both doors and check that three thicknesses of edge veneer will just slip down the gap between them.

With the doors shut, use a straight edge to mark a line across their tops, exactly in line with the tops of the door jambs. Mark the bottoms in the same way, in line with

the top of the notch for the kick rail.

Remove both doors and re-mark those lines right round the tops and bottoms with a knife cut. Saw and plane away the waste. Finish the closing edges of the door only with iron-on edge veneer, see page 146. Rub down all the faces and edges of the doors and finish to match the rest of the wardrobe.

Rehang the doors. Mark out and fix the door handles. Fix the magnetic catches to the underside of the top frame front rail and their counter plates to the inside surface of the doors.

figure 13

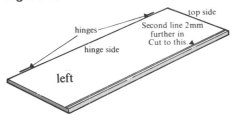

Single Cupboard with Drawers

The construction of this unit differs slightly, depending on whether you plan to add it on to the double wardrobe or to build it as a free-standing unit in its own right. To make things absolutely clear, we will describe the system for adding on first, then show how the design differs for the free-standing unit.

Making the Add-On Cupboard

When you add on the single cupboard unit to the wardrobe, the side panel labelled A in **figure 14** forms a common wall between the two cupboards. The single unit is therefore built without a left-hand wall and its top and bottom frames are screwed directly into side A.

To give an unbroken look to the whole piece, the original kick rail is removed from the wardrobe and replaced by a longer rail B which spans both units.

All the parts for the add-on version of the single unit can be cut from two standard 2440×1220mm boards, one of veneered chipboard or blockboard and the other of 6mm plywood. Dimensions are given in **figure 15**.

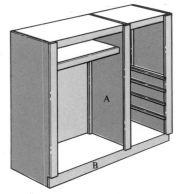

figure 14

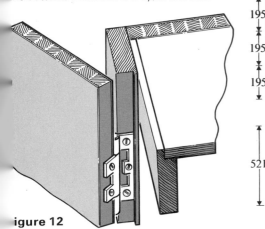

figure 12

figure 15

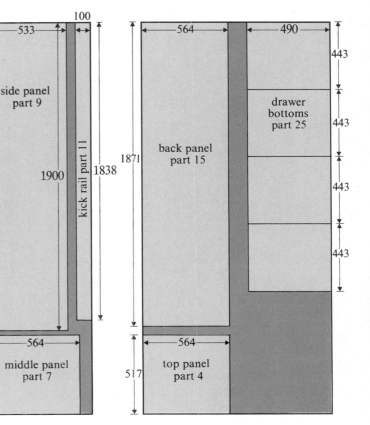

veneered board

6mm plywood sheet

Bedroom Storage Range

If you decide from the start that you are going to build the combined unit shown in **figure 14**, you can save money by making side panel A out of 18mm plain chipboard, rather than the more expensive veneered board. If, however, you decide six months after you built the double wardrobe that you would like to add the single cupboard on, it is probably not worth replacing side panel A with chipboard as you will have to dismantle one side of the wardrobe and rehang one of the doors.

The construction of the single unit has much in common with the double wardrobe. Read through the instructions for the double wardrobe before starting work.

Mark the top and bottom rectangular frames exactly as for the double wardrobe and pin the top and bottom panels in position. Mark out the inside surface of the new side panel (9), omitting the line for the shelf, since the cupboard does not have one. Mark the outside surface of the right hand side panel of the double wardrobe in the same way, but leave out the front corner fillet. Reference to **figure 17** will show that the door jamb on the left is already incorporated in the wardrobe, so the corner fillet has no function. Cut the 2·5 × 2·5mm rebate in the front face side edge of the side panel.

the combined kick rail which spans both units, allowing for irregularities in the floor.

Reference to **figure 18** shows that the door jamb (17) projects inwards on the right-hand side. This means that the new side panel (9) cannot be used to support the drawers and it is necessary to fit a false side panel (18) to carry the drawer runners. To bring the false side panel flush with the inside edge of the jamb, a spacer batten (19) is fixed between the front corner fillet and the false side panel. On the left-hand side the drawer runners are simply fixed to the side panel of the wardrobe.

Cut the false side panel to size and check that it fits exactly between the inside of the plywood back and the inside of the door jamb. Hold the panel with its outer face flush with the edge of the jamb and check that the space between it and the front corner fillet is 14mm. If not, adjust the thickness of the spacer battens to suit, making back and front the same. Glue and screw the spacer battens to the corner fillets — when you drill for the screws, make sure that you avoid those already in the corner fillets.

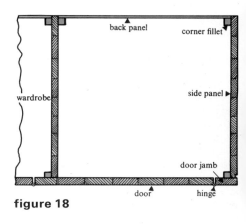

figure 18

Mark out the false panel for the drawer runners as shown in **figure 19**, working from the bottom upwards. The 196 and 146mm dimensions comprise the finished height of the drawer sides plus 1mm clearance.

Screw the drawer stop (21) temporarily in place, flush with the back edge of the false panel. Drill and countersink each drawer

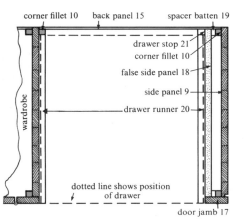

figure 17

Drill the screw holes in all three corner fillets, then screw and glue the single back corner fillet on to the side of the wardrobe, 6mm from the back edge. Lay the single cupboard side panel face downwards on the floor and screw and glue the front and back corner fillets in position. Cut and rebate the single door jamb and screw it to the front corner fillet.

Screw the top and bottom frames to the side panel, then stand the cupboard assembly against the wardrobe end, line up the top and bottom frames with the marks on the wardrobe end and screw the frames to it. Add the plywood back panel. Stand the combined unit up in the place where it will eventually be kept, remove the kick rail from the wardrobe and replace it with

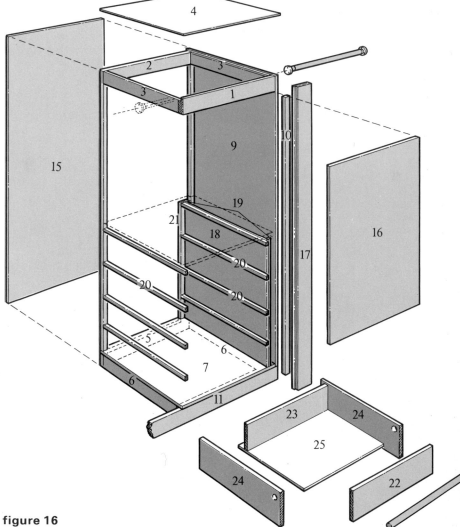

figure 16

44

runner (20) at its centre point and about 50mm from each end to take 1" No. 8 countersunk woodscrews. Screw each runner in place between the marked lines and butting against the drawer stop—the front ends of the runners should project 21mm beyond the front edge of the false panel, that is the thickness of the door jamb. Remove the drawer stop, place the false panel in position and glue and pin it to the spacer battens front and back, then screw the drawer stop permanently in position.

The drawer runners on the other side are screwed direct to the side panel of the wardrobe. Mark out the side panel with the positions of the runners and screw them on with their back ends butting up to the back corner fillet. Check that the top runners are an equal distance from the cupboard floor on each side.

Cut the middle panel (7) to size and glue and cramp its lipping to its front edge. When the glue is dry, plane the lippings flush with the panel faces. Cut three of the corners away with 21 × 21mm notches to leave room for the corner fillets. Drop the panel into place over the left top drawer runner and the top of the false side panel. There is no need for screws or glue: it will sit there quite happily under the force of gravity.

Cut the hang rail to length and screw the thimble end centrally to each side panel.

Measure the horizontal distance between the two door jambs (do not measure into the rebate) and check that the jambs are parallel from top to bottom. Saw and plane the door so that it is 2mm narrower than the gap and has straight edges. Follow the hanging instructions given for the wardrobe, with the exception that the bottom edge of the door is marked and cut to finish a couple of mm above the top drawer runners. Finish the door to match the rest of the wardrobe.

The cupboard is now complete except for the drawers, but first we shall look at the constructional difference in the free-standing cupboard.

Making the Free Standing Cupboard

Because the free-standing version has two side panels, it will need four corner fillets and two door jambs. For the same reason you will need two false side panels to support the drawers and four spacer battens. The presence of the extra door jamb means that the door is narrower than in the add-on cupboard and a short kick rail 600m long is used at the base. Most of these changes are reflected in **figure 20** and in the cutting list. With these exceptions, construction is as for the add-on cupboard.

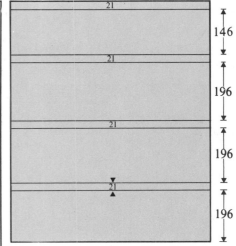

figure 19

Making the Drawers

Note that the top drawer is 50mm shallower than the other three drawers.

Cut each drawer side (part 24) slightly overlength and plane its width so that it slides freely between its pair of runners. The four drawers are made up from 20 parts and it is very easy to get them mixed up unless you label each part clearly from the start. Label each drawer side Right 1, 2, 3 and 4 and Left 1, 2, 3 and 4 respectively. On each drawer side mark the side which will become the outside of the drawer as the face side and the bottom edge as the face edge.

Trim each drawer side to length and square its ends with a plane so that when the back end is butted up to the back corner fillet, the front end is flush with the front face of the door jamb. Measure between the two false side panels (or between the false side panel and the wardrobe if adding on) to find the exact width of the drawers. Deduct 1mm for clearance. From that dimension

No.	Part	Material	Qty	Length	Width	Thickness
1	Top frame front rail	Hardwood	1	564	77	21
2	Top frame back rail	Softwood	1	564	71	21
3	Top frame sides	Softwood	2	485	71	21
4	Top panel	Plywood	1	564	517	6
5	Bottom frame front/back rails	Softwood	2	564	71	21
6	Bottom frame side rails	Softwood	2	467	71	21
7	Bottom and middle panels	Veneered board	2	564	521	18
8	Bottom and middle lippings	Hardwood	2	564	19	6
9	Side panel	Veneered board	1	1900	533	18
10	Corner fillets	Softwood	3	1705	21	21
11	Combined kick rail	Veneered board	1	1838	100	18
15	Back panel	Plywood	1	1871	564	6
16	Door	Veneered board	1	964	509	18
17	Door jamb	Hardwood	1	1800	71	21
18	False side panel	Chipboard	1	818	527	18
19	Spacer battens	Softwood	2	818	21	14
20	Drawer runners	Hardwood	8	527	21	15
21	Drawer stop	Softwood	1	818	21	21
22	Drawer front (top)	Veneered board	1	480	145	18
	Drawer front (others)	Veneered board	3	480	195	18
23	Drawer back (top)	Softwood	1	480	120	15
	Drawer back (other)	Softwood	3	480	170	15
24	Drawer sides (top)	Softwood	2	527	145	15
	Drawer sides (other)	Softwood	6	527	195	15
25	Drawer bottoms	Plywood	4	443	490	6

Cutting List for the add-on cupboard with drawers. See figure 16

Note: Remember the cutting list gives *finished* sizes only. See Buying Timber, page 109. For varying size, see note at foot of cutting list for free-standing single cupboard.

Other Materials

5 lengths of 18mm dia. chrome plated steel tube, 562mm long, for hang rail and drawer handles
2 thimble ends for hang rail, complete with screws
1 pr. 65mm plated flush hinges with ¾" screws to match
1 magnetic catch and plate complete with screws
1 door knob
700mm of iron-on edge veneer
4 × 1500mm lengths of wooden or plastic drawer slip, if being used

2" No. 10 countersunk steel woodscrews
1¼" No. 8 countersunk steel woodscrews
1" No. 8 countersunk steel woodscrews
¾" No. 6 countersunk steel woodscrews
½" No. 6 countersunk steel woodscrews
1" and 2" panel pins
PVA glue
Contact adhesive
Finishing materials

Bedroom Storage Range

deduct the combined thicknesses of the two drawer sides and cut the drawer fronts (22) and backs (23) to that exact length. It will probably differ marginally from the dimension given in the cutting list.

Mark the outside surfaces of the fronts and backs as the face sides and their bottom edges as the face edges. As you make the parts, label them front 1, front 2, back 1, back 2, and so on.

Mark two lines down the inside face of each drawer side, one 88mm from the front and one 20mm from the back, as shown in **figure 21**. These mark the positions of the drawer front and back. Also drill out the hole for the drawer handle, using an 18mm flat bit and placing a spare piece of softwood under the work to prevent splitting out. A drill stand should be used for this operation, see page 124.

On the same face, mark and cut the groove for the bottom. This is 4mm wide and 5mm deep and is stopped 5mm in front of the 88mm line, **figure 21**. Also cut a matching groove on the inside surface of the front. This is not stopped, but runs through the whole length of the front. For the technique of cutting grooves, both run through and stopped, Techniques Section, page 155.

There too you will find the groove cutting jig with the power drill shown in the television programme.

If you wish, you can avoid cutting the grooves by using standard drawer slip section made of wood or plastic. If fitting wooden drawer slips, cut one length for each drawer side to stretch from the back end to the 88mm line as in **figure 22**. Mitre the front end. For mitreing see page 148. Cut another piece, with mitres at both ends, to the exact length of the drawer front. You will also need to cut away the curved top part of the drawer slip on the sides at the 20mm mark to make room for the drawer back, **figure 22**. Glue and pin the slips to the sides and front flush with their bottom edges.

Plastic drawer slips are fitted with their top edge 20mm from the bottom of the front and sides. Mitre their ends and pin and glue them in position.

You should now drill the screw holes in the face side of each drawer side in preparation for assembling the drawers. Dimensions are given in **figure 23**. Countersink for 1¼" No. 8 woodscrews.

Assemble the four drawer parts in their marked sets. Butt the inside face of the front

up to the 88mm line and the outside edge of the back up to the 20mm line, **figure 24**. Cramp the parts together. Note that the back sits on top of the groove in the sides to leave room for the plywood bottom. Drill pilot holes and screw each drawer together.

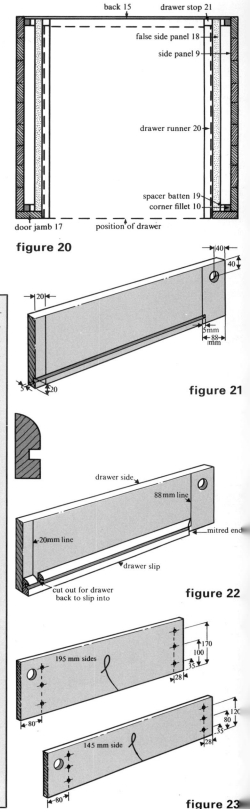

figure 20

figure 21

figure 22

figure 23

No.	Part	Material	Qty	Length	Width	Thickness
1	Top frame front rail	Hardwood	1	564	77	21
2	Top frame back rail	Softwood	1	564	71	21
3	Top frame side rails	Softwood	2	485	71	21
4	Top panel	Plywood	1	564	517	6
5	Bottom frame front/back rails	Softwood	2	564	71	21
6	Bottom frame sides	Softwood	2	467	71	21
7	Bottom and middle panels	Veneered board	2	564	521	18
8	Bottom and middle lippings	Hardwood	2	564	19	6
9	Cupboard side panels	Veneered board	2	1900	533	18
10	Corner fillets	Softwood	4	1705	21	21
11	Kick rail	Veneered board	1	600	100	18
15	Back panel	Plywood	1	1871	564	6
16	Door	Veneered board	1	964	456	18
17	Door jambs	Hardwood	2	1800	71	21
18	False side panels	Chipboard	2	818	527	18
19	Spacer battens	Softwood	4	818	21	14
20	Drawer runners	Hardwood	8	527	21	15
21	Drawer stops	Softwood	2	818	21	21
22	Drawer front (top)	Veneered board	1	427	145	18
	Drawer front (others)	Veneered board	3	427	195	18
23	Drawer back (top)	Softwood	1	427	120	15
	Drawer back (others)	Softwood	3	427	170	15
24	Drawer sides (top)	Hardwood	2	527	145	15
	Drawer sides (others)	Hardwood	6	527	195	15
25	Drawer bottoms	Plywood	4	443	437	6

Cutting List for free-standing cupboard with drawers. See figures 16 and 20.

Notes: Remember the cutting list gives *finished* sizes only, see Buying Timber, page 109. This cutting list refers to a cupboard which is 600mm wide overall. If you wish to make it wider, say 700mm, add 100mm to the length dimensions of parts 1, 2, 4, 5, 7, 8, 11, 22, 23 and 26. Add 100mm width dimension to parts 15, 16, and 25.

Other Materials

As for add-on cupboard. A larger number of 1¼" No. 8 woodscrews will be needed.

Cut the drawer bottoms (25) to size, making sure they are square. Note that they will be smaller than shown in the cutting list for drawers which are fitted with slips. To determine the exact width, measure between the grooves in the sides. The length of the bottom is the dimension from the inside of the groove in the drawer front to the extreme end of the drawer side. Slide the bottoms into the grooves and secure them with three screws running through them and into the bottom edge of the backs.

Clean up all the faces of the drawers and finish the fronts to match the rest of the cupboard. Finally apply adhesive to one of the handle holes, pass the tubular handle through the other hole and into and just beyond the glued one. Glue the second hole and push the tube back into it. Wipe off all excess adhesive and allow to dry.

Fit the drawers. It may be necessary to ease them slightly with a sharp, smooth plane to achieve a final fit. Lubricate the drawer sides and runners by rubbing a candle over them.

The Dressing Table

The dressing table consists of a shelf of melamine veneered chipboard, a louvred light box which carries the neon strip, and a 2mm thick mirror held in place by two retaining battens (45). See **figure 25**. The illustration at the start of this chapter shows that the dressing table is suspended between the small cupboard with drawers and a second double wardrobe. This is only one arrangement: it can stretch between any two cupboards or between a cupboard and the wall, depending on the local situation. Its great virtue is that it may be varied in width as required. The cutting list gives dimensions for a unit 1000mm wide, but it is an easy matter to change the dimensions to suit your particular needs. However, if you intend to increase the width, you should user wider section timber in the construction of the frames.

Making Instructions

The construction of the shelf is very similar to that of the top frame of the wardrobe, with the exceptions that the back rail projects upwards to help support the mirror and that there is a lap joint between the front and side rails.

Cut a rebate 18mm deep along the inside top edge of the shelf front rail (40) leaving an 8mm wide upstand, as in **figure 26**. The melamine veneered top panel (43) may be a little thicker than the 18mm stated

figure 24

figure 25

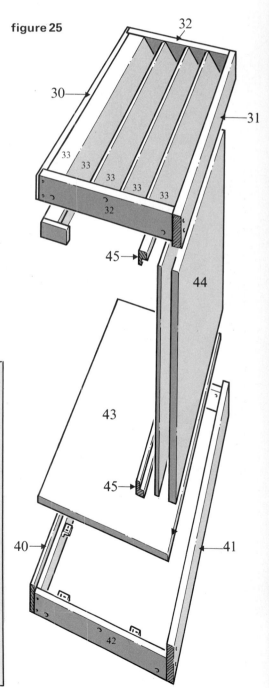

Cutting List for dressing table. See figure 25						
No.	**Part**	**Material**	**Qty**	**Length**	**Width**	**Thickness**
30	Light box front rail	Hardwood	1	1000	96	21
31	Light box back rail	Softwood	1	1000	121	21
32	Light box side rails	Softwood	2	504	96	21
33	Louvres and light hood	Softwood	5	958	121	15
40	Shelf front rail	Hardwood	1	1000	71	21
41	Shelf back rail	Softwood	1	1000	96	21
42	Shelf side rails	Softwood	2	504	53	21
43	Shelf top panel	Melamine veneered chipboard	1	1000	504	18
44	Mirror back	Chipboard	1	1000	1000	12
45	Mirror retaining battens	Hardwood	2	1000	46	15

Note: Remember the cutting list gives *finished* sizes only, see Buying Timber, page 109.

Other Materials

piece of 2mm thick glass mirror, cut to fit
900mm flourescent light fitting with tube and fixing screws, complete with pull switch.
Electrical cable as required
table stretcher plates with round headed screws to match

2″ No. 12 countersunk steel woodscrews
1½″ No. 8 countersunk steel woodscrews
1¼″ No. 8 countersunk steel woodscrews
2″ panel pins
PVA glue
Finishing materials

Bedroom Storage Range

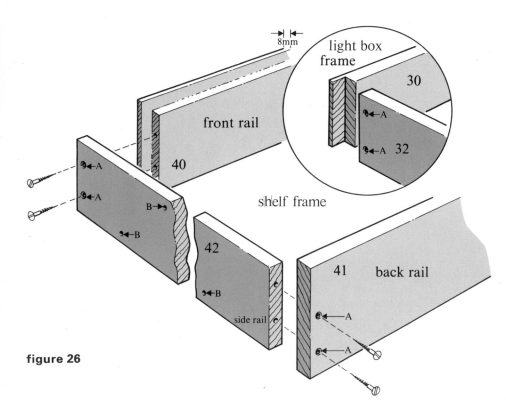

figure 26

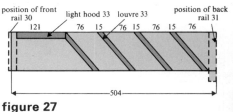

figure 27

The Wardrobe and Single Cupboard as Built-in Units

Built-in storage units vary from the free-standing ones in that they take much of their strength from being attached to adjoining walls. No backs are required. They are usually much cheaper to make but have the disadvantage that it is very difficult to remove them if you change houses.

The basic constructional system of the units shown on the previous pages can be readily adapted to be built-in. The following instructions apply to units which include floor to ceiling storage assuming a ceiling height of not more than 2500mm—this makes use of standard 2440mm long sheet material. If you should wish to build higher than this it will be necessary to make each side panel (9) in two parts, a lower one which runs from floor to mid-way on the intermediate frame, and the upper one which starts there and rises to the ceiling. See **figure 28**.

Bulky skirting boards can be a problem when fitting built-in furniture. In such cases their removal is well worth considering. The time taken in stripping them out and making good the wall is often more than repaid by the resulting simplified construction of the units. However, since most modern houses have skirtings of between 75 and 150mm in height, building around them will be no problem and the following instructions take these into account.

Planning the Units

To begin with, measure the space you have available and decide on the combination of units you will be making. Draw a plan to scale on a piece of paper as a guide to the number of uprights, frames and doors you will require. Remember when planning to make the most economic use of sheet materials. Two panels will have to be cut from the width of 1220mm. Therefore avoid making either the side panels (9) or the doors (16) more than about 605mm wide. Economic cuts were considered in the cutting lists of the free-standing units, so use them as a guide to your plan.

If you are building the unit around an existing shallow skirting, adapt the height of the kick-rail (11) and its cut out on the side panels to match it exactly. This gives the unit a continuous horizontal line at door-bottom level which exactly follows the top of the remaining skirtings, giving the

in the cutting list. If so, deepen the rebate accordingly and plane down the side rails (42) to match.

Cut away the ends of the front rail in line with the upstand to form a lap joint with the sides. (Lap joint, page 148.) Drill the holes in each side rail and in the ends of the back rail to take No. 10 countersunk woodscrews. Countersink holes A in **figure 26** from the face side and holes B from the reverse side.

Stand all the parts on a flat surface, drill pilot holes and screw the frame together with all bottom edges flush. Check that the frame is square.

Screw two equally spaced table stretcher plates to the inside faces of the four shelf frame members; to the front rail with their tops lining up with the bottom of the rebate, to the side rails with their tops flush with the top of the rail, and to the back rail along a line joining the top edges of the side rails.

Cut the shelf panel (43) to fit inside the frame. Try it for fit, but do not fix it yet.

The light box frame is made in the same way as the shelf frame, except that there is no rebate on the front rail, **figure 26**, and the back rail projects downwards rather than upwards. The inside surface of the side rails is marked out as shown in **figure 27**. When the frame is complete, screw the fitting for the fluorescent tube to the inside of the front rail, then pin and glue the louvres and light hood into position. Do not fit the fluorescent tube until the whole unit is firmly attached between adjacent cabinets.

Screw the light box to the wardrobe or cupboard on one side, making sure all the edges are flush and using 1¼″ No. 10

countersunk woodscrews. Screw the shelf in position with the top edge of the front rail 675mm from the floor. Check dimensions to ensure that it is level, then screw the light box and the shelf to the cupboard on the other side. Slip the shelf top panel into place and secure it with screws passing through the stretcher plates into its underside.

Cut the mirror back (44) to fit exactly between the shelf top panel and the underside of the light box side rails. This length may be slightly less than the 1000mm given in the cutting list. Screw the mirror back to the back rails of the light box above and the shelf below.

Rebate the top and bottom mirror retaining battens (45) to a depth of 15mm and a width equal to the thickness of the mirror. Screw the battens to the top and bottom of the mirror back in four equally spaced positions, avoiding the rebate. Measure between the edges of the battens and add 30mm to find the exact height of the mirror; its width is the distance between the adjacent cabinets. Deduct 2mm from both dimensions for clearance. Remove only the top retaining batten to fit the mirror, then screw it back in place.

The 2mm mirror must be handled with great care when carrying or positioning it. Once in place, the chipboard back will support it well. If you wish to fit a more robust mirror, but at considerably higher cost, buy one made from 6mm float glass. Have the short edges ground and increase the rebate in the retaining battens to take the extra thickness of glass.

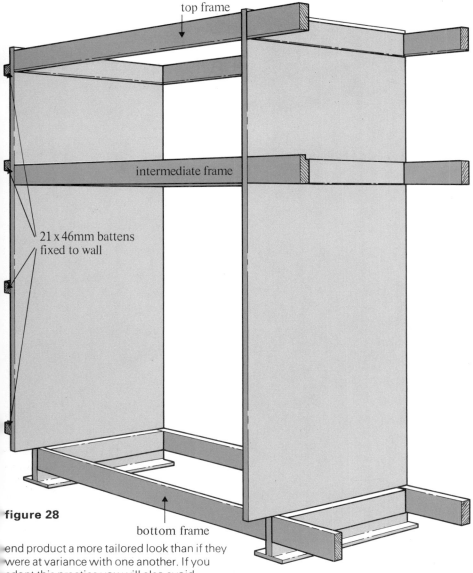

top frame

intermediate frame

21 x 46mm battens
fixed to wall

figure 28

bottom frame

end product a more tailored look than if they were at variance with one another. If you adopt this practice you will also avoid constructional difficulties which might occur if the skirtings were to rise above the level of the wardrobe floors. Remember to make all bottom frames narrower than the intermediate and top ones by the thickness of the skirtings otherwise they will stick out and nothing will go together. Do not fix the bottom shelf until the whole carcase is together. It has to be cut to fill the overall space up to the wall and access for the fixing screws from frame sides to panels is necessary.

Construction

Mark the position of the front of the unit on the floor. Use a long, straight piece of timber as a straightedge and remember to allow for the thickness of the skirting board when setting out, **figure 29**. If you have removed one of the larger type skirtings then no allowance is required. Continue that mark vertically up the wall at the end. Use a spirit level and the longest straightedge possible to ensure accuracy.

With built-in furniture the main assembly fixing is fairly quick after the initial donkey work of fixing the first pieces is done. In this case the first piece is the side panel which is fixed to the wall. If this is not fitted upright and square, the rest will not go together correctly.

To achieve correct alignment, the side panel is not fitted directly to the wall but to spacer battens which are adjusted to take up variations in the wall surface.

At a point halfway between the line on the wall and the plastered corner, use a straightedge and spirit level to test the wall to see how flat and plumb it is. If it is out of true, and most are, mark the highest spot on the wall with a pencil.

Cut an odd scrap of 21mm thick batten and stick it on to the high spot with double-sided self-adhesive tape. Re-erect the straightedge in the same position but on to the block. Cut and fix another block to the floor or skirting of such a size that when the straightedge touches both blocks it is standing vertically, **figure 29**.

Now cut four 21 × 46mm battens 10mm shorter than the width of the side panel. (This reduction in length allows the battens to be fitted slightly away from the plastered corner, to clear the normal rounding there, without forcing the other end beyond the front edge of the panel when fixed.)

Fix the four battens to the wall, each with two 2½" No. 10 countersunk woodscrews. Screw one just above the top of the skirting (or 200mm above the floor), another about 300mm below the ceiling, one at the height of the intermediate frame and the last between that and the lowest one. Do not tighten the screws completely.

Replace the straightedge between the two blocks to check that all the battens are vertically in line, **figure 29**. Some adjustment will be required. Do this by inserting slivers of wood behind the battens next to the screw position.

At this stage is is also necessary to check that those battens are at 90° to the line of the unit fronts (the line on the floor). A large try square is required for this.

Use additional packing, or shave off the wall battens to correct them for the right-angle and tighten the screws. Cut the end panel to size, allowing about 50mm gap between it and the ceiling for easy movement, and scribe it to the rear wall and skirting. Screw the panel to the wall battens—checking that its front edge is in line with, and 21mm behind, the line on the wall.

Now mark the positions of the intermediate panels on the floor. Use the straightedge and spirit level to check the floor level. Note any hollows or bumps where the panel marks occur. Add packing strips to the floor where there are hollows so that the panel will stand level. See **figure 28**. Cut off the bottom of panels which are standing on bumps to achieve the same result.

The intermediate panels should stop short of the ceiling by 20–30mm for ease of positioning. This leaves room for a couple of small G cramps to hold the top frames in position while fixing. The frames themselves can sit a further 20mm below the top edge of the panel, again to allow plenty of hand room whilst driving in the screws securing them to the panels. The resultant gap showing at the front is covered by the scribing pieces, which should be cut to the ceiling line and secured by screws from the inside. Only the door jambs and the scribing pieces actually touch the ceiling. See **figure 30**.

From this point the assembly of the units follows the approximate order of the free-standing ones. Screw the bottom intermediate and top frames to the wall-fixed panel, then add a dividing panel and so on to complete the main carcase. Make additional screw fixings through the back rails of the bottom intermediate and top

Bedroom Storage Range

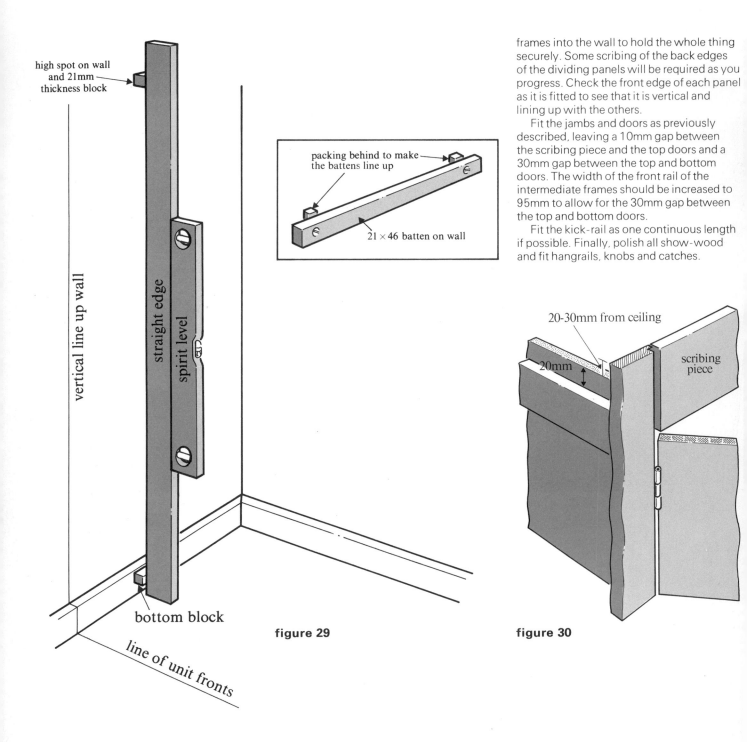

high spot on wall and 21mm thickness block

vertical line up wall

straight edge

spirit level

bottom block

figure 29

line of unit fronts

packing behind to make the battens line up

21 × 46 batten on wall

frames into the wall to hold the whole thing securely. Some scribing of the back edges of the dividing panels will be required as you progress. Check the front edge of each panel as it is fitted to see that it is vertical and lining up with the others.

Fit the jambs and doors as previously described, leaving a 10mm gap between the scribing piece and the top doors and a 30mm gap between the top and bottom doors. The width of the front rail of the intermediate frames should be increased to 95mm to allow for the 30mm gap between the top and bottom doors.

Fit the kick-rail as one continuous length if possible. Finally, polish all show-wood and fit hangrails, knobs and catches.

20-30mm from ceiling

20mm

scribing piece

figure 30

DINING TABLE and CHAIRS

Brian Davey

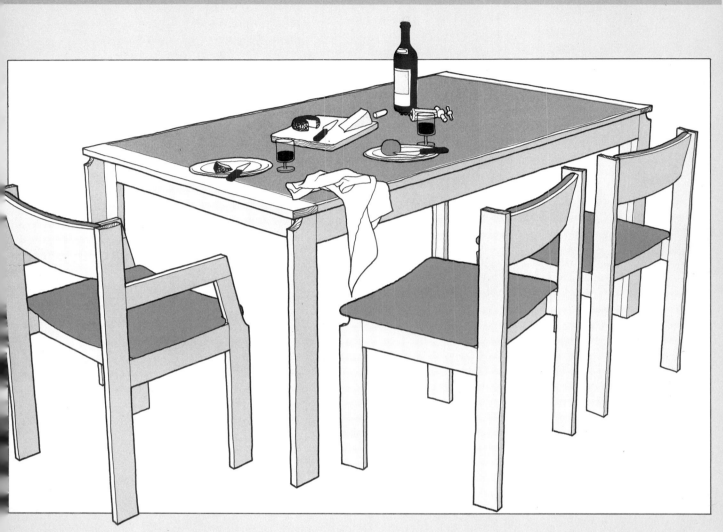

Many Do-It-Yourself enthusiasts who would happily set to work on a shelving unit or a built-in cupboard, hesitate at the idea of building tables and chairs. It seems altogether too difficult and demanding. My prime objective in designing this dining set was to convince the doubters that even seemingly complicated furniture can be quite simple and straightforward, once the basic techniques have been mastered.

The dining table is intended to seat six people comfortably and eight at a squeeze. To achieve this, the traditional 'leg at each corner' principle has been used, a form of table construction which is also the easiest to make. The design is a versatile one, and with a little pre-planning you should be able to choose materials which will ideally complement your home. The dining set was originally built in solid elm, with a cork top for the table and brown fabric seats and backs for the chairs. Variations which we made were a teak table with a teak veneered blockboard top and black PVC chair seats; and a kitchen set in pine, where the table top was white plastic laminate and the backs and seats of the chairs were made of plywood and painted white. Throughout the text we give instructions for the elm and cork version. Some suggestions for the teak and pine variations are given at the end.

The Dining Table
Making Instructions

Bring all components to correct width and thickness. *Some should be left overlength— see below.* Mark all pieces with face side and face edge—see Keeping Square, page 145.

The Underframe

When you bring the timber home from the yard, you will probably find it has been rapidly cross cut with a blunt blade, causing breakout and splitting at the ends, so it is best to allow for a little waste at each end which can be trimmed off cleanly with a tenon saw.

Leave the leg flats and leg returns— parts 1 and 2—10mm to 15mm overlength. Make a mark a few mm from one end of each and square round with a try square. This will be the bottom of the leg. From this line measure up exactly 740mm and square round again. This marks the top of the leg.

On the face edge of the leg flats (1) measure down and mark a line 75mm from the top. This marks the area covered by the side rail after assembly. You can choose which joint to use between the side rail and the leg. I prefer a mortice and tenon, but a dowel joint is a perfectly acceptable alternative. See mortice and tenon joint,

page 153 and dowel joint, page 150.

The marking out for both mortice and tenon and dowel joints is given in **figure 2**. For the dowel joint, mark and bore two holes in the centre line 45mm apart to take 10mm dia. dowels 25mm deep. Alternatively, draw and chop out a mortice 60×13mm to a depth of 46mm.

Cut the leg flats to length, leaving a minimum of 2mm over at the top. This is removed with a plane after assembly of the table frame.

To make the tenons, leave the side rails— part 3—at least 15mm overlength. Mark out the shoulder lines of the tenons, working out from the centre line as shown in **figure 3**. Offer up the respective ends of the rail to the mortices previously made in the legs and mark off the tenons, as shown in **figure 4**. This will ensure that each joint is a good fit. Number each mortice and tenon 1–1, 2–2, etc. as you proceed. This will help you to 'keep your place' during final assembly.

For the dowel joint, cut the side rails (3) exactly to length and mark out and bore 10mm dia. holes 26mm deep in the end grain to match those in the leg flat. Use a dowel jig if possible and number each joint as before.

The dowel joint is the joint of choice between the leg return (2) and the end

Dining Table and Chairs

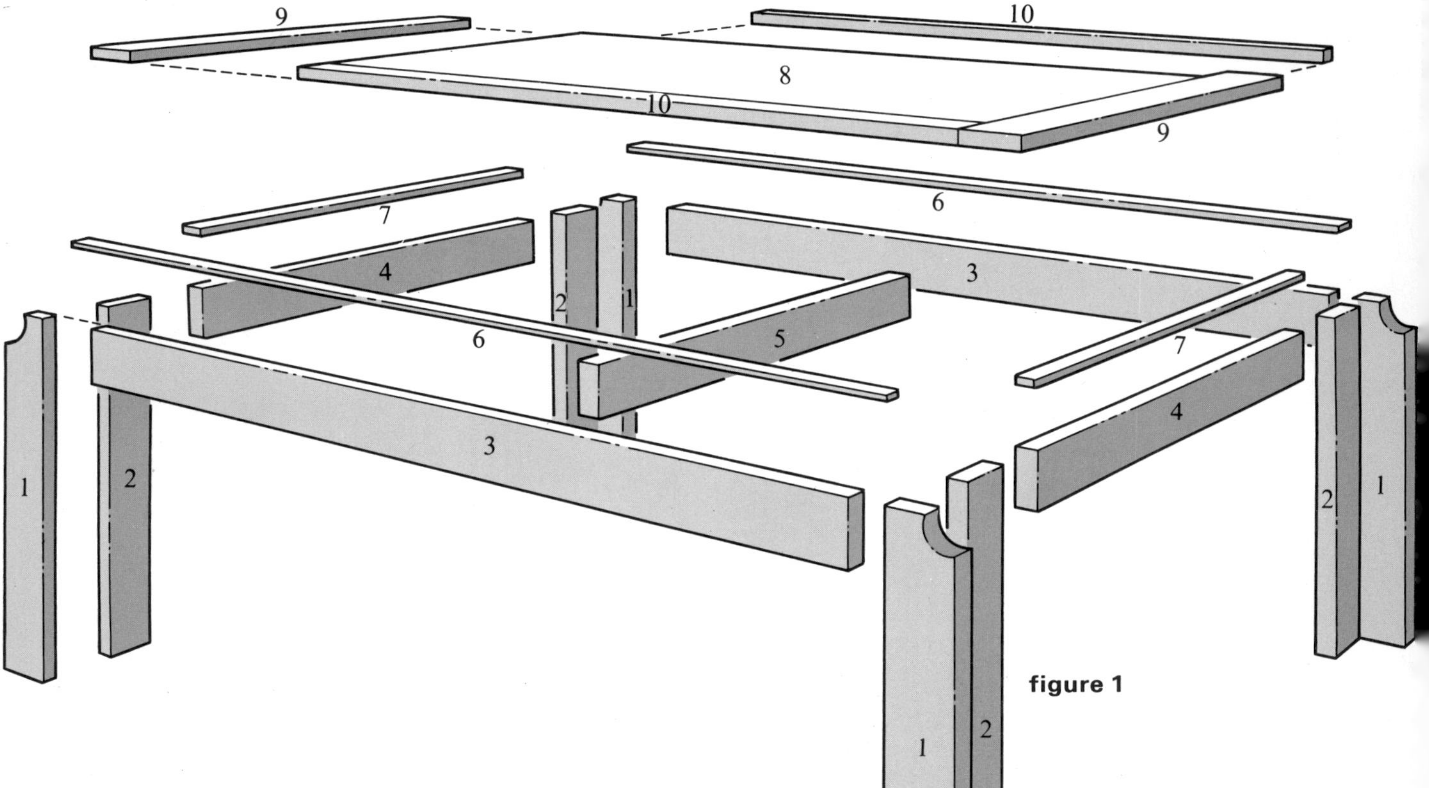

figure 1

rails (4). Mark the bottom and top lines as you did for the leg flat and square round. Mark and bore the dowel holes on the face edge of the leg return and on the ends of the end rails. Cut the leg returns to length, leaving 2mm at the top as before.

The centre rail, part 5, is marked and bored out in the same manner as the end rails.

Finally, mark out the scallop detail on the top of the leg flat. To assist in this job, make yourself a circular template of stiff card, 50mm in diameter, with a cross marked through the centre. Hold it against the top of the leg as shown in **figure 5** and mark the curve with a pencil. Do not cut out the curve until the side frame is assembled, then remove the scallop with a coping or bow saw (Cutting Curves, page 119), and finish with garnet paper wrapped round a short length of broom handle. Start with 80 grit and use both a turning and a side-to-side action, then finish off with 120 grit, using the turning motion only.

Each leg consists of an L-section made out of one leg flat (1) and one leg return (2). Lay out the leg components in pairs and make sure you know which are the left-hand legs and which the right. Label the pairs A–A, B–B and so on. Each pair of components is dowelled together as shown in **figure 6**. Mark and bore four 8mm holes 20mm deep in the inside face of the leg flat and in the edge of the leg return (Dowel joint, page 150). Clean up both pieces thoroughly and check for fit and squareness whilst still dry. Take apart and carefully glue both surfaces and each dowel, then set up in 150mm G cramps with softwood blocks to protect the surfaces, as shown in **figure 7**. Wipe off excess glue with a clean damp rag.

When the glue has dried, remove the assembled leg from the cramps and plane lightly along the external faces until flush. Take care that the edge of the leg flat remains square, as this carries the mortice or dowel joint. Check repeatedly with a small try square whilst planing. Repeat this procedure for each leg assembly.

Take two of the completed legs and one side rail and joint them up dry to check for squareness. Cramp up in a 1·8m sash cramp as shown in **figure 8**, again using softwood

Cutting List. See figure 1

No.	Part	Material	Qty.	Length	Width	Thickness
1	Leg flat	Elm or other hardwood	4	740	75	28
2	Leg return	Elm or other hardwood	4	740	50	28
3	Side rail	Elm or other hardwood	2	1596	75	28
4	End rail	Elm or other hardwood	2	764	75	28
5	Centre rail	Elm or other hardwood	1	864	75	28
6	Side spacers	Elm or other hardwood	2	1600	24	4
7	End spacers	Elm or other hardwood	2	764	24	4
8	Top	Chipboard or Blockboard	1	1500	900	16 (chip) 18 (block)
9	End cap	Elm or other hardwood	2	920	75	21 (chip) 23 (block)
10	Side lipping	Elm or other hardwood	2	1500	21 or 23	10

Note: Remember the cutting list gives *finished* sizes, see Buying Timber, page 109.

Other Materials

15 cork tiles 300 × 300 × 5mm. (If the ones you buy are not 5mm thick, modify the thicknesses of the end caps and side lippings accordingly)
8mm diameter dowels 40mm long for the end caps and leg sections
10mm diameter dowels 50mm long for the main frame joints

17 right-angled steel table stretcher plates
34 × ½″ No. 8 round headed screws, black Japanned
PVA adhesive
Contact adhesive

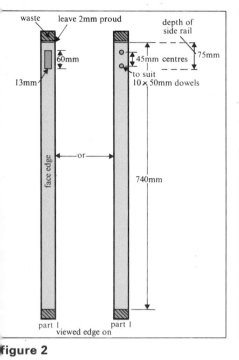

waste | leave 2mm proud

depth of side rail

60mm

13mm

45mm centres

75mm

to suit 10 × 50mm dowels

face edge

-or-

740mm

part 1 | part 1

viewed edge on

figure 2

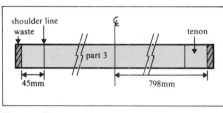

shoulder line
waste

part 3

tenon

45mm

798mm

figure 3

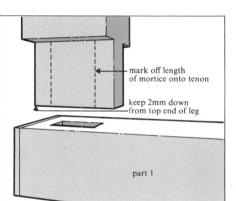

mark off length of mortice onto tenon

keep 2mm down from top end of leg

part 1

figure 4

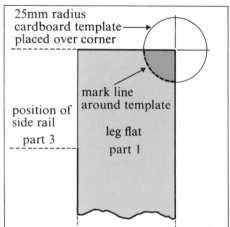

25mm radius cardboard template placed over corner

mark line around template

position of side rail

part 3

leg flat

part 1

figure 5

blocks. If you do not own long sash cramps, they may be hired quite cheaply over a weekend. See Cramps, page 127. A stick cut to the shoulder length of the side rail and placed between the bottom ends of the two legs will allow you to check whether the legs are parallel and to make a quick adjustment, if necessary, whilst cramping up.

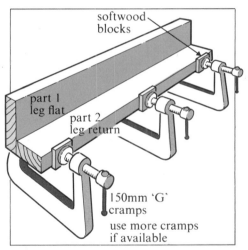

leg flat

part 1

leg return

part 2

dowel

figure 6

softwood blocks

part 1 leg flat

part 2 leg return

150mm 'G' cramps

use more cramps if available

figure 7

Now take the frame apart, carefully glue each joint and re-assemble in the cramp, again checking for squareness. Wipe away all excess glue with a damp, clean cloth. If the glue gets on to the metal of the sash cramp bar, there will be a chemical reaction which may stain the wood. To prevent this, lay a piece of paper over the cramp bar and under the joint line.

When the side frame is dry, remove from cramps and plane the exterior of the joint flush, using a sharp plane worked diagonally to the line of the joint.

Assemble the whole underframe dry, joining the two side frames together with the centre (5) and end (4) rails. Make sure the underframe is standing on a clean, level floor while you do this. Checking for square at this stage is vitally important, using a try square and a measuring stick, see Keeping Square, page 145.

When you are sure that the table is square, take it apart and glue up. Be sure to prepare everything you need for this operation in advance, because the sheer size of the table can create its own problems if everything required is not to hand. For the same reason, it is a good idea to have a friend give you a hand with putting on the cramps, checking for square and so on. Three sash cramps are used in the final assembly and they should be positioned as shown in **figure 9**, so that the top of the table is completely clear. If this is not done, you will not be able to use the stick for checking square. Two more sticks, cut to the shoulder length of the end rails (4) will be useful to ensure that the legs remain square in this dimension, **figure 9**. When

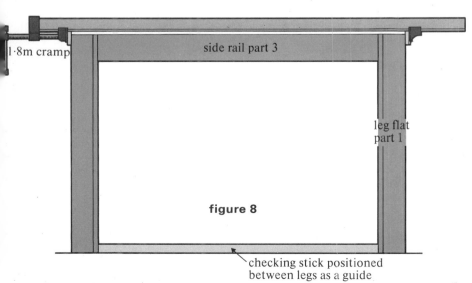

1·8m cramp

side rail part 3

leg flat part 1

figure 8

checking stick positioned between legs as a guide

Dining Table and Chairs

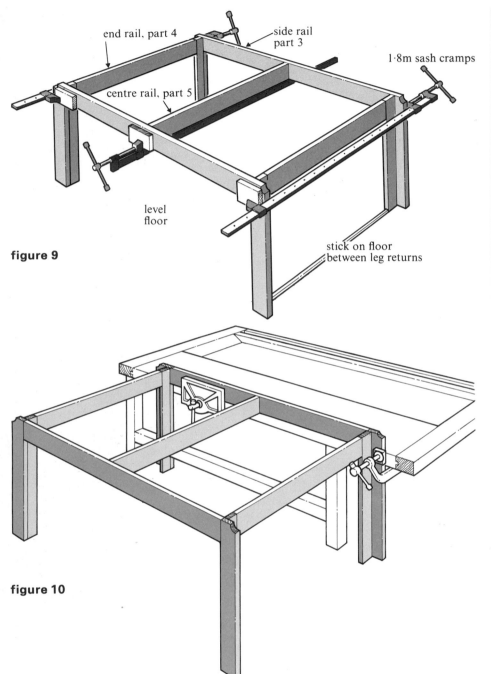

end rail, part 4

side rail
part 3

centre rail, part 5

1·8m sash cramps

level
floor

stick on floor
between leg returns

figure 9

figure 10

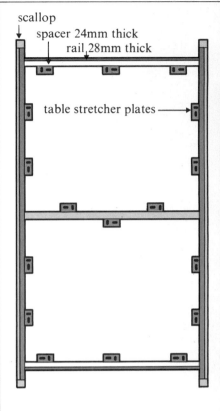

scallop

spacer 24mm thick

rail 28mm thick

table stretcher plates

figure 11
The Table Top

The top (part 8) is made from a solid piece of chipboard or blockboard 1500×900mm covered with cork tiles. Its edges are protected with solid elm end caps (9) and side lippings (10). Unless you are very experienced, buy the chipboard or blockboard finished exactly to size. Ask the supplier to make sure the edges are square.

The finished thickness of the end caps and side lippings depends on whether you use chipboard 16mm thick or blockboard 18mm thick, and on the thickness of the cork tiles. For example, if you use blockboard and the tiles are 5mm thick, then the thickness of the end caps and side lippings will be $18+5=23$mm.

The end caps are dowelled on to the ends of the top. Bore four 8mm dia. holes 20mm deep in each end of the top, equally spaced along the width, to receive these dowels.

You are now ready to cover the top with the 300mm square cork tiles. You will need 15 of these to complete the job and they are available from Do-It-Yourself shops, usually in packs of 9. The moisture content of cork varies, so you should if possible leave the tiles loose in the room where they will be used for a few days to allow them to stabilise. The day before using them, seal the upper surface of each tile with a coat of polyurethane. This will minimise swelling and subsequent shrinkage when fixed to the table top.

you are sure the frame is square, wipe off all surplus glue and leave in cramps overnight, which will give plenty of time for the glue to harden.

When the frame is dry, clean up the top surface with a plane. Try not to be too energetic about this, as too much effort can cause flexing of the frame and possible fracture of the joints. If possible, cramp the underframe to the bench, as in **figure 10**.

The next job is to attach the spacer strips—parts 6 and 7—which are used to create a visual break between the underframe and the top. This break also means that any minor variations in accuracy can be 'lost' when lining up the edge of the table top with the side of the underframe.

Glue and pin the spacer strips as shown in **figure 11**. The spacers go up as far as the scallop, so that they can help to support the end caps on the table top. As usual, be careful to wipe the work clean of all excess glue.

Figure 11 also shows the approximate positions of the 17 table stretcher plates which are used to secure the top on the underframe. **Figure 12** shows that they must be set about 1mm below the top edge of the rails, so that they will pull down the top when screwed in position.

To complete the underframe, rub down with 120, followed by 240 grit garnet paper on a softwood block. Then polish as desired. See Finishing Techniques, page 158.

Above *Brian Davey's elegant dining set seats six people in comfort. This version is made in solid elm and the top is covered with cork tiles.*

Far Left *The dining chair has an upholstered seat and back. Note that the back is upholstered on one side only.*
Left *The carver chair has a fine sturdy look to it. It is a modification of the standard chair design in which the front leg has been extended upwards and an arm added between it and the back.*

Dining Table and Chairs

Above *A handsome variation with a sol[id]
teak underframe and a teak-veneered
chipboard top. The heavy grain figure in
the underframe is unusual for teak and ha[s]
meant that the match with the top is not a[s]
good as it might have been. This could
have been avoided by buying all the
materials at the same place at the same
time. Note that if you only want to build
the table, you can still buy chairs to suit
it, as in this picture.*

Left *A practical version for children's
breakfast time with a wipe-clean plastic
laminate top. The chairs have been left
unupholstered and the seats and backs
have been covered with white gloss pain[t]*

Upholstered Wooden Seating

Upholstered Wooden Seating

Above *The two-seater from Peter Cornish's upholstered wooden range (see overleaf). It can be built by itself as a sofa, and with its small back cushions it looks good in a traditional fabric.*
Right *Detail of the arm unit fitting. Note dowel plug on the front face of the upright. This does not appear if flush mounts are used (see chapter 6).*
Far Right *The single seater is really capacious. A child could curl up in it!*

Right *Pine takes coloured wood stain very well, to give dramatic variations like this one, upholstered in canvas.*

To cover the top, use contact adhesive and lay the tiles one by one, being careful to set them flush with the edge of the top. Since you are using contact adhesive, the tile will bond to the surface immediately it touches it. To give yourself extra manoeuvrability, put a sheet of clean brown paper between the tile and the top, as in **figure 13**, and remove it gradually as you position the tile. Remove any excess adhesive with petrol or lighter fuel. Take care to avoid naked flames, otherwise all your work could be rapidly wasted! When the tiles are dry, trim off excess with a sharp craft knife, so that the edges are flush all round.

The side lippings (10) should be completely finished and sanded down at this stage. If you leave finishing till the lippings are attached to the top, you may damage the cork. Leave the lippings a little overlength, until they have been glued to the long edges. This will ensure a little more freedom to get the faces flush with the top when cramping up and will guarantee the length when trimmed off.

Apply a coat of glue carefully to each of the long sides of the top and to the unfinished face of each side lipping. Put up in cramps as shown in **figure 14**, using softwood battens to protect the lipping, and leave to dry. Take special care to see that the top edge of the lipping is exactly flush with the cork tiles. When the lippings are dry, trim off flush with the ends.

Now bore out four 8mm dowel holes 20mm deep in the end caps to match those already bored in the end of the top.

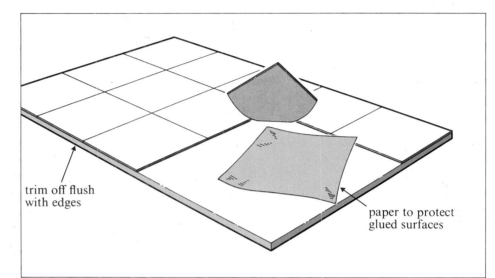

figure 13

trim off flush with edges

paper to protect glued surfaces

Mark the dowel hole positions *carefully* before drilling. These holes will be off centre because the end caps have to cover the edge of the cork *plus* the edge of the top — see **figure 15**. Again it is necessary to thoroughly finish and sand the end caps before assembly to avoid damage to the cork later. Check the joint fit while still dry, then glue up and put in cramps. These cramps will run in the opposite direction to those in **figure 14**.

When the top is dry, polish the wood to match the underframe, then apply a thin coat of polyurethane over the whole top, wood and cork together.

Final Assembly

Place a blanket or dust sheet on to the clean level workbench, or similar surface capable of supporting the whole table. Lay the top on it, face down, and then place the underframe, upside down, on to the top, Position the frame with thumb and fore-

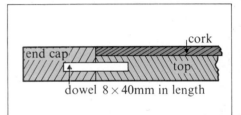

cork

end cap

top

dowel 8 × 40mm in length

figure 15

finger, evenly distributing any variations in size between the two sides. With a bradawl make shallow pilot holes in the top, using the holes in the stretcher plates as a guide. Do not make these too deep, particularly if you are using a chipboard top; there may be insufficient material for the screw to bite into. In some hardware shops you may obtain special screws for chipboard, otherwise use $\frac{1}{2}$″ No. 8 round headed screws.

Return the upright table to the floor and dust off all surfaces. The job is now complete.

figure 12

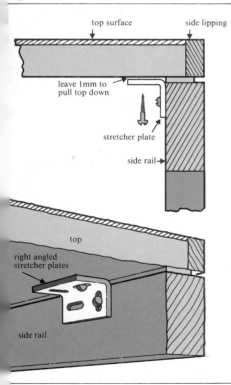

top surface   side lipping

leave 1mm to pull top down

stretcher plate

side rail

top

right angled stretcher plates

side rail

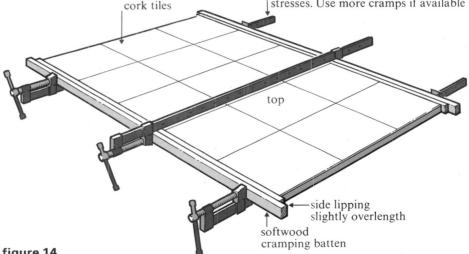

alternate sash cramps to even out stresses. Use more cramps if available

cork tiles

top

side lipping slightly overlength

softwood cramping batten

figure 14

The Dining Table and Chairs

Table Variations

These are very much a matter of personal choice and of what appearance will best suit the room where the table is to be used. Practically any hardwood can be used, from pale woods with little grain, like beech, to strongly figured woods like walnut or teak cut 'through and through'. Supplies of hardwood (and consequently prices) vary greatly over the country and it would probably be best to take the cutting list to your local timber yard to find out what woods are available and at what cost.

The table can also be happily made out of pine and this has the advantage of taking coloured wood stain well (as does beech), opening out another set of colour possibilities.

The cork tiles on the top can be replaced by any other material that takes your fancy, for example marble or 'solid' colour PVC sheet or tiles. The wooden side lippings are only there to protect the edges of the tiles and if you use other materials to cover the top, you can dispense with them. For example, there is a wide variety of veneered blockboards and chipboards available, but do make sure that you get a decent match between the veneer on the top and the hardwood for the frame, as wood colours may vary considerably. *If the side lippings are left off, increase the width of the top from 900 to 920mm.*

Another possibility is to buy plain block-board or chipboard and then to cover it with plastic laminate. This has the advantage of being tough and wipe-clean, and there are truly hundreds of colours and designs available. *The board width in this case should be 917mm*, allowing 3mm over all for the thickness of the laminate on the long edges.

The Dining Chair
Making Instructions

Bring all the components to size and mark the face edge and face side, see 'Keeping Square, page 145. *Read these instructions right through before starting work, as some parts are left temporarily overlength.* It would also be a help to read the instructions for the table if you have not made it, as many of the construction techniques are common to both table and chairs.

Side Frames

Leave the front and back legs — parts 1 and 2 — about 12mm overlength. Mark one end and square off with a try square. Measure up from this line on the face edge 357mm, which marks the bottom of the mortice, and square round. Finally measure up and mark the finished length of the leg — 430mm for the front and 775 for the back — and square round again. See **figure 17**.

The side frames are joined together with a mortice and tenon joint, see page 153. Mark out a mortice 13 × 46mm on the face edge of each leg and chop out to a depth of 64mm on the back legs and 44mm on the front legs. Now cut the legs to size, leaving about 2mm on the top of the front legs only. This will be planed off flush with the side rail after assembly. Chamfer the bottom of the legs to a depth of 2–3mm. This will prevent splitting of the wood if the chair is dragged across the floor. Place the front and back legs together in pairs. If you are making more than one chair, be careful at this stage not to get the parts mixed up.

The side rails — part 3 — should also be left about 12mm overlength. Mark the centre point of the rail and measure away

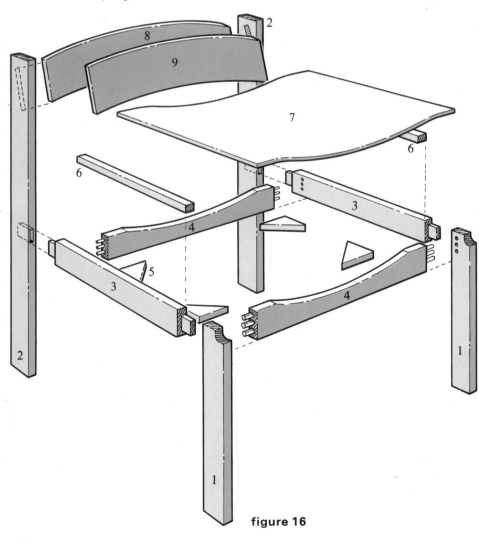

figure 16

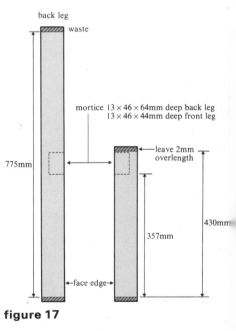

figure 17

from it to give the shoulder line and length of tenon, as shown in **figure 18**. Offer up the respective ends of the side rail to the mortices already made in the front and back legs and mark off the width of the tenons, as in **figure 4**. Cut the tenons and take off the waste at the ends. Number each mortice and tenon 1–1, 2–2 and so on, to aid identification later.

Once you have made all four joints, assemble the left and right side frames dry, following the numbers on the joints. Check for fit and squareness. If the joints are satisfactory, take the frame apart.

Before gluing up the side frame there is one more job to do, that is to cut the mortice on the inside of the back leg. This will receive the plywood back (8) at a later stage. It is best to do it now, as the assembled side frame is too cumbersome to manage later.

Measure 130mm down from the top of the leg on the inside face and 12mm in from the face edge (front), to mark the lower front corner of the mortice, as in **figure 19**. Place a second mark 32mm down from the top and 27mm in from the face edge and join the two points with a sliding bevel, see page 135. Mark the width of the mortice using an 8mm chisel and draw another line for the other side of the mortice using the same bevel setting, then square off at each end. Chop out the mortice to 16mm depth.

It is very important to mark each of the pair of back legs Left and Right and to make sure the mortices slope the right way — they should be mirror images of each other — otherwise it will be impossible to fit the back during final assembly.

You can now go on to assemble the side frames. Carefully glue both parts of the joint with PVA adhesive and set up each side

figure 19

figure 20

27mm
12mm
32mm
130mm

back leg
part 2

← face edge

2mm on front
legs only

side rail
part 3

← face edges

figure 18

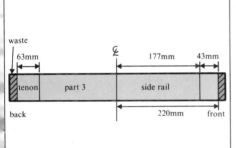

waste
63mm
₵
177mm
43mm

tenon | part 3 | side rail
back
220mm
front

4mm ply skin
to former

← centre line

figure 21

620mm   550mm

space out
intermediate
members equally

side member

halving
joints

figure 22

Cutting List. See figure 16

No.	Part	Material	Qty	Length	Width	Thickness
1	Front leg	Elm or other hardwood	2	430	64	21
1A	Carver front leg	Elm or other hardwood	2	574	EX150	21
1B	Carver arm	Elm or other hardwood	2	347	36	21
2	Back leg	Elm or other hardwood	2	775	64	21
3	Side rail	Elm or other hardwood	2	440	64	21
4	Front and back rails	Elm or other hardwood	2	450	76	21
5	Corner block	Elm or other hardwood (triangular)	4	75	75	21
6	Seat batten	Elm or other hardwood	2	285	21	21
7	Seat lamina	Plywood	3	496	380	4
8	Back lamina	Plywood	3	486	140	4
9	Back pad	Plywood	1	450	140	4

Note: Remember the cutting list gives *finished* sizes only, see Buying Timber, page 109.

Other Materials

Rubber carpet underlay 495 × 380 × 6mm for seat pad

Fabric 595 × 480mm for seat cover

8 × 1¼" No. 8 countersunk steel woodscrews for attaching seat to battens

8 × 2" No. 10 countersunk steel woodscrews for corner blocks

¼" blue steel tacks or staples for upholstering

PVA glue

Contact adhesive

frame in a sash cramp, as in **figure 20**. Be careful to wipe off all excess glue with a clean damp rag, or it will spoil the finish later.

When the glue has set, remove the assembled side frame from cramps and if necessary plane the joints flush, working diagonally to the joint line. Now secure the side frame vertically in a bench vice and plane off the 2mm waste from the top of the front leg, so that it is flush with the top of the side rail. Lastly, cut out the scallop from the top of the front leg, using a 50mm dia. cardboard template, as described for the table leg on page 52.

Seat and Back Former

The seat and back have a built-in curve, and to make them you will need the former shown in **figure 21**, built from 25mm softwood, shaped and covered with a 4mm ply skin. The overall dimensions of the former are given in **figure 22**. The softwood members which cross over each other use

The Dining Table and Chairs

halving joints, page 149, and the frame round the outside uses pinned and glued butt joints, page 147.

The curved members of the former must be cut from pieces of softwood 550×75mm using a bow saw, coping saw or powered jig. The pattern for the curve is given in **figure 23**. Rule up your piece of softwood in a 25mm square grid then carefully copy on to it the full size shape of the curved member, square by square, from **figure 23**. You need only go through this procedure once: after that you can use the member you have already cut out as a pattern to trace out the remaining three shapes. When you have cut out all 4 curved pieces, hold them together in a vice or in G cramps and lightly sand them down till they all have exactly the same contour.

Now turn your attention to the five pressure bearers. These are 640mm lengths of 65×45mm softwood which are used to hold the back or seat in the curve of the former while the glue is drying, as shown in **figure 24**. The bearers overhang the former by 10mm at each end. Measure in 20mm from each end of the bearers and drill a hole to clear a No. 10 screw.

The last job is to cover the top of the former. Use a 620×550mm sheet of 4mm plywood and pin and glue this to the former, starting at the centre line and moving outwards. Make sure the grain direction of the plywood allows for the curve, as shown in **figure 25**. The pressure bearers come in useful to hold the top of the former in its curve while the glue is drying. Lay each of the bearers in position and mark through the screw holes on to the ply. Drill 2mm dia. pilot holes in the former with a hand drill or bradawl, then screw the bearers to the former, using 3½″ No. 10 wood screws.

When the glue is dry, remove the bearers and check that no pin heads are protruding

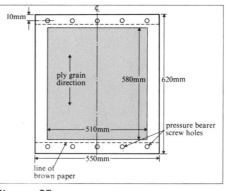

figure 25

from the surface of the ply. If so, punch down and fill them. Sand the finished former to remove all blemishes which could damage the surface of the back or seat when the former is in use. Finally draw a line along the centre of the curve, as in **figure 21**.

Constructing the Seat Back

The seat and back are made together from 3 sheets of 4mm plywood 580×510mm laminated together with PVA adhesive. The backs are simply made by cutting off a panel 150mm wide after gluing. The waste at the other end of the laminate is used as a curve pattern for the front and back rails, **figure 27**.

Make sure the grain is running in the correct direction in each sheet of ply and mark each with a centre line as in **figure 25**. Cut a sheet of clean brown paper 595 × 550mm and lay it on the top of the former, to protect it from glue. Take the first sheet of ply and liberally cover the whole of one surface with PVA adhesive, then lay it on top of the brown paper, keeping clear of the screw holes and matching up with the centre line on the former, **figure 25**. Repeat with

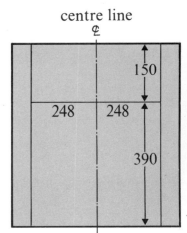

figure 26

each sheet of ply until you have a sandwich of three pieces lying on top of each other. Now cramp the ply down over the curve using the pressure bearers, working out from the centre and making sure the sheets stay square with each other. Use 3½″ No. 10 screws for this operation. Leave to set.

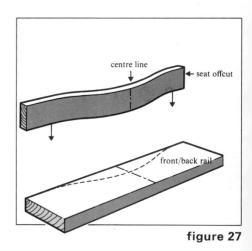

figure 27

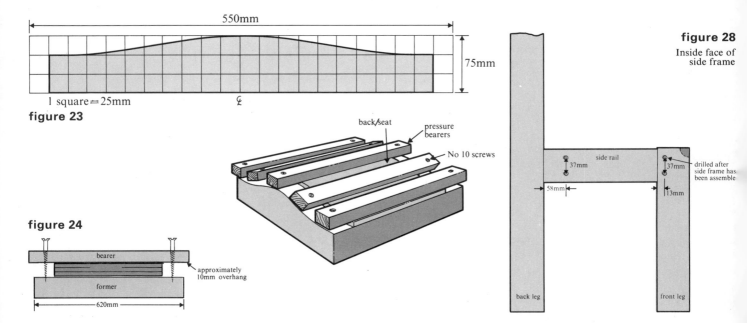

figure 23

1 square = 25mm

figure 24

bearer

former

approximately 10mm overhang

620mm

back/seat

pressure bearers

No 10 screws

figure 28

Inside face of side frame

side rail

37mm

58mm

37mm

13mm

drilled after side frame has been assemble

back leg

front leg

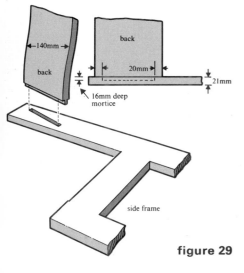

figure 29

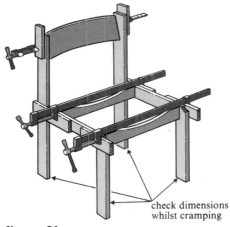

figure 31

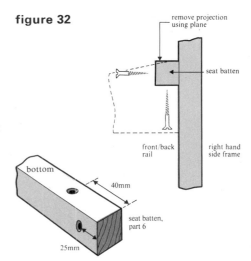

figure 32

Having removed the curved panel from the former, you now have to cut the seat and back to size. Start by measuring out 248mm, to one side from the centre line, as shown in **figure 26**. Plane this edge square and parallel to the centre line, checking frequently with a try square. From this face edge, square across, mark and saw along the cutting lines to give rough cut pieces 150mm and 390mm long respectively, **figure 26**.

The rough cut seat and back must now be brought to the finished sizes of 486×140mm for the back and 496×380mm for the seat. In each case start by planing one of the long edges at 90° to the face edge to give a reference point. Measure and mark the width from this edge and plane to size. Note that the 248mm dimension is exactly half the finished length of the seat but that the back is slightly shorter.

Remove all sharp edges, using garnet paper and a sanding block unless you intend to veneer the chair (see later) when the edges should be left square. Do not remove the centre line marks.

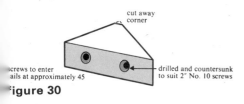

figure 30

Final Assembly

The front and back rails—part 4—need to be curved to accept the seat which rests upon them. See **figure 16**. Take the front and back rails already cut to length and mark a centre line on each. Offer up to each the curved pattern piece cut off from the laminated plywood, matching centre line with centre line as shown in **figure 27**. Mark the curve with a pencil and cut out with a coping or bow saw or an electric jigsaw. Finish off to the line with a spokeshave.

The front and back rails are connected to the side frames with a dowel joint, page 150. Mark out the dowel hole positions on the side frame as shown in **figure 28** and drill them out to a depth of 16mm using an 8mm bit. Transfer the same positions to the ends of the front and back rails and drill out to a depth of 25mm. Use a dowel jig if possible.

Now cut tenons in the ends of the ply back to fit the mortices in the back legs, offering up the tenon to the mortice as you did for the side frame, **figures 4** and **29**. *Be careful to cut each tenon 20mm up from the bottom edge of the back,* or the back will not be level when you assemble the chair, **figure 29**.

Drill and countersink two holes to suit No. 10 screws in each of the corner blocks (5) as shown in **figure 30**.

Now assemble the whole chair dry, working on a flat, level bench or table, and using sash cramps with softwood blocks as shown in **figure 31**. With the feet square on the level surface, check all internal angles for squareness.

When you are sure all is square, dismantle the chair, then carefully re-assemble it, gluing each joint with PVA adhesive as you go. Check again for squareness with a measuring stick and adjust as necessary, see Keeping Square, page 145. Wipe off all excess glue with a clean damp rag. Leave in cramps overnight.

Cut the seat batten (6) to length and drill and countersink two screw holes 25mm from each end (to hold the batten to the chair frame) and two more 40mm from the end (to hold the seat to the batten) as shown in **figure 32**. Hold the batten in position between the front and back rails, and you will see that there is a corner of the batten projecting, owing to the curvature of the rail—**figure 32**. Mark the curve with a pencil and plane the batten down to the line before fixing with 1¼" No. 8 countersunk steel screws.

To complete the chair frame, rub down with 120 grit and finally 220/240 grit garnet paper, all those areas exposed, and particularly those seen and polished. Always sand *with* the grain, never across, as the scratches will show after polishing. A sharp cabinet scraper can be useful for getting into corners. Finish the chair frame as desired.

Seat and Back Pads

Read the relevant part of the Upholstery section, page 162, before starting work.

The seat is covered with rubber underlay and fabric before it is screwed to the frame, whereas the back pad is made up on a 4mm ply base, then stuck to the chair back with contact adhesive. This is to conceal the ragged edges of the fabric.

Seat. Chamfer all round the top edges of the seat panel with plane and sand paper. Cut the rubber underlay exactly to size and coat its jute undersurface and the top surface of the seat panel with contact adhesive. When the adhesive has had time to go off, stick the underlay to the seat panel, using a sheet of brown paper to aid manoeuvrability as described for the table top. Trim off any excess underlay with a sharp knife.

Lay the fabric face downwards on the bench and place the seat upside-down on top of it. Pull the fabric taut with both hands along the centre of the curve, **figure 33**, and tack or staple in position. Now pull the opposite two sides taut and fix these in position. Moving outwards from these centre points, tack each of the flaps alternately, keeping the tension even throughout, **figure 34**.

At the corners, pull both flaps together and at the same time inwards, towards the centre of the seat, as in **figure 35**. Secure either side of the fold with a tack or staple and cut away the excess fabric, being careful to leave enough fabric to cover the corner itself. If a stapler is used, apply a few staples diagonally across the join, neatly securing the rest of the fabric to the underside of the seat. Repeat at all four corners.

The Dining Table and Chairs

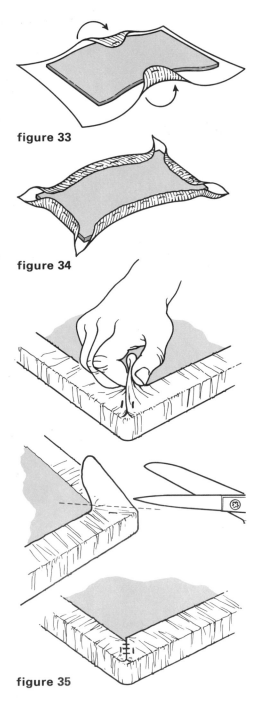

figure 33

figure 34

figure 35

Place the upholstered seat on the chair frame and, using 1¼" No. 8 countersunk screws, secure in position by screwing up through the seat battens.

Back Pad. Upholster the 4mm ply back pad (9) in the same way as the seat, making sure the grain of the ply runs across the short width of the piece to allow for bending, but using contact adhesive throughout, rather than tacks or staples. The fabric is glued in turn both to the face of the underlay and to the back of the ply. The ply should be flexed when the fabric is applied, so as to create tension when it tries to return to its normal state. In this way it will imitate more closely the curve of the chair back.

When the pad is dry, apply contact adhesive to the back of the chair and to the ply surface of the pad. When the adhesive is touch dry carefully apply the pad as in **figure 36**, using even pressure with the palm of the hand until all edges are well laid.

Chair Variations

As in the case of the table, a very wide variation of appearance is possible. The seat can be covered in any heavy duty fabric or PVC material — or if you are feeling very proud, you can be extravagant and use leather. Alternatively there is no need to upholster the seat and back; the chairs to match the pine and white table (see photograph, page 56), were finished with white gloss paint. If you choose a pre-veneered board for your table top, you may wish to use a matching veneer on the chair seat and back. This is applied early on, when you are laminating the seat and back from ply sheets. Insert previously cut and jointed pieces of veneer between the brown paper and the first sheet of ply, **figure 37**. This can be glued in exactly the same way and trimmed back afterwards. For the chair back, it will be necessary to lay a second piece of veneer between the last sheet of the ply and another sheet of brown paper. Put a last sheet of 4mm ply on top of this to protect the veneer and spread the pressure from the bearers evenly. This sheet can be used again.

In order to cover the ply laminations along the edge of the back and seat, veneer can be applied using urea formaldehyde one-shot glue and a hot iron. Pre-glued edging strips should be available from the supplier of the pre-veneered board and is 'ironed on' in much the same way. Because of the curve it may be easier to use ordinary veneer and glue, as a wider strip can then be applied and trimmed after. Use brown paper between the edge veneer and the iron.

Carver Chair

See **figure 38** and colour photograph page 55.

A carver is simply a dining chair with arms, obtained in this case by extending the front leg upwards. The scallop at the top of the front leg disappears and is blended into the line of the arm, **figure 39**.

The carver front leg—part 1A—is cut from a 21mm board apx. 575×150mm, **figure 41**, and extra material is also required for part 1B, the carver arm. To make the carver front leg, rule a grid with 25mm squares on to the 600×150mm board, then carefully copy the pattern from **figure 41** on to it square by square. Pin the board for the other arm to it through the waste, then cut out the two arms together with a bow saw, coping saw or powered jig saw. Finish off with a small block plane and spokeshave before sanding. When finished

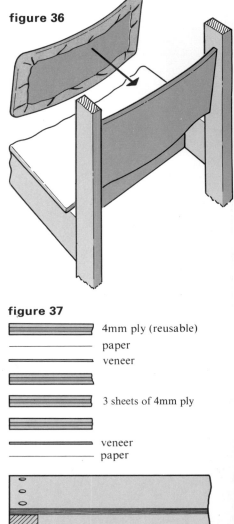

figure 36

figure 37

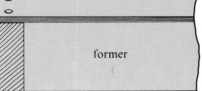

	4mm ply (reusable)
	paper
	veneer
	3 sheets of 4mm ply
	veneer
	paper

former

figure 38

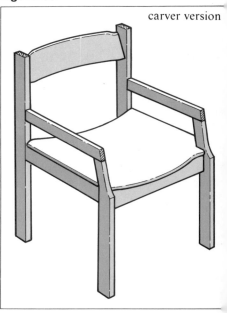

carver version

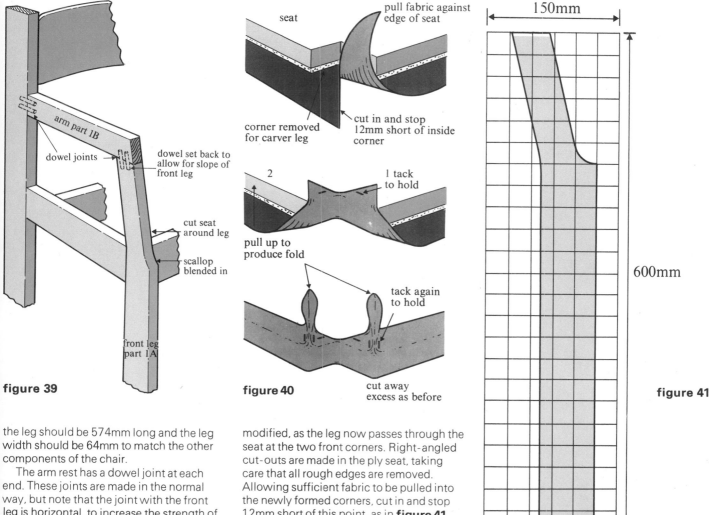

figure 39

labels in figure 39: arm part 1B · dowel joints · dowel set back to allow for slope of front leg · cut seat around leg · scallop blended in · front leg part 1A

figure 40

labels in figure 40: seat · pull fabric against edge of seat · corner removed for carver leg · cut in and stop 12mm short of inside corner · 2 · 1 tack to hold · pull up to produce fold · tack again to hold · cut away excess as before

figure 41

labels in figure 41: 150mm · 600mm · 64mm · 1 square = 25mm

the leg should be 574mm long and the leg width should be 64mm to match the other components of the chair.

The arm rest has a dowel joint at each end. These joints are made in the normal way, but note that the joint with the front leg is horizontal, to increase the strength of the arm. When the arm rest is jointed in position, you will have to plane off the top corner to maintain the line of the leg, so be careful to set the front dowel back from the edge far enough to allow for this. See **figure 39**.

The upholstery will also have to be modified, as the leg now passes through the seat at the two front corners. Right-angled cut-outs are made in the ply seat, taking care that all rough edges are removed. Allowing sufficient fabric to be pulled into the newly formed corners, cut in and stop 12mm short of this point, as in **figure 41**. Pull the fabric in towards the centre against the edge of the ply and staple or tack in position. Repeat with the opposite flap, again pulling hard to keep a clean line. Staple the two external corners, cut off the waste and staple down as described earlier for the dining chair seat.

Peter Cornish

The aim of this design was to produce a simple upholstered chair which could be extended to a two- or even three-seater arrangement and which, although of very basic construction, would not look downright primitive — a strong possibility when the designer is striving at all costs to eliminate 'the tricky bits'.

The result is a tough yet comfortable range of seating that will stand up to the knocks of life with a young family. We made it in natural pine with blue denim cushions, but it looks good in any fresh-coloured fabric or print and the pine can be stained any colour you wish. Another variation, I fancy, is a work or gaffer's chair in natural canvas, entirely covered in pockets and loops, to carry all the paraphernalia of a hobby.

Single Chair
Making Instructions

Read these instructions carefully all the way through before starting work.

Start by building the basic frame shown in **figure 2**. Cut the four legs—part 1—to length and mark the face side and face edge, page 142. Measure down from the top of each leg 510mm and mark and square round. This is the line at which the top edge of the seat rail—part 2—meets the leg. Carefully mark out and bore three 9mm diameter holes 28mm deep for the dowel joints, see page 150; using a dowel jig if possible. Number the joints 1—1, 2—2 and so on as you go, as shown in **figure 2**. This will help you 'keep your place' during final assembly.

Assemble the frame dry, check for square and that the outside surfaces of the joints are flush. If all is well, dismantle and clean up all inside surfaces with medium grit sandpaper on a softwood block. It is also a good idea at this stage to chamfer off the outside

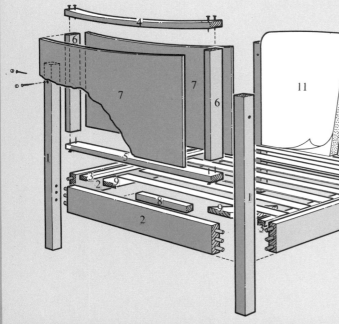

figure 1

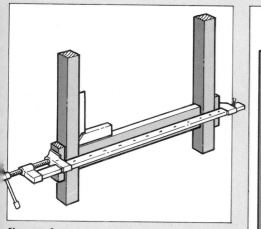

figure 4

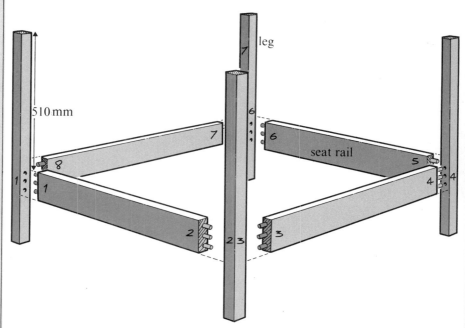

510 mm

leg

seat rail

figure 2

corners of the legs and the ends of the seat rails, using a sharp plane. This 'expresses the joint' as shown in **figure 3** and helps to disguise any slight inaccuracy and any subsequent timber shrinkage.

If you have only two sash cramps available, assemble the basic frame in two stages. First glue up and cramp opposite pairs of legs with their seat rail as shown in **figure 4**. Check carefully for squareness with a try square. When the glue has set, remove from cramps, then glue and sash cramp the remaining two seat rails between these end frames to assemble the complete frame. Again check for square, using a

diagonal measuring stick, see Keeping Square, page 145. While the frame is still in cramps, glue and screw in position the four corner blocks part 9. Note that these are set down 23mm from the top edge of the seat

rails to leave room for the webbing supports, **figure 5**.

When the frame is out of cramps, screw and glue in position the two side seat fillets, part 8, using two 1½" No. 8 screws each. They lie flush with the top edge of the seat rails as shown in **figure 5**.

Before installing the seat fillets, you should bore the 4mm diameter hole for the screw which will later fix the arm in position. This is counter sunk and don't forget to position the side fillet with the countersink on the underside. Similarly there are two countersunk holes in the back webbing support to fix the back sub-frame.

figure 3

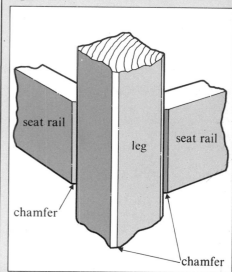

seat rail

leg

seat rail

chamfer

chamfer

Cutting List. See figure 1

No.	Part	Material	Qty	Length	Width	Thickness
1	Leg	Softwood (Pine)	4	760	45	45
2	Seat rail	Softwood (Pine)	4	610	95	22
3	Webbing support	Hardwood (Pref. beech or birch)	2	600	45	22
4	Arm and back frame top	Softwood	3	605	EX150	22
5	Arm and back frame bottom	Softwood	3	605	45	22
6	Arm and back frame sides	Softwood	6	464	45	22
7	Arm and back frame cladding	Hardboard	6	620	508	3
8	Seat side fillets	Softwood	2	200	22	22
9	Corner blocks	Softwood	4	150	45	22
10	Seat cushion	D10 polyether foam	1	650	600	125
11	Arm and back cushion	D7 polyether foam	3	1065	610	25

Note: Remember that the cutting list gives *finished* sizes only, see Buying Timber, page 109.

Other Materials

1 bag polyether foam crumble
to fill loose back cushion

24 × 9mm multigroove beech dowels, 50mm long

3 pieces fabric 1100 × 660mm (finished size including seam allowance)
to cover the arm and back

1 piece of fabric 600 × 1550mm (finished size including seam allowance)
to cover the seat cushion

2 pieces fabric 650 × 125mm (finished size including seam allowance)
for the seat cushion borders

1 piece of fabric 400 × 650mm (finished size including seam allowance)
to make the loose back cushion

Staple gun and staples (or use tacks)

14 × 1½" No. 8 countersunk steel screws
16 × 2" No. 10 countersunk steel screws
¾" upholstery tacks
5m × 50mm standard rubber webbing

All on one roll

Upholstered Wooden Furniture

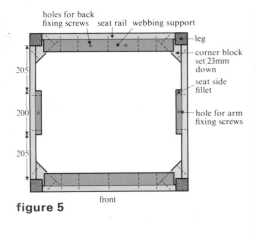

figure 5

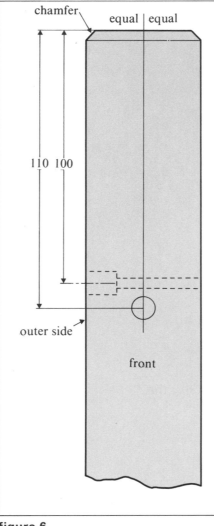

figure 6

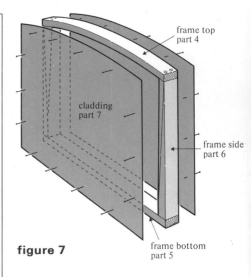

figure 7

Now screw and glue the front and back webbing supports – part 3 – flush with the top of the seat rails, using five 2″ No. 8 screws each. The supports should be well rounded on the inside top edge and will hold tacks better if they are made from beech, birch or similarly dense hardwood.

The last job, before finishing the frame, is to make the counterbored holes, at the top of each leg, through which the back and arms will be screwed and firmly held in place. Mark the centre line of the leg and measure down 110mm on the front and back faces of the legs and 100mm down on the side faces of the back legs. The reason for this is shown in **figure 6**. Two screws pass through the back legs—one to hold the back and one to hold the arm. Obviously if they were at the same height, they would collide with each other. Bore each hole with a 9mm wood bit to a depth of 12mm. Then with a 4mm twist drill, pick up the centre of the larger diameter hole and continue to drill right through the leg.

After rubbing down the whole frame with a fine glass paper and making a chamfer around the tops and bottoms of the legs **figure 6**, give the whole frame a sealer coat of polyurethane lacquer, using a clean one inch brush. When perfectly dry, rub down again with some spent paper to take off any knibs and apply the second coat, leaving in a dust-free area to dry.

Arm and Back Frames

The arm and back units are identical in shape and size, so for an armchair you will need to make three similar frames, the structure of which is shown in **figure 7**.

The only tricky job is making the curved top – part 4. To do this, take a 22mm thick softwood board 600×150mm and mark it up with a grid of 50mm squares. Then carefully copy the curved shape of the top rail from **figure 8** on to the wood. Secure the board to a bench with G cramps, leaving the marked shape projecting over the edge, then cut out with a coping saw or preferably

an electric jigsaw or a drill with a jigsaw attachment.

Once you have cut out the first curved top piece, it can be used as a template for the others. Simply place on a wide board of 22mm thick softwood and trace out the shapes with a pencil, nesting them together for economy, **figure 9**. This is particularly useful if you are making the 2-seater as well as the armchair, when you will need a total of seven curved pieces.

Using the top and bottom rails, parts 4 and 5 and the sides, part 6, screw and glue together as shown in **figure 7**. When you have completed the frame, you will notice that the top of the side pieces juts out on the inside surface, because the top rail curves away from it. Remove this with a plane, as shown in **figure 10**.

1 square = 50mm   **figure 8**

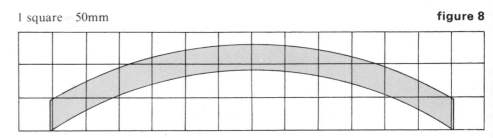

figure 9

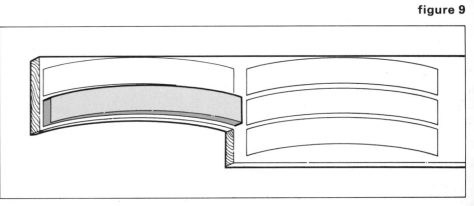

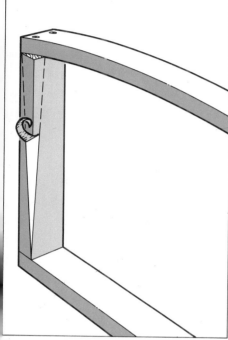

figure 10

The completed frame will still be 'wobbly' and will easily go out of square. Normally when you are cladding a frame like this, you can use the cladding to hold the frame square. This is not possible here because of the curve at the top, so you will need to build a simple jig. Take any piece of spare timber or chipboard about 800mm square and nail to it two 25×50mm softwood battens, exactly 464mm long with their outside edges

exactly 605mm apart. It is important to get these dimensions right.

The frame fits over the jig as shown in **figure 11**. The jig holds the frame square while you pin and glue on to it the hardboard cladding (7). This is best accomplished by pinning first along the flat bottom edge and then working outward from the centre point of the curved rail, finishing by running down each of the straight sides. Because it has to allow for the curve at the top, the hardboard will be oversize at the bottom. Trim off the surplus with a tenon saw.

Having clad the outside face, remove the frame from the jig and clad the inner face in a similar way, starting with the bottom row of pins. Press the hardboard down to meet the curved rail at its centre point and work towards its end. As pinning proceeds, roll the frame along its top curved rail. This will ensure it is supported by the bench and also that the pins are square to the face in the particular area being worked.

Finish by pinning along both sides, trim off surplus hardboard and chamfer all edges. The once flimsy frame, like the seven stone weakling, will now be seen to have gained quite incredible strength.

Webbing the Seat

When the frame is dry, and not before, web the seat using standard grade 50mm rubber webbing. Webs should be placed 25mm apart across the seat area. Obviously you will need to put some tension on the webs if

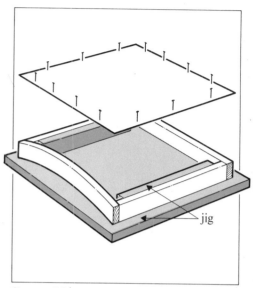

figure 11

they are to support someone sitting down. Most makes of webbing recommend 10% pre-tension.

Start by tacking the free end of the webbing to the rear web support bar, **figure 12a**. Note how the tacks are patterned to spread the load on the web evenly. Now pull the webbing over to the front web support and tack loosely. Measure the web up to the inside of the seat rail — it should be around 600mm and you want 10% pre-tension, so reduce the 600mm by 60mm to 540mm and make a mark. Now pull the web taut until this mark touches the inner edge of the front web support and tack the web down firmly **figure 12b.** Cut the rubber flush with the seat rail **figure 12c**. Continue this he-man stuff until all eight webs are in place.

Foaming the Arms and Back

Let us now embark upon the magic of upholstery. See Upholstery Section, page 162.

Take one of the arm and back cushions (11) and lay it flat on the bench. It is best if it is a little oversize at this stage — say 1100×660mm. Coat one side evenly with a contact adhesive. Using the same adhesive also coat the inside, outside and top faces of one arm frame. Leave the adhesive to go off according to maker's instructions.

When both surfaces are touch dry, lay the arm frame on one end of the foam, its concave face up and towards the centre of the foam, leaving 25mm margin around the sides. Rock the frame from side to side, as shown in **figure 13**, to make the foam stick to its convex face.

When that has stuck, gently fold the foam over the frame without stretching it and press it down over the concave face. Finally trim the foam flush with the edges of the frame. This is the moment to buy the wife that long promised electric meat knife, but if this is not possible an ordinary bread

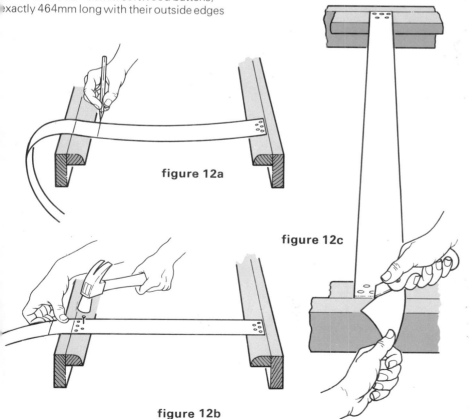

figure 12a

figure 12c

figure 12b

Upholstered Wooden Furniture

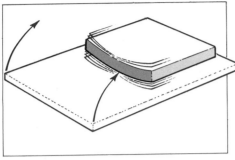

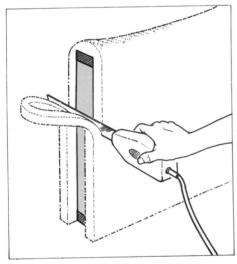

figure 13

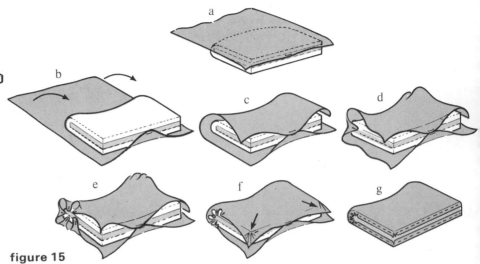

figure 15

knife with a toothed blade will have to do. In either case trim the foam flush by holding the blade flat against the sides of the frame, as in **figure 14**. Repeat for the other two frames.

figure 14

Covering the Arms and Back

You will probably have bought the fabric for the arms, back and two seat cushions all in one roll. Clear the bench of all glue pots, clagging sticks and ticky-tacky. Cover it with clean brown paper and unroll the fabric. Mark with chalk a rectangle 1100 × 660mm. When cut off the roll, this piece of fabric will cover one of the arm/back frames in a similar way to the foam and will be stapled or tacked to the sides and bottom edge of the frame.

Lay the foam-covered frame on the bench, concave side down and top edge away from you. Lay the fabric over the frame face side up, and line up one of the short edges with the bottom edge of the frame. Let it overlap by 25mm and hold it with one staple in the centre of the bottom edge, as in **figure 15a**.

Brush the fabric with the palm of the hand up towards the curved top of the frame, turn it over and continue to brush the fabric down the inner concave face to the bottom rail, whilst keeping the fabric edges parallel with the edges of the frame, **15b**. Put another staple at the centre of the bottom rail to hold fabric position and tension, **15c**.

Now, taking the loose fabric at the end of the top curve, pull this down and hold with one vertical staple, **15d**. Continue to work out the fullness of the cover at each end of the top by taking small pleats or tucks and stapling them down in a radial pattern, which allows closer packing of staples, **15e**.

When you have done both ends of the top and before you work down the sides, strain the cover out towards each bottom corner at 45° and tack down, **15f**. Only now can the side edges of the fabric be pulled round the sides of the frame with *even* tension and stapled off. Uneven tension will result in 'tack bites' or dimples along the edges. You can give the fabric a more even strain by 'friction tensioning' it with the whole hand held flat against the fabric.

Finally, staple along the bottom edges, **15g**. You may find it necessary to remove staples initially placed at the centre points. All surplus fabric should be trimmed close.

Fitting the Arms and Back

When you have upholstered both arms and the back, you are ready to move on to fitting them into the main frame. If you were not

figure 16

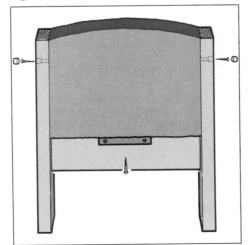

careful to make the main frame square, this is where you will find difficulty!

Hold one of the arms at an outward angle from the main frame and locate its bottom corners between the front and back leg at seat height. Holding the arm firmly between the legs, swing it up into a vertical position, so that its back and front edges are flush with the inside and outside faces of the legs and its bottom edge flush with the side rail. Without moving the arm frame, insert a bradawl through the front leg counterbored hole and bore a pilot hole in the side of the arm frame. Follow this up with a 1½" No. 8 screw and screw firmly in position. Repeat at the back and finally up through the seat side fillet (8) as shown in **figure 16**.

figure 17

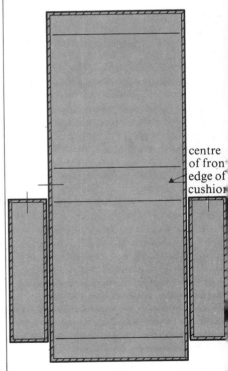

centre of front edge of cushion

This procedure should be repeated for the remaining arm and back. Plug the screw holes in the legs with pieces of 9mm dowel 12mm long glued in position. Trim the dowel end flush with the leg face using a sharp plane and sandpaper, then touch up the finish with polyurethane lacquer.

Its a good idea to tuck a piece of card between the leg and the upholstery to prevent the polyurethane getting on to the fabric. Any fabric caught between the arm/back and the main frame should be tucked in neatly with a bodkin, or failing this a blunt table knife.

Making the Seat Cushions

Take the polyether seat cushion—part 10—and check between the arms and back, where it should be found to fit with a compression of approx. 10mm side to side. The next job is to make its cover. Lay out the fabric face down and mark on its back face a rectangle exactly the width and length of the foam. Add another length of the foam and two thicknesses, as shown in **figure 17** adding another 5mm all round. These dimensions will give a good tight fit when 10mm allowance is taken at the sewing stage (see later).

Cut out the side borders the same dimensions as the side section of the cushion. Measure the centre point of the front edge of the foam cushion and mark it on the front panel of the cover and on the borders, as shown in **figure 17**. This will allow you to line up the fabric pieces correctly.

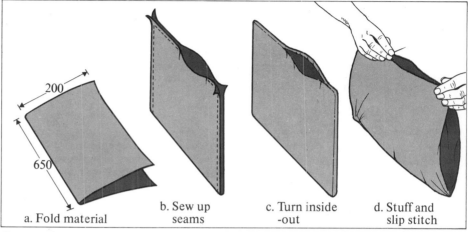

a. Fold material
b. Sew up seams
c. Turn inside-out
d. Stuff and slip stitch

figure 18

Pin the pieces of the cover together inside out in their final relationship and sew together on a machine inside the 10mm seam allowance, using a stitch length something between 8–10 stitches to the inch. Leave the back end open.

With the cover fresh from the sewing machine still inside out, locate its front corners on to the front corners of the foam block, then gradually pull the fabric case over the foam, turning the case face side out as you cover the foam. If all has gone according to plan, the cover will be tight and will take a little time and effort to fit. The case is finished by slip stitching along the centre line of the back edge. Slip stitch, page 165. This will give you the opportunity to remove any slack in the fabric as the case is closed.

The loose back cushion is made from a piece of fabric 400 × 650mm. Fold the fabric face side in, as shown in **figure 18**, and sew up, leaving a gap of about 100mm at the top. Turn this sewn envelope inside out, to reveal the face side of the fabric and stuff it with loose crumble foam, which may be bought for exactly this purpose. Close the gap with slip stitching.

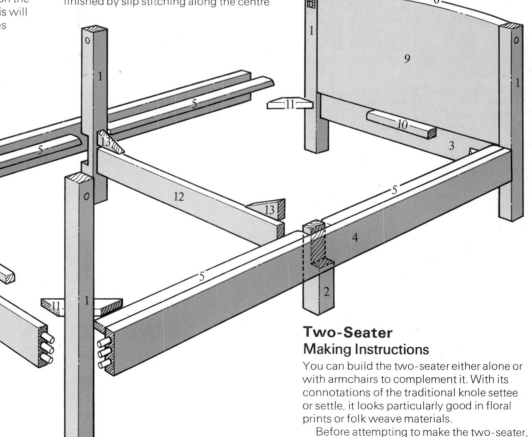

Two-Seater
Making Instructions

You can build the two-seater either alone or with armchairs to complement it. With its connotations of the traditional knole settee or settle, it looks particularly good in floral prints or folk weave materials.

Before attempting to make the two-seater, read carefully through the instructions for

figure 19

71

Upholstered Wooden Furniture

Cutting List. See figure 19.

No.	Part	Material	Qty	Length	Width	Thickness
1	Long leg	Softwood (pine)	5	760	45	45
2	Short leg	Softwood (pine)	1	248	45	45
3	Side seat rails	Softwood (pine)	2	610	95	22
4	Front/back seat rails	Softwood (pine)	2	1265	95	22
5	Webbing supports	Hardwood	4	600	45	22
6	Arm/back frame top	Softwood	4	605	EX150	22
7	Arm/back frame bottom	Softwood	4	605	45	22
8	Arm/back frame sides	Softwood	8	464	45	22
9	Arm/back frame cladding	Hardboard	8	620	508	3
10	Seat side fillets	Softwood	2	200	22	22
11	Corner blocks	Softwood	4	150	45	22
12	Centre stretch rail	Softwood	1	610	75	22
13	Centre braces	Softwood Triangular	2	90	50	22
14	Seat cushion	D10 polyether foam	2	650	645	125
15	Arm/back cushion	D7 polyether foam	4	1065	610	25

Note: Remember that the cutting list gives *finished* sizes only, see Buying Timber, page 109.

Other Materials

28 × 9mm diameter multigroove dowels, 50mm long

23 × 1½″ No. 8 countersunk steel screws

18 × 2″ No. 10 countersunk steel screws

¾″ upholstery tacks

Staple gun and staples (or use tacks)

2 prs. flush mounts

10m × 50mm standard rubber webbing

2 bags polyether crumble foam for loose back cushions

4 pieces of fabric 1100 × 660mm (finished size) to cover the arms and backs

2 pieces of fabric 600 × 1550 (fin) to cover the seat cushions

4 pieces of fabric 650 × 125mm (fin) for the seat cover borders

2 pieces of fabric 400 × 650 (fin) to make the loose back cushion covers

Finished sizes include seam allowance

All on one roll

the armchair, as the method is almost exactly the same. The only additions are an extra long leg, a short leg and a centre stretch rail to support the increased length.

Start by making two end frames comprising two long legs (part 1) and a side seat rail (part 3) using dowel joints as for the armchair. Cut a lap joint, see page 148, on the front of the short leg (part 2) as shown in **figure 20** and screw and glue it to the centre point of the front seat rail (4). Cut a housing joint, see page 148, in the back surface of the remaining long leg (1) and screw and glue this to the centre point of the back seat rail. Make dowel joints, page 150, between the inside surfaces of the long and short legs and the centre stretch rail (12). Dowel holes should be 9mm diameter and 28mm deep. Glue and sash cramp these pieces to form an H shape, **figure 21**.

When the H shape is dry, glue and cramp on the two end frames you have already made, using dowel joints again. While the frame is still in cramps, screw in the webbing supports (5), with their inside edges well rounded, the seat side fillets (10), the corner blocks (11) and the centre braces (13). Web the seat as for the chair, using 16 lengths of standard rubber webbing.

Prepare and finish the timber as for the armchair, making counterbored holes in the long legs for both arms and one back. Make four of the upholstered arm/back frames as for the chair and screw both arms and one

back in position. It is not possible to screw mount the remaining back, as there is no room to attach it to the central long leg, so use flush mounts (see page 140) for this job. See **figure 22**. Fix a male half of the flush mount on each side of the back frame, 40mm from the top edge. Screw female halves of the flush mount in matching positions on the centre and corner leg. Then slide the back frame down between the legs, on to the flush mounts. Screw up through the back webbing support to fix the bottom edge of the back frame. You can, of course, use flush mounts for all the arm/back fixings, which disposes of the counterbored screws and means that no dowel plug is seen at the top of the arm.

figure 20

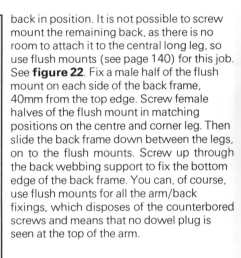

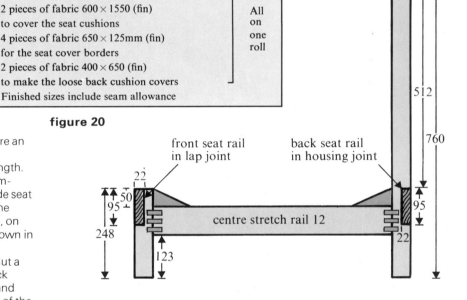

front seat rail in lap joint

back seat rail in housing joint

centre stretch rail 12

figure 21

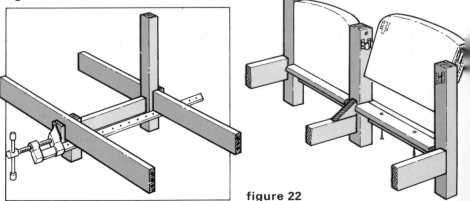

figure 22

72

FULLY UPHOLSTERED MODULAR SEATING

Peter Cornish

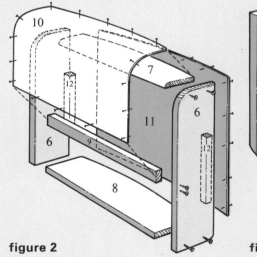

This range of seating consists of three modules—a single seater, a two-seater, (both of which can be built with or without arms), and a corner table. One arrangement of the modules is shown above.

One of the problems of fully upholstered seating in the home is scuffing of the area between the cushions and the floor. It is for this reason that I have covered the base with carpet, hoping that you will have some scraps left over from a recent flooring job. The use of carpet makes the range blend in very pleasantly with the floor, and if you make the cushions a different colour to the carpet, they will give the appearance of 'floating' above the floor.

The design is certainly demanding for the complete beginner but I felt I had had enough of the sort of DIY design which is so simple that it always provokes the comment 'very nice, make it yourself did you?' Each module consists of a wooden carcase with the cushions on top, attached by Velcro tape. The cushions are made of laminated foam, and making these and their covers does take a little time and patience, but the carcase has a hidden bonus. You can make it from cheap flooring quality pine and hardboard, and it doesn't matter if some of the joints are a bit untidy because they are all covered over in the end.

figure 2

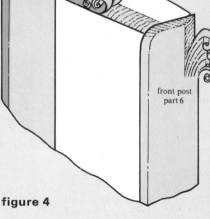

figure 4

Single Seater Module with Arm
Making Instructions

Arm and Back
Figure 2 shows the construction of these units. For convenience, I shall describe how to make the arm only. The back is made in exactly the same way but is a little higher.

The first job is to cut the curves on the arm top board (part 7) and bottom board (part 8). The patterns for the curves are given on the grids in **figure 3**. Carefully copy them on to 22mm thick softwood, using 50mm squares as described for the upholstered wooden range, page 68. Cut out with a bow saw or jig saw. Now take the arm front and back posts—part 6—finished to size with the top inside curve cut and butt

Fully Upholstered Modular Seating

join them to the top and bottom boards with glue and screws. Make sure the frame is square at the corners. Only now should you plane away the inside edge of the top board, as shown in **figure 4**. Finally curve off the outside vertical edge of the front and back posts, **figure 4**.

Screw and glue in position the arm centre rail (9), 156mm up from the inside face of the bottom board and flush with the inside edge of the front and back posts. Also screw and glue in the arm side fillets (12), setting them back 3mm from the outside edge of the front and back posts and 100mm up from the bottom, as shown in **figure 5**.

You are now ready to clad the arm unit. With the frame lying flat on the bench, inside surface downwards, run a bead of glue along the two side fillets and along the edges of the top and bottom boards. Pin the outer hardboard panel (11) to them.

The inner arm cladding panel (10) must be bent over quite a severe curve and the hardboard will snap if you work with it dry, so half an hour before you use it, thoroughly damp the front and back of the area that must bend. At the end of this time, lay the

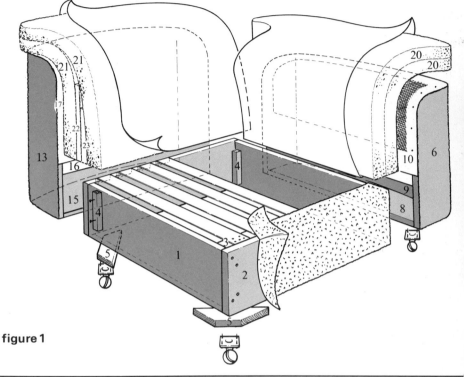

figure 1

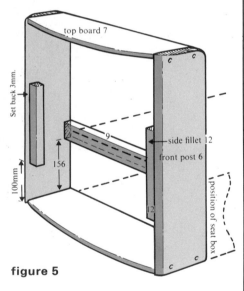

figure 5

frame on the bench with the curved outside face downwards and run a bead of glue all round the edges of the inner surface. Line up the bottom edge of the hardboard panel with the centre line of the arm centre rail and pin in position. Pin up the side edge as far as possible, then take the complete assembly and stand it upright on the floor. With firm pressure across its width, bend the hardboard over the top of the arm frame. Sit on it, to hold it down while you finish pinning. When finished, trim off and chamfer all edges. Mark centre lines at the top and bottom of the panels, as in **figure 10**.

Cutting List. See figures 1, 2 and 6

No.	Part	Material	Qty	Length	Width	Thickness
1	Seat side	Plywood	2	624	200	18
2	Seat front/back	Plywood	2	660	200	18
3	Webbing support	Beech or birch	1	600	45	22
4	Seat corner fillet	Pine	4	150	22	22
5	Castor block	Pine	2	200	45	22
6	Arm front/back post	Pine	2	470	145	22
7	Arm top board	Pine	1	612	EX140	22
8	Arm bottom board	Pine	1	612	EX174	22
9	Arm centre rail	Pine	1	612	45	22
10	Inner arm cladding	Hardboard	1	420	618	3
11	Outer arm cladding	Hardboard	1	470	625	3
12	Arm side fillet	Pine	2	200	22	22
13	Back side post	Pine	2	650	145	22
14	Back top board	Pine	1	612	EX140	22
15	Back bottom board	Pine	1	612	EX174	22
16	Back centre rail	Pine	1	612	45	22
17	Inner back cladding	Hardboard	1	600	618	3
18	Outer back cladding	Hardboard	1	650	625	3
19	Seat cushion	D10 polyether foam	1	560	500	130
20	Arm cushion	D14 polyether foam	2	600	700	40
21	Back cushion	D14 polyether foam	2	900	700	40
22	Large lumbar support	D14 polyether foam	1	320	700	20
23	Small lumbar support	D14 polyether foam	1	160	700	20

Note: Remember the cutting list gives *finished* sizes only, see Buying Timber, page 109.

Other Materials:

Fabric: From one roll of 1200mm wide fabric
    Arm piece 950mm long
    Seat piece 1650mm long
    Back piece 1450mm long
Carpet: Arm piece 970 × 470mm
    Back piece 970 × 650mm
    Seat piece 656 × 260mm
Finished sizes. Larger piece
needed to start with

Apx. 70 × 1½″ No. 8 countersunk steel screws
Apx. 6 × 2″ No. 10 countersunk steel screws
4m of 50mm wide standard rubber webbing
1·2m Velcro hook and loop tape 12·5mm wide
½″ panel pins
¾″ upholstery tacks
4 plate-fixed castor wheels
PVA glue
Contact adhesive

Above *Two double units and a corner unit are used in this variation of Peter Cornish's upholstered modular range. The bamboo coffee table shows how the most un-likely things will go together if only you have the courage to try them.*

Left *A very luxurious version in patterned velour. The use of matching carpet on the base integrates the chair into its setting.*

Stationery Cabinet and Desk

Above Left *Stationery cabinet designed by Bill Brooker. The shiny red chipboard carcase contrasts well with the natural pine drawers.*

Top Right *The drawers are built in the same simple way as the drawers in the bedroom storage range, chapter 4.*

Above Right *The bottom drawer is of double depth to allow room for hanging files. For the same reason, a double front is used.*

Left *Two of the stationery cabinets, slightly modified, plus a veneered chipboard top, make an imposing desk.*

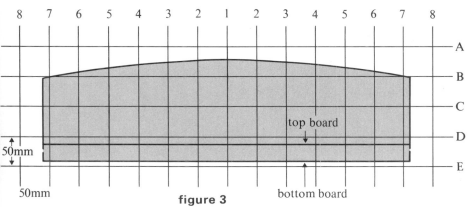

figure 3

50mm

50mm

top board

bottom board

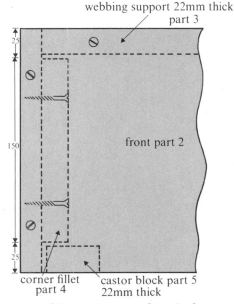

webbing support 22mm thick
part 3

front part 2

corner fillet
part 4

castor block part 5
22mm thick

part of the seat box, seen from the front

figure 7

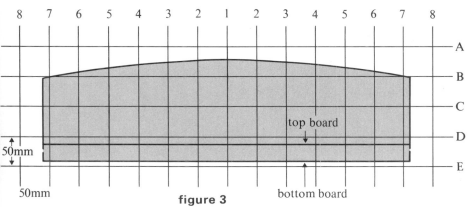

R   L

L   R

figure 8

figure 6

Seat Box

The seat box carries both arms and back and is therefore, though simple, very robust. See **figure 6**. First make the basic square frame from the front, back and sides—parts 1 and 2—with screwed and glued butt joints, as you did for the arm frames. Screw and glue in the corner fillets (4), making sure the frame is square. Note that the fillets are set 25mm away from the top and bottom edges of the box to leave room for the webbing support (3) and the castor blocks (5). See **figure 7**. Screw and glue the castor blocks (5) in position.

One point worth mentioning about castors—some are designed to work best fitted left and right, although one cannot determine this from the actual shape of the castor. Check by examining the body of the castor and if an R is seen, it is a 'right-hander' if an L a 'left-hander'. They should be fitted as in **figure 8**. The webbing support rail is fixed to the front of the box only and should be made of beech, birch or hardwood of similar density, as it has to take considerable strain. Round off the top inside edge well to stop it cutting into the webbing. It's a good idea to round off the inside edge of the seat back (2) for the same reason. Screw and glue the webbing support in position as shown in **figure 6**.

Use eight strips of webbing 25mm apart, fixing them with ¾" upholstery tacks and 10% pre-tension as described for the upholstered wooden range, page 69. Note that there is no back webbing support in this design since the back of the seat frame is further strengthened when screwed to the back. Because of this, the webs can be tacked directly to the rear face of the seat

frame, as in **figure 9**, thereby increasing the web's operational length and providing greater resilience and comfort.

Covering with Carpet

Cut the carpet well over the finished sizes given in the cutting list, and if it is rubber or foam backed, strip this off. Clear the bench completely and lay the piece of carpet for the arm face down upon it. Mark its centre line with a felt tip pen, then coat the back of the carpet liberally with contact adhesive. Coat the front, back and outside faces of the arm unit with contact adhesive too. When the adhesive is touch dry (see manufacturer's instructions), take the arm unit and lower it carefully on to the carpet, ensuring that the centre lines of the carpet and the frame coincide, as in **figure 10**. Rock the frame from side to side until the carpet adheres to the main curve, then firmly wrap the carpet round to cover the ends. Trim all the edges of the carpet flush with the frame, using a sharp knife.

Repeat as above for the back unit. Finally attach the piece of the carpet to the front of the seat box,

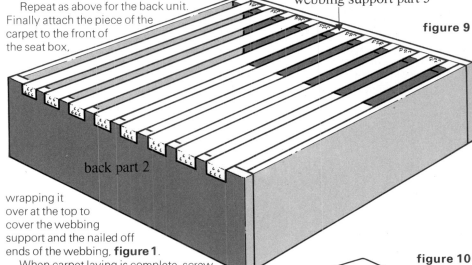

webbing support part 3

figure 9

back part 2

wrapping it over at the top to cover the webbing support and the nailed off ends of the webbing, **figure 1**.

When carpet laying is complete, screw the arm and back to the seat box as shown in **figure 11**, using 1½" No. 8 screws. You will need to bore countersinks for these before assembly. Staple the hook side of the 12·5mm wide Velcro tape 600mm long along the top curve of the arm and back, **figure 11**. Add the four castors and the basic frame is complete.

figure 10

Fully Upholstered Modular Seating

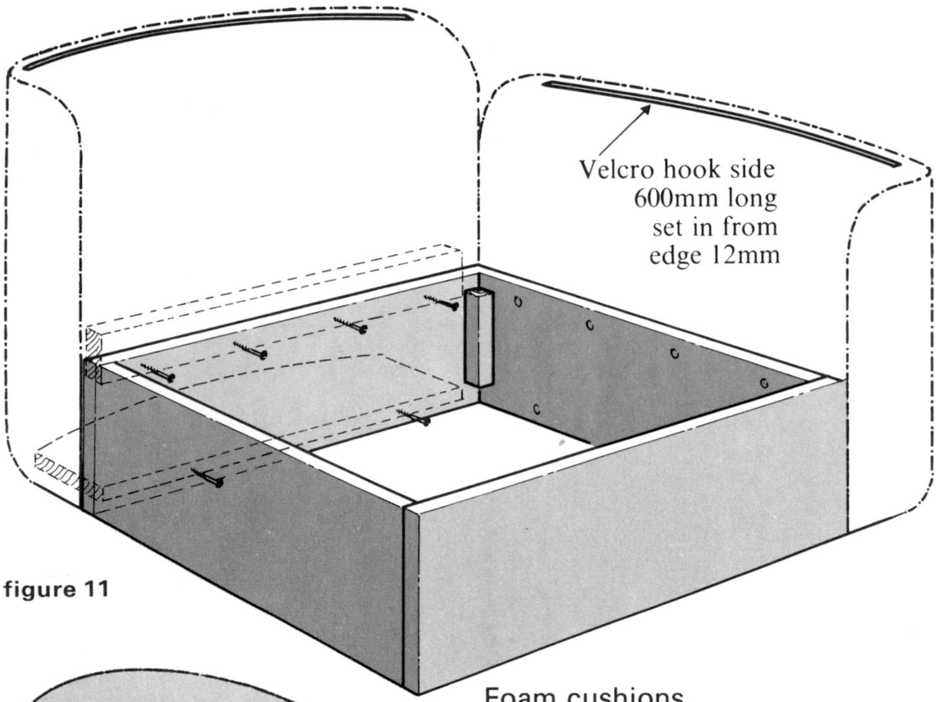

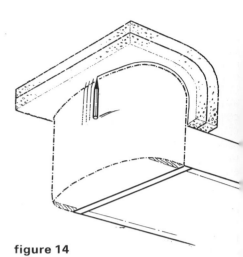

figure 11

Velcro hook side
600mm long
set in from
edge 12mm

figure 14

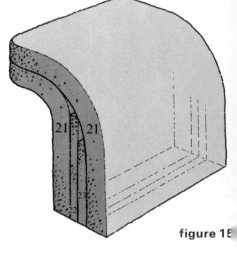

figure 15

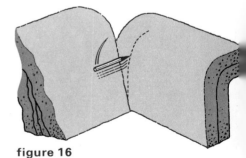

figure 16

figure 17

projected
joining line

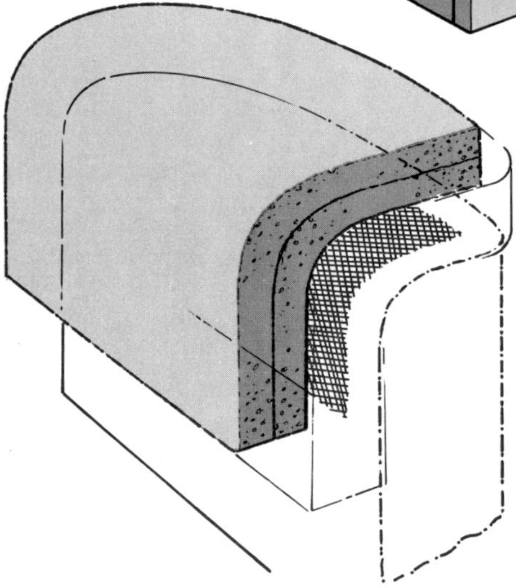

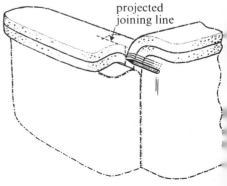

figure 12 *The arm cushion is made from two layers of foam laminated together. Note the piece of hessian lying underneath.*

figure 13

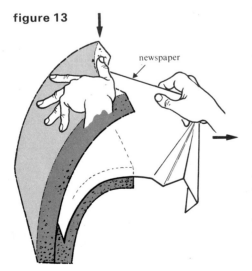

newspaper

Foam cushions.

See Upholstery Section, page 162. The arms and back are made from sheets of soft density polyether foam, laminated together to give the curves which fit the basic frame. Do not react badly to this idea of laminating foam; we are, don't forget, trying to make something better than 'your average Do-It-Yourself'.

As with all lamination, it is the 'glue lines' which do the work of holding the material in shape, and the more lines the better. In this design two glue lines are used, one between the two layers of foam and one between the foam and a piece of hessian or lining fabric. See **figure 12**.

Start with one of the arm cushions. Cut a piece of hessian to cover the inside surface of the arm and suspend it from the top of the arm with double-sided adhesive tape. Coat its surface liberally with contact adhesive. Paint one side of the foam arm cushion (20) similarly with contact adhesive.

When the adhesive is dry to the touch, lay a sheet of clean newspaper over the hessian to prevent it making premature contact with the foam. Position the foam on the inside of the arm, one of its long edges tight down on to the side of the seat box.

While holding the foam in position, gradually remove the paper and push the foam down on to hessian, without stretching it, until both adhesive surfaces meet.

A few drawing pins pushed through the edge of the first layer of foam will ensure that nothing moves while its top face and the second layer of foam are coated with adhesive. Again leave till touch dry, then stick down the second layer of foam as you did the first one with a sheet of newspaper between the layers for greater control, see **figure 13**. Remove the drawing pins.

Now mark the underside of the foam with a felt tip pen, using the carpetted surface of the arm as a guide, as in **figure 14**. Remove the arm by pulling the hessian off the double-sided tape, then draw another line on the foam 25mm outside the one you have already drawn. This extra 25mm allows for compression of the foam inside its cushion cover and an overhang of the finished cushion beyond the arm frame. Using an electric meat knife with the skill of a surgeon, cut along the outside line, keeping the blade at 90° to the surface of the foam.

The back cushion is made the same way, except that there are two extra pieces of foam – parts 22 and 23 – laminated in to provide a lumbar support. Their positions are shown in **figure 15**. Mark the completed cushion as above – trim with the meat knife.

The arm cushion will not fit into the chair properly until it has a notch in it to accommodate the thickness of the back cushion. To do this, place the arm cushion in the chair and slide the back cushion up to it. Using the front face of the back cushion as a guide, mark the arm cushion with a felt tip pen, as in **figure 16**. Now pull the arm cushion forwards and slide the back cushion in behind it. As in **figure 17** mark the back edge of the arm cushion using the side of the back cushion as a guide. Project this line across to meet the first mark and cut out the notch with the electric knife. The back will now nest into the arm.

The seat cushion foam is bought cut to size and needs no preparation. It will appear too large at this stage, because its dimensions allow for slight compression by the

cushion cover. This helps to stop the cover wrinkling in use.

Making the Cushion Covers

The next move is to cut out and sew the fabric cushion cases. Equipment should include a sewing machine and operator.

Figure 18 gives the shapes needed for one arm and one back cover, including a 10mm seam allowance all round. Draw a 50mm grid on a large sheet of brown paper and carefully copy the shapes from **figure 18** on to it. Label each piece, then cut them out with scissors.

Unroll the fabric, right side up, on to a clean flat surface. Pin the pattern pieces to the fabric in the correct relationship to any design on the fabric, but nesting them as closely together as possible for economy.

figure 18a

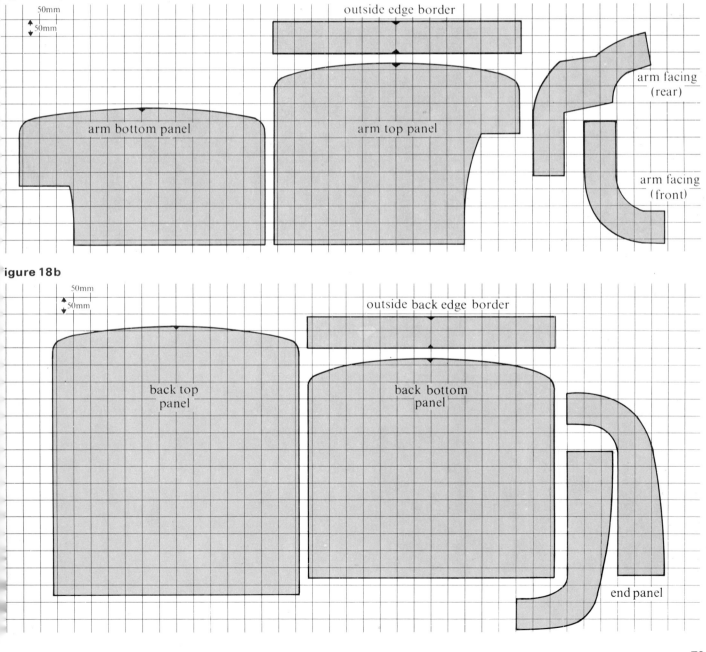

figure 18b

Fully Upholstered Modular Seating

I feel this is important, since I suggest you use as durable and expensive a fabric as your pocket will allow. I once went to considerable trouble to re-cover an antique chair in cheap Belgian flat weave fabric and was disappointed when serious wear was seen less than twelve months later.

Cut round the paper patterns, following the edge closely. Mark with chalk on the reverse side of each piece of fabric its description and any centre marks, then remove the paper pattern. Only cut one arm or back pattern out at a time, as all fabrics behave differently and any adjustments to the pattern to suit the fabric you have chosen can be made at this stage.

Having cut out the pieces for one arm cushion in this way, take all the borders and pin them end to end, face to face in their correct sequence. **Figure 19** shows the relationship of the various cover pieces. Place all the pins at right angles to the seam line, so that when the pieces are machined, the needle will run over them without harm. Sew all the border pieces together, taking up the 10mm seam allowance.

Next line up the centre mark on the arm edge border with the centre mark on the arm top panel and pin the two pieces together face to face, using pins apx. 75mm apart, but closer at the corners. Repeat the process with the arm bottom panel. It is a good idea at this stage to check the assembly by turning it inside out (avoiding the pins!) to see if its general configuration is as expected. If it is, turn it back again to expose the reverse of the fabric and, working away from the centre marks, complete the sewing of the case, again using a 10mm seam allowance, and leave the bottom edge open.

The last job on the case before filling is to sew a 600mm length of 12·5mm Velcro (loop side) to the arm bottom panel 25mm in and parallel to the arm side border. Now stuff the foam arm cushion into the cover. This is a job that can take several minutes' heavy breathing before it is accomplished.

Repeat the whole process for the back cushion, again leaving the bottom edge open.

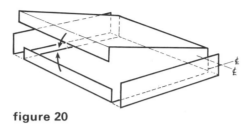

figure 20

Now lay out the fabric for the seat cushion, reverse side upwards. Mark on it a rectangle, the short side of which is the exact width of the foam cushion. The length of the rectangle is made up of twice the depth of the cushion (front to back) and twice the thickness. This piece of fabric will wrap right round the cushion and meet at the mid line of the back edge. See **figure 20**. Mark the centre point of the front edge of the cushion. See **figure 17** of the upholstered wooden range, page 70. Cut out the rectangle of fabric, adding 5mm all round.

Mark the side borders to the same dimension as the side section of the cushion and again mark the centre point of the front edge. Cut the two side borders out, again adding 5mm.

Pin the borders and the rectangle together inside out, matching up the centre lines and sew them together with a 10mm seam allowance, using a stitch length between 8–10 stitches to the inch.

With the cover fresh from the sewing machine and still inside out, locate its front corners on to the front corners of the foam seat cushion and turn the sewn case right side out as it is worked over the foam. Once again, leave the bottom edges open.

Assemble all cushions into the main chair frame and after checking that they are satisfactory, take each cushion in turn and with light tension only, tuck in the fabric along the bottom and slip stitch it to close. (Slip stitching, page 165.) Slip stitching gives the opportunity to remove any slack in the fabric as the cover is closed.

Corner Table

The matching corner table is very easily made and provides a means of utilising an awkward corner while at the same time providing visual continuity. It may, of course, be used free standing. If you are going to use it with the seating modules, you can save money by leaving two of the faces bare of carpet. I have recommended glass for the top, but other materials, such as slate, marble or wood could be used. A particular favourite of mine is antique mirror, an expensive material which gives the fantastic effect of petrol on water.

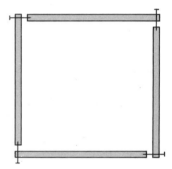

figure 21

Making Instructions

Take the four side pieces and glue and nail their ends together, always allowing the left hand panel to overlap the right as in **figure 21**. Run a bead of glue around the

figure 22

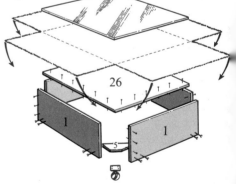

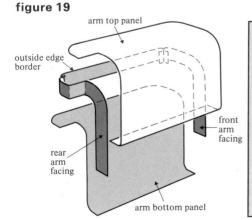

figure 19

Labels: arm top panel, outside edge border, rear arm facing, arm bottom panel, front arm facing

Cutting List. See figure 22.

No.	Part	Material	Qty	Length	Width	Thickness
1	Side	Chipboard	4	644	350	12
5	Castor block	Softwood	4	200	45	22
26	Top	Chipboard	1	656	656	12

Note: Remember the cutting list gives *finished* sizes only, see Buying Timber, page 109.

Other Materials

4 plate fixing castors
6mm thick mirror 580mm square, all edges ground and polished
PVA glue
Contact adhesive

Carpet: 4 pieces 656 × 362mm (fin) for the sides
1 piece 656 × 656mm (fin) for the top or, better, 1 piece apx. 1500mm square
Apx. 16 × 1½″ No. 8 countersunk steel screws
1″ panel pins

top edges of the box and pin down the top. Make sure that the top is square and that the fairly flexible frame below is held flush with its edges.

Once the top is fitted, turn the whole box upside down and glue in the castor blocks flush with the bottom edge. Attach each block with four 1½" No. 8 screws, two through each side panel. With a sharp jack plane, put a chamfer on all edges.

Now for the covering with carpet. If you have a remnant big enough—about 1500mm square—place the carpet face downwards and place the box upside down roughly in in the middle. Mark with a felt tip pen around the edges, then roll the box over on to its side and mark around that. Repeat on the other three sides and cut out the developed cross shape, **figure 22**.

With the carpet still face down, spread contact adhesive over its back face and also the top and sides of the box. When touch dry, lay a piece of clean brown paper over the carpet, but be sure to leave two sides of the central square visible to act as guide lines. Position the up-turned box on the central square and carefully remove the brown paper without disturbing the alignment of the box.

Now, pulling outwards and upwards, lay the carpet on each of the box's sides. Screw the castors on to the centre of each corner brace and turn the table over. The final touch is to lay the piece of glass in position. It will settle into the pile under its own weight with about 75mm all round.

Two-Seater Module with Arm Making Instructions

The two-seater is made in exactly the same way as the single seater, except that the front and back panels of the seat box are longer and that there is a stretcher bar across the centre. **Figure 23** gives the one-arm version which joins up with the corner table. The addition of a second arm makes a comfortable sofa.

Read the instructions for the single seater module for the basic method.
Build the seat box from 18mm ply as before. Add the corner fillets (4) and castor blocks (5). Mark the centre lines of the seat front and back panels and position the central stretcher bar (24) on them, its top edge 100mm from the top edge of the seat box. Screw and glue it with two 1½" No. 8 screws, as shown in **figure 23** adding the 2 angle braces (25)

Next position the long hardwood webbing support (3), screwed through the front face of the ply. The box is webbed as before, using 16 lengths of 50mm standard webbing. The arm and two back units are made and fixed as described previously.

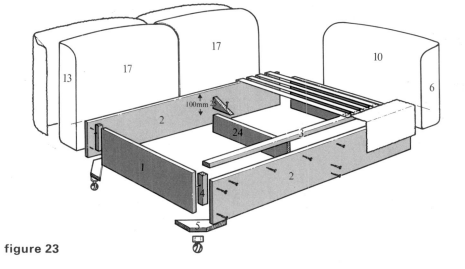

figure 23

Cutting List. See figure 23.

No.	Part	Material	Qty	Length	Width	Thickness
1	Seat side	Plywood	2	624	200	18
2	Seat front/back	Plywood	2	1332	200	18
3	Webbing support	Beech or birch	1	1210	45	22
4	Seat corner fillet	Pine	4	150	22	22
5	Castor block	Pine	2	200	45	22
6	Arm front/back post	Pine	2	470	145	22
7	Arm top board	Pine	1	612	EX140	22
8	Arm bottom board	Pine	1	612	EX174	22
9	Arm centre rail	Pine	1	612	45	22
10	Inner arm cladding	Hardboard	1	420	618	3
11	Outer arm cladding	Hardboard	1	470	625	3
12	Arm side fillet	Pine	2	200	22	22
13	Back side post	Pine	4	650	145	22
14	Back top board	Pine	2	612	EX140	22
15	Back bottom board	Pine	2	612	EX174	22
16	Back centre rail	Pine	2	612	45	22
17	Inner back cladding	Hardboard	2	600	618	3
18	Outer back cladding	Hardboard	2	650	625	3
19	Seat cushion	D10 polyether foam	2	560	500	130
20	Arm cushion	D14 polyether foam	2	600	700	40
21	Back cushion	D14 polyether foam	4	900	700	40
22	Large lumbar support	D14 polyether foam	2	160	700	20
23	Small lumbar support	D14 polyether foam	2	100	700	20
24	Stretcher bar	Pine	1	618	95	22
25	Angle brace	Pine	2	150	75	22

Note: Remember the cutting list gives *finished* sizes only, see Buying Timber, page 109.

Other Materials

Fabric: From one roll of 1200mm wide fabric
    Arm piece 950mm long
    Seat piece 1650mm long
    2 Back pieces each 1450mm long
Carpet: Arm piece 970 × 470mm
    2 Back pieces 970 × 650mm
    Seat piece 1332 × 260mm
Finished sizes. Larger piece
needed to start with.

Apx. 60 × 1½" No. 8 countersunk steel screws
Apx. 10 × 2" No. 10 countersunk steel screws
8m of 50mm wide standard rubber webbing
1·8m Velcro hook and loop tape 12·5mm wide
½" panel pins
¾" upholstery tacks
4 plate-fixed castor wheels
PVA glue
Contact adhesive

STATIONERY CABINET and DESK

Bill Brooker

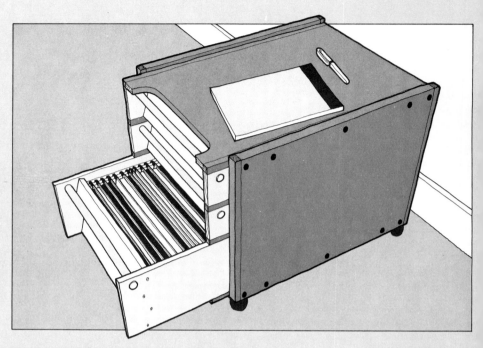

Here is a handy little cabinet which will hold all your bills, letters and personal stationery and which also has a convenient working surface on the top. It is mounted on castors so that you can pull it up to your favourite armchair and there's a deep filing drawer at the bottom to hold your accounts.

The cabinet is easy on the pocket because it is made for the most part of fine grain chipboard with a hardboard back. Solid timber lippings are added to the edges of the chipboard to protect it against knocks in use. You can decorate the cabinet any way you like. We stained the hardboard and chipboard a deep red and left the drawer fronts in natural pine with bright chrome handles.

By building two cabinets in veneered chipboard and adding a top of the same material you can make a fine desk. We used teak veneered board for the top and pedestal carcases and birch plywood for the drawers, which were stained black to contrast with the bright chrome handles.

Making Instructions

Read these instructions carefully and make sure you understand them before starting work.

The first job is to construct the chipboard carcase. Take the bottom panel (part 1), cut accurately to size and plane all the edges square. The top and bottom lippings (part 4) should be slightly longer and wider than the finished size in the cutting list, say 620× 20×15mm. Apply a coat of glue to the long edges of the bottom panel and to one side of each of the lippings and set up in cramps as shown in **figure 3**. When the glue is dry, plane the lippings down flush with the chipboard and saw off the ends.

Repeat this process for the top panel. The front edge of the top panel is cut back to allow access to the top drawer handle. The pattern for the cut away is given in **figure 4**. Mark out both sides of the top panel to the dimensions given, then cut out with either a jig saw or coping saw, keeping to the waste side of the line. Clean down to the line with a half round rasp and spokeshave, then finish with fine grade garnet paper. Take time doing this, working from both sides of the board to prevent chipping of the edges. Remove all sharp edges with garnet paper wrapped around a cork block.

The top and bottom lippings also serve as drawer runners (see later) and therefore

must be made of a hardwood, such as utile. The side lippings (6) do not have this function, so they can be made of pine, which roughly matches the colour of the chipboard side panels.

Leave the side lippings overlength and overwide as before and glue them to the side panels (2) in cramps. When dry, cut and plane to size.

When the side panels are complete, label one as Left and one as Right, remembering that these will eventually be *mirror images* of each other, as in **figure 5**.

On the *inside* face of each side panel, mark out the positions of the top and bottom panels, drawer runners (5) and back corner fillets (7). It is very important that the space for the large drawer side – 280mm – is exact. If it is any less, there will be no room for the suspended file. It is possible that the drawer runners may have been left a mm or two overwidth by your supplier. If so,

don't bother to plane them down, just adjust the heights of the two small drawer sides to suit.

On the *outside* surface of the two side panels mark the positions of the five screw

figure 1

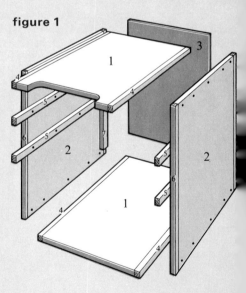

figure 2

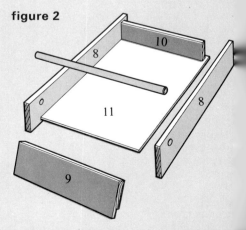

figure 3

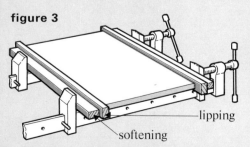

lipping

softening

figure 4

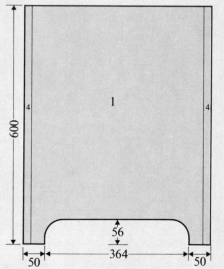

600

4

1

4

56

50

364

50

holes shown in **figure 5** in the top and bottom. These take the $1\frac{3}{4}$" No. 8 countersunk securing screws and after assembly screw covers are used to mask the otherwise visible screw heads. Each screw cover is a two-part plastic moulding, consisting of a collar which fits under the screw head and a cap which snaps over the head and into the collar when the screw has been finally tightened. To house the screw covers flush with the surface of the board, drill a 16mm dia. hole using a flat bit to a depth of appx. 5mm, then change to a $\frac{5}{32}$" bit and bore clearance holes through the remaining thickness of the chipboard, placing a piece of softwood under the chipboard to stop it fragmenting. For screw cap and cups see page 139.

Turn each board over and pin and glue the back corner fillet (7) to the side panel, 6mm in from the back edge and stopping 26mm short of the top and bottom edges.

Drill and countersink the four screw holes in the drawer runners, using a $\frac{5}{32}$" bit. Butt the back ends up to the back corner fillets and screw and glue them in position, using four 1" No. 8 countersunk steel screws per runner.

Before assembling the carcase, it is advisable to apply the finishing lacquer to its

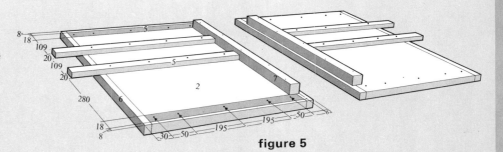

figure 5

components, that is the top, bottom, two sides and hardboard back. The best finish to show the texture of the chipboard is coloured gloss polyurethane. This seals the chipboard permanently and is extremely hardwearing. Be sure to thoroughly sand all surfaces beforehand with fine garnet paper and apply a minimum of four coats of lacquer to obtain an even finish. Do not lacquer the inside of the carcase, as this will make the drawers stick.

When the lacquer is thoroughly dry, assemble the carcase one corner at a time, using a sash cramp to hold the boards in place while you line them up and drive in the screws. See **figure 6**. Note that no glue is used. Make sure to line up the top and bottom panels exactly with the marks you made

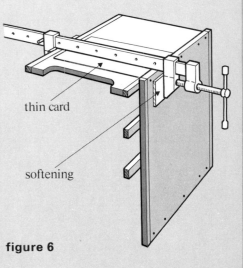

thin card

softening

figure 6

on the side panels. They should be parallel and exactly 8mm from the top and bottom edges of each side, otherwise the drawers will not run properly. Put a sheet of thin card under the bar of the sash cramp to protect the laquer as shown in **figure 6**.

Pin and glue the hardboard back panel (3) to the back corner fillets and to the back edges of the top and bottom panels, with the rough side inwards. Use four $1\frac{1}{4}$" panel pins evenly spaced along the top and bottom edges and five 1" pins along each side.

Check before fitting that the back panel is exactly to size and that all four corners are square. This provides the final alignment and rigidity of the carcase.

When the back is on, screw the castors to the four corners of the cabinet.

The drawers of the cabinet are built of solid pine and use the same basic method of construction as those in the bedroom storage range. For making instructions see page 45. The only differences are that the fronts have been tilted backwards to give a more decorative effect, and that part of the drawer sides project beyond the front edge of the carcase.

The lower drawer is approximately double the depth of the others so that it can take a standard suspension filing system. Its components are shown in **figure 7**. The depth of the sides and back given in the cutting list are not generally available in 15mm thick pine, so you will have to join 2 boards 600 × 145mm edge-to-edge.

Start by holding the two pieces of timber

Cutting List. See figures 1 and 2

No.	Part	Material	Qty	Length	Width	Thickness
1	Top and bottom panel	Fine grain 650 density chipboard	2	600	434	18
2	Side panels	Fine grain 650 density chipboard	2	590	520	18
3	Back panel	Hardboard	1	582	464	6
4	Top and bottom lippings	Utile	4	600	18	15
5	Drawer Runners	Utile	4	600	20	15
6	Side lippings	Pine	4	590	18	15
7	Back corner fillets	Pine	2	438	20	20
8	Small drawer sides	Pine	4	580	109	15
9	Small drawer fronts	Pine	2	434	118	15
10	Small drawer back	Pine	2	434	92	15
11	Large and small drawer bottoms	Hardboard	3	520	448	6
12	Large drawer sides	Pine	2	580	*280	15
13	Large drawer fronts	Pine	2	434	145	15
14	Large drawer back	Pine	1	434	*260	15
15	Large drawer batten	Pine	2	410	20	15

*To be made from 2 pieces of timber (see text)

Note: Remember that the cutting list gives *finished* sizes only, see Buying Timber, page 109.

Other Materials

3 lengths 18mm dia. chrome tube 464mm in length for handles

4 twin wheeled castors 50mm dia.

2 lengths aluminium strip 410 × 19 × 3mm

20 brown plastic screw covers

8 × $1\frac{1}{4}$" panel pins for the carcase back

10 × 1" panel pins for the carcase back

20 × $1\frac{3}{4}$" No. 8 countersunk steel screws for securing carcase

30 × $1\frac{1}{4}$" No. 8 countersunk screws, brass or steel for drawer sides

6 × 1" No. 8 countersunk screws, brass or steel for the large drawer batten

8 × $\frac{1}{2}$" No. 4 countersunk screws (chrome or bright zinc) for aluminium strip

18 × $\frac{1}{2}$" No. 6 round headed screws, steel for drawer bottom

PVA glue

Stationery Cabinet and Desk

figure 7

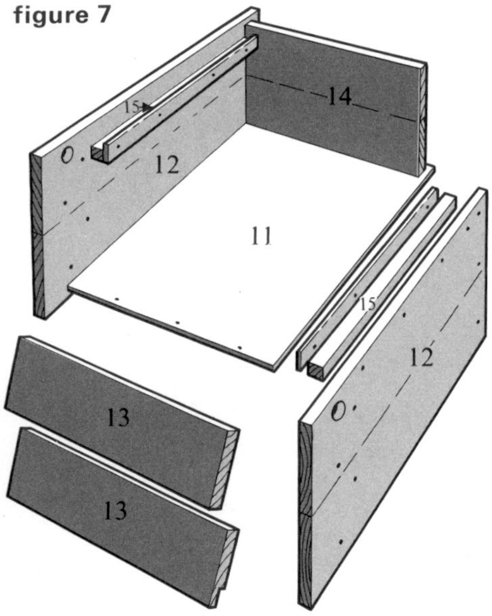

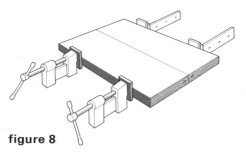

together in a vice and plane the edges to be glued. After planing, apply glue to both edges, remove from the vice and set up in sash cramps as shown in **figure 8**. Note the arrangement of the annual rings in the end grain labelled A in **figure 8**. Arranged this way, the timber will not distort unduly when in use.

When the glue has set, remove the board from cramps and plane both sides flat. Saw off any waste and plane both edges to the finished sizes shown in the cutting list. Note that the sides are 280mm deep but that the drawer back is only 260mm deep.

Before you cut the back to its finished length, put the two sides inside the carcase and measure the distance between them. If this is not exactly 434mm, adjust the back to allow for the discrepancy.

Figures 7 and **9** show that there are two sloping drawer fronts, only the lower one of which receives the drawer bottom. Because the drawer front slopes backwards, the groove used in the bedroom drawers, page 45, is replaced by a rebate 15×7mm cut in the lower drawer front only. See Cutting Grooves and Rebates, page 155.

Lay each side piece flat on the bench with its face side uppermost and mark out the positions of the drawer fronts, back and bottom and the batten to support the filing system (part 15) as shown in **figure 9**.

Mark and drill the holes in the side panel

figure 8

84

shown in **figure 9** using a $\frac{5}{32}$" bit. These are the clearance holes for the screws which will fix the back and fronts to the sides and also support the drawer batten (15). Now turn the board over and countersink the holes.

Finally cut a groove 8mm up from the bottom edge of each side panel to a depth of 7mm and 4mm wide. Because this groove stops at the drawer front, **figure 9**, a plough or combination plane cannot be used and you will need a groove cutting attachment on an electric drill. See bedroom drawers, page 45 and Cutting Grooves, page 155.

Don't forget to drill the holes to take the chrome handle with a $\frac{3}{4}$" flat bit. Hold both drawer sides together and flush at their edges with a piece of softwood underneath. Drill straight through both sides and into the softwood. Thoroughly sand all the interior faces of the drawer before assembly.

Take the two aluminium strips 410×19× 3mm and drill 4 holes in each using a $\frac{1}{8}$" bit, one near each end and two equally spaced along its length. Make sure these holes do not coincide with the screws which will fix the batten in the drawer. Screw the aluminium strip to the batten using $\frac{1}{2}$" No. 4 countersunk chrome screws. Now glue and screw the battens to the side panels working from the outside surface of the panel and using three 1" No. 8 countersunk screws on each side.

The drawer needs to be assembled carefully to ensure a good fit in the cabinet but the difficulty is that when you are putting in the screws you cannot see the marking out on the side panels. Nevertheless there are some tips that can make the job easier.

Start by fixing the sides to the drawer back. Take one of the sides and fix a softwood batten to it with two G cramps so that the batten is exactly flush with the inside line of the marking out for the back. Lay the back against this as shown in **figure 10** and adjust it till it is just above the groove in the side panel. Drive three 1$\frac{1}{4}$" No. 8 countersunk screws in position, then turn the work over and repeat with the other side.

Take the back and two sides and stand them up with the back downwards as shown in **figure 11**. Place a sash cramp with gentle pressure over the free ends, then slide the two fronts into position. You should be able to adjust the pressure on the cramp to hold them in position, then tap them lightly with a hammer till they line up exactly with the marks on the side panels.

Screw the front panels in position, then remove the cramps and slide in the drawer bottom (11). This is secured by three $\frac{1}{2}$" round headed screws in the front and three in the back, as shown in **figure 12**. $\frac{1}{8}$" dia. holes should be drilled for these in the hardboard prior to assembly.

Rub down the fronts of the drawer and the parts of the side which project beyond the carcase with fine garnet paper and

figure 9

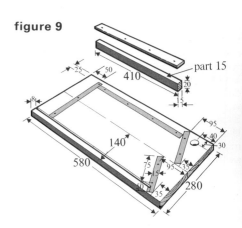

finish with at least 3 coats of clear gloss polyurethane. When dry, fit the chrome tube handle with a spot of glue at each end.

The two small drawers are made in the same way as those in the bedroom storage range, page 45. To fix the angle of the drawer fronts, take all four drawer sides (8) finished to size and lay them on the bench with their edges flush and the bottom edge uppermost. Measure 35mm along this edge with a try square and mark a line across all four pieces. Now take one of the drawer sides, lay it flat on the bench with the inside face uppermost and mark a point 95mm back along the top edge. Join the two points together with a sliding bevel.

This is the line against which the faces of the drawer fronts should be set. Use the bevel to mark another line 7–8mm behind it. This is the line for the screw clearance holes. Use the bevel to mark out the other 3 drawer sides in the same way.

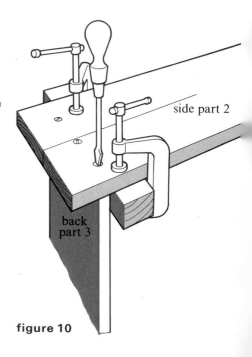

figure 10

Drill four $\frac{5}{32}$" holes in each side for the fixing screws, turning each board over and countersinking on the outside surface. Assemble as for the large drawer, using $1\frac{1}{4}$" No. 8 screws throughout. Again finish the drawer fronts and the portion of the sides which project beyond the carcase with 3 coats of clear gloss polyurethane. Do not lacquer the rest of the drawer, as this will make it stick. For details of drawer fitting, see bedroom storage range.

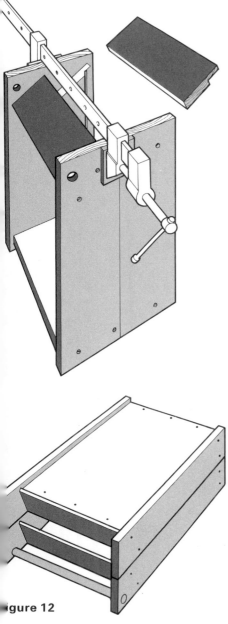

figure 11

figure 12

Desk

In the desk version, each of the pedestals is our old friend the stationery cabinet, thinly disguised. The castors have been removed and the sides and back have been extended below the bottom panel, as shown in **figure 13**. The gap at the front between the bottom panel and the floor is filled in by a plinth, part 8.

Because the pedestal is not mobile and therefore not so prone to knocks, the solid timber lippings on the side panels have been replaced by iron-on veneer, see page 146, which is also used on the front and back edges of the top and bottom panels. The plastic screw covers look a bit out of place in this design too, so I have replaced them with brass screw covers which simply screw into the head of the retaining screws.

Making Instructions

The basic method of construction for the two pedestals is the same as for the stationery cabinet. Read carefully through the instructions for the cabinet before starting work on the desk.

Reference to **figure 13** will show that the main difference between the pedestal unit and the stationery cabinet is that the pedestal unit is not mobile and that the castors have been replaced by a plinth (8), whilst the sides and back run down to the floor. Also there are 4 small drawers rather than 2 plus a large filing drawer.

Start with the side panels, cut to size with the edges planed square and apply the iron-on veneer to the front, back and top edges only. Then mark out, drill and assemble the side panels as shown in **figure 16**. Note the extra screw hole at the bottom of each panel for fixing the plinth.

Stationery Cabinet and Desk

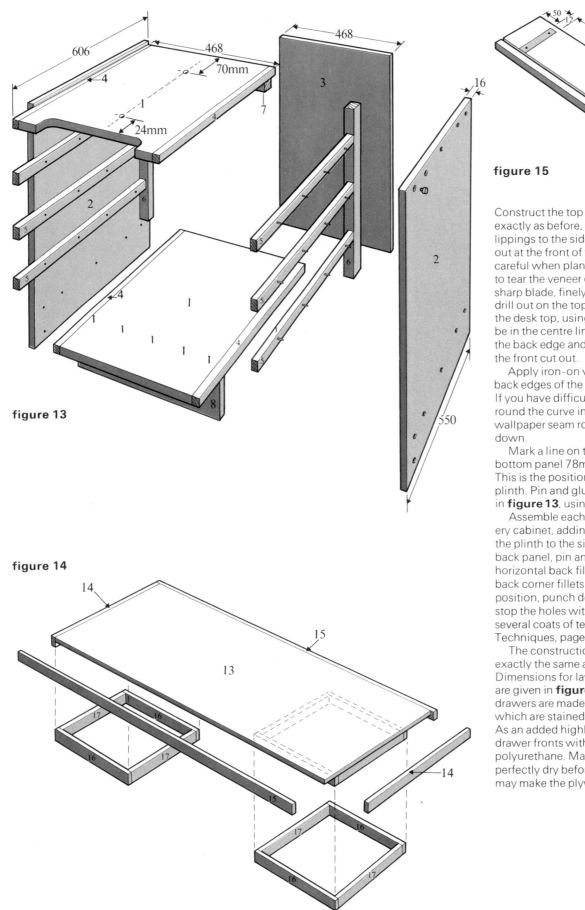

figure 13

figure 14

figure 15

Construct the top and bottom panels exactly as before, applying solid hardwood lippings to the sides and removing the cut-out at the front of the top panel. Be very careful when planing down the lippings not to tear the veneer on the panels. A really sharp blade, finely set, is essential. Also drill out on the top panel the holes for fixing the desk top, using a $\frac{3}{16}$" bit. These should be in the centre line of the panel, 70mm from the back edge and 24mm from the edge of the front cut out.

Apply iron-on veneer to the front and back edges of the top and bottom panels. If you have difficulty in laying the veneer round the curve in the top, try using a wallpaper seam roller to press the lipping down.

Mark a line on the under surface of the bottom panel 78mm from the front edge. This is the position of the front face of the plinth. Pin and glue it in position as shown in **figure 13**, using five $1\frac{1}{2}$" panel pins.

Assemble each carcase as for the stationery cabinet, adding that extra screw to fix the plinth to the sides. Before adding the back panel, pin and glue in position the horizontal back fillet (7) in line with the two back corner fillets. Pin and glue the back in position, punch down the pin heads and stop the holes with wood filler. Finish with several coats of teak oil. See Finishing Techniques, page 158.

The construction of the drawers is exactly the same as in the stationery cabinet. Dimensions for laying out the drawer sides are given in **figure 15**. The fronts of the drawers are made of 12mm birch plywood, which are stained black prior to assembly. As an added highlight we finished the drawer fronts with 3 or 4 coats of clear gloss polyurethane. Make sure that the stain is perfectly dry before fitting the drawers, as it may make the plywood swell slightly.

figure 16

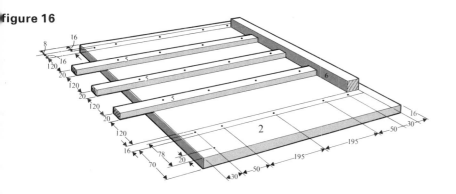

figure 17

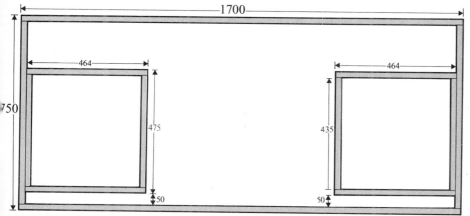

Desk Top

The top of the desk is a sheet of veneered chipboard with a solid hardwood lipping round the edges to give it strength and rigidity. It is fixed to the two pedestals by two softwood locating frames stained black and glued to the underside of the top. Dimensions for the top and the locating frames are given in **figure 17**.

The method of attaching the lippings to the top is similar to that used for lipping the panels in the stationery cabinet and pedestals. Start with the end lippings (14). Leave them slightly overwidth and over-length and glue them to the ends of the top, holding in position with sash cramps. When dry, plane flush with the top, again being careful to protect the veneer, and cut off the waste from the ends with a tenon saw. Repeat this for the side lippings (15).

When the lippings are dry, sand all the surfaces which show and remove all sharp edges with a small plane.

Cut the long and short locating battens (16 and 17) to length and make sure their ends are square. Pin and glue them to make the 2 locating frames, using two 2″ oval nails per corner. When they are dry, clean the frames up all round and stain all faces black, excepting the edges that will be glued to the desk top.

Lay the desk top face downwards on a clean table, bench or carpet and pin and glue the frames in the positions shown in **figure 17**. Use 1¼″ panel pins driven in at an angle, being careful not to let them come through the top face. Leave to dry.

Place the two pedestals in the position that they will occupy in your room and locate the top between them. The softwood frames should slot between the upwardly projecting side panels of the pedestals and the front rail of the top should line up with the fronts of the pedestals. Fix the top in position by screwing up through the two holes in the top panels of the pedestals into the softwood frames, using two 2″ No. 10 screws for each pedestal. Finish the top with several coats of teak oil, as for the pedestals.

Cutting List. See figures 13 and 14

No.	Part	Material	Qty	Length	Width	Thickness
1	Top and bottom panel	Veneered chipboard	4	606	444	16
2	Side panel	Veneered chipboard	4	650	550	16
3	Back panel	Veneered chipboard	2	626	468	16
4	Top and bottom lippings	Hardwood	8	606	16	12
5	Drawer runners	Hardwood	12	570	20	12
6	Back corner fillet	Pine	4	520	20	20
7	Horizontal back fillet	Pine	2	468	20	20
8	Plinth	Veneered chipboard	2	468	70	16
9	Drawer side	Birch ply	16	570	120	12
10	Drawer front	Birch ply	8	444	130	12
11	Drawer back	Birch ply	8	444	100	12
12	Drawer bottom	Hardboard	8	510	454	3
13	Desk top	Veneered chipboard	1	1660	710	16
14	End lippings	Hardwood	2	710	45	20
15	Side lippings	Hardwood	2	1700	45	20
16	Long locating batten	Pine	4	464	45	20
17	Short locating batten	Pine	4	435	45	20

Note: Remember that the cutting list gives *finished* sizes only, see Buying Timber, page 109.

Other Materials

pieces of 18mm dia. chrome tube 468mm long for the handles

×2″ No. 10 countersunk steel screws for fixing the desk top

×1½″ No. 8 countersunk screw Woodfit No. CH200 for securing carcase

×13mm dia. brass screw covers Woodfit No. CH050

2×1¼″ No. 8 countersunk steel screws for drawer sides

48×1″ No. 8 countersunk steel screws for drawer runners

24×½″ No. 6 round headed steel screws for drawer bottoms

10×2″ panel pins for plinth

Apx. 100×1¼″ panel pins

15 metres iron-on edge veneer

Teak oil

PVA glue

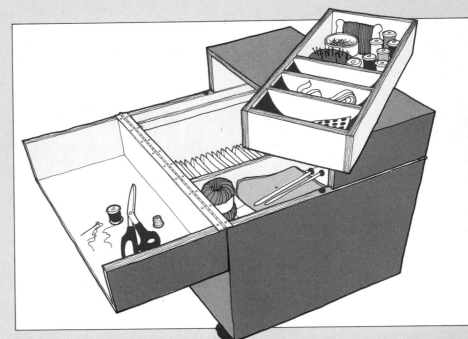

Both these little cabinets are made from the same basic structure – a sealed box made of 15mm plywood for the sewing box and 15mm mahogany veneered chipboard for the drinks cabinet. As shown in **figure 1**, the top is cut off the box and divided in half to make two closely fitting lids.

The two cabinets differ mainly in their internal construction. The drinks cabinet has a slide-out tray for glasses and the space underneath it is used for bottle storage. The sewing box has two trays running at right angles to each other and one of them is divided into small compartments for storing thimbles, buttons, pins and the like.

Both units are mobile on castors, so that they can be moved about the house at will.

Sewing Box

The sewing box is covered with a beautiful rosewood plastic laminate which makes a very effective contrast to the inside surfaces, which are lacquered with polyurethane to show the natural grain of the plywood. The two lids swing outwards on piano hinges to give a working surface and besides the two trays there is space in the well of the box for storing fabric.

Making Instructions

Start by cutting out the pieces for the plywood box. This measures 600 × 500 × 590mm overall. 15mm ply is sold in sheets 2440 × 1220mm (8' × 4') and **figure 3** shows how this can be cut with the minimum of waste. This a large board to get home in one piece, but most suppliers have a free delivery service. You could have the large piece of waste sawn off one end in the yard or have the sheet split down the middle, but I don't like to leave the more accurate cutting to final sizes to the supplier. The only safe way is to do it yourself.

Cut the sheet up with a large tenon saw, panel saw or power saw, cutting through the 5mm waste (or kerf) shown in **figure 3**. When you have cut all the pieces out, clean them down to the line with a plane, check-

ing frequently with a try square to make sure the edges stay square. See Planes and Planing, page 120, and Try-Square, page 134.

Mark the face edge and side on each of the parts and then carefully rub down the opposite side to the face side on each part. These faces will form the inside of the box and they will be difficult to clean up once it is made.

Pin and glue the box sides (3) inside the front and back (2) to give a rectangular frame, using 1½" panel pins 50mm apart. Check again that the top (1) is square at its corners. Label it for future reference, then pin and glue it to the top of the frame, pulling the frame flush with the edges of the top. Finally turn the box upside-down and pin and glue the bottom. It is important to get the top and bottom on quickly before the glue has set. If necessary, save time by leaving some of the panel pins out until the top and bottom are fixed in place, putting the remaining pins in afterwards.

Punch all the pin heads down and when the glue has set, fill all pinholes, grain and cracks with grain filler. Thoroughly sand the whole box to a fine finish.

Measure down 130mm from the top of the box and square a line all round it. Draw another line from front to back along the centre line of the top to mark off the two lids. Number the sides of the box as in **figure 4** so that you do not get them mixed up when you have sawn them.

Saw off the top with a large tenon, panel or power saw. Clean up the edges with a smoothing plane and re-fit the top, ensuring that it does not rock. Saw the top along the marked line into two equal pieces, but do not clean up the edges at this stage.

Each of the two lids is fixed to the box with a piano hinge. This hinge is ideal for long horizontal joints, especially as it does not require to be let into the wood, which would be difficult with plywood. It is available only in 1800mm (6 ft) lengths, so the two hinges will have to be cut to

figure 1

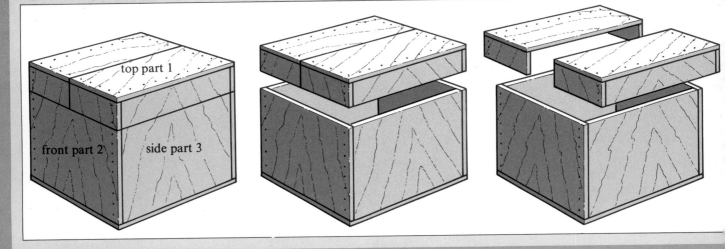

top part 1

front part 2 side part 3

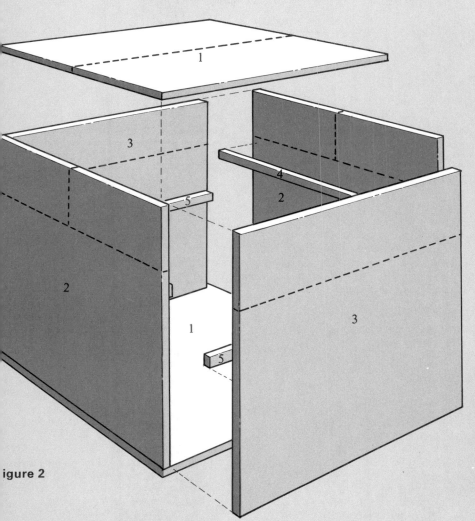

figure 2

size with a junior hacksaw before use.

Take one of the two lids and match it up with the main carcase, using the numbers marked on the wood earlier. Fix it in the open position on the side of the box, using two G cramps, as shown in **figure 5**. Because the box will eventually be covered in plastic laminate, put two spare pieces of the laminate between the lid and the box to allow for its thickness, otherwise the lid will not open flat when the box is finished.

Open the hinge and lay it with the knuckle of the hinge accurately centred over the gap between the lid and the box. Bore pilot holes with a hand drill, then screw the hinge temporarily in position using only six $\frac{1}{2}$" No. 4 countersunk chrome screws, evenly spaced, as the lid will have to be removed again soon. Repeat the operation with the other lid.

Where the lids meet in the closed position, the sawn edges should now be planed. The best way to do this is to take them off the

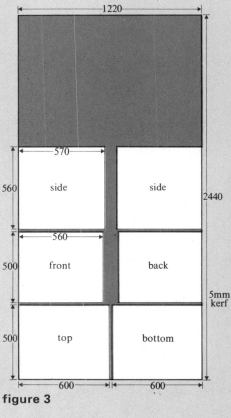

figure 3

figure 4

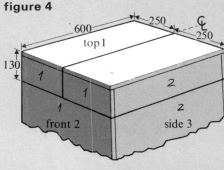

Cutting List. See figures 2, 6 and 7

No.	Part	Material	Qty	Length	Width	Thickness
1	Top and bottom	Birch plywood	2	600	500	15
2	Front/back	Birch plywood	2	560	500	15
3	Side	Birch plywood	2	560	570	15
4	Upper tray runners	Hardwood	2	470	20	15
5	Lower tray runners	Hardwood	2	570	20	15
6	Upper tray sides	Birch plywood	2	560	64	12
7	Upper tray ends	Birch plywood	2	200	64	12
8	Upper tray dividers	Birch plywood	3	200	60	9
9	Upper tray panels	Plastic laminate	3	240	80	1
10	Upper tray bottom	Birch plywood	1	560	224	6
11	Lower tray sides	Birch plywood	2	460	100	12
12	Lower tray ends	Birch plywood	2	256	100	12
13	Lower tray bottom	Birch plywood	1	460	280	6

Note: Remember that the cutting list gives *finished* sizes only, see Buying Timber, page 109.

Other Materials

× 50mm twin wheeled castors
lengths of chrome piano hinge 570mm long
× 12mm dia. rubber buffers 3mm thick
pieces of rosewood laminate 505 × 1800mm
and 605 × 1200mm
× $\frac{1}{2}$" No. 4 countersunk chrome screws
r piano hinges
× 1" No. 8 countersunk steel/brass screws
r tray runners

$\frac{1}{2}$ kilo $1\frac{3}{4}$" panel pins
$\frac{1}{2}$ kilo $1\frac{1}{4}$" panel pins
$\frac{1}{4}$ kilo 1" panel pins
7 metres whitewood iron-on edge veneer
PVA glue
Contact adhesive
Polyurethane lacquer

Sewing Box and Drinks Cabinet

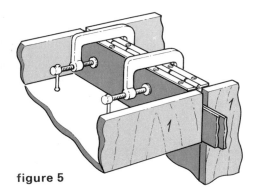

figure 5

box again and to hold them in a bench vice. Replace the lids temporarily to check the fit and remember to leave an adequate gap for the application of the iron-on edge veneer, plus a working clearance.

Pin and glue the drawer runners in position. The lower tray runners (part 5) are situated 160mm down from the top edge of the box sides (3) and the upper tray runners (4) are 20mm down from the top edge of the front and back (2).

Making the Trays

The trays are made from 12mm ply, pinned and glued at the corners. To ensure good jointing on simple structures like these, it is essential that each part is cut exactly to length and that all the ends are exactly square. Always mark out with a pencil the correct centre line for your pins and do not use too much glue.

Start with the lower tray, **figure 6**. Pin and glue the two ends (12) between the two sides (11), then pin and glue on the bottom (13), pulling the frame square on it as you do so. When the tray is dry, carefully plane and sand the outside surfaces and remove all sharp edges with a sanding block. Fit it into the box and check that it moves freely on its runners. To finish, apply three coats of clear polyurethane lacquer, drying and rubbing down between coats.

The structure of the upper tray is shown in **figure 7**. It has 3 small compartments separated by dividers (8) and each compartment has a curved floor made from the plastic laminate panel (9). The curved panel makes it easier to pick up small sewing items such as buttons, press studs, etc which tend to get stuck in corners.

Mark out on the tray sides (6) the position of the three dividers (8) 80mm apart. As shown in **figure 8**, the edges of curved panels are held in a narrow V-shaped groove on the inner surfaces of the tray sides. Mark and cut the groove 3mm wide, 5mm down from the top edge of the tray side, using a sharp chisel.

Pin and glue the ends (7) and the sides (6) as you did for the lower drawer and pin and glue its bottom (10) in place. Check the dividers for fit, then pin and glue them in position, pinning through the tray sides and following the marked positions. Plane and rub down and check fit in the box. Apply three coats of polyurethane as before.

Cut the plastic laminate panels to size, making sure that the grain on the back follows the width rather than the length. When the tray is dry, place each laminate piece centrally over its intended compartment and press firmly in the centre to snap in position. We found that cream coloured laminate looked very attractive here.

Once you have completed the trays, you can go on to cover the outside with rosewood plastic laminate. In order that the grain pattern shall go the right way on the box, it is important that the laminate is cut and fitted as shown in **figure 9**. Note that the sizes given for the laminate in the cutting list allow a few mm each way for trimming.

Mark out the laminate, numbering each piece with a chinagraph pencil (or anything else that will wipe off afterwards) as shown in **figure 9**.

Hold a metal straight edge along one of the lines and score down it several times with a craft knife fitted with a laminate cutting blade, then holding the laminate down with one hand on the straight edge, pull the free end upwards until the laminate snaps along the line. This can be an alarming procedure for the uninitiated, especially since the laminate makes a loud noise when it snaps. If it doesn't work with moderate tension, score the line a few more times.

The plastic laminate is stuck to the carcase with contact adhesive, see page 131. Start by removing the lids once again and lay them together on the bench. Always work on adjacent surfaces when applying the laminate to ensure a perfect grain match. Fix the two top panels (4) and (5) first, then the sides of the lids (2) (3) (6) and (7), ending with the front and back of the box, (1) and (8). Fixing the laminate in this way prevents any misalignment appearing on the top faces. As each panel is laid, clean off round the edges with a smoothing plane or one of the branded makes of edge trimmer.

The hinged sides of the box faces can now be covered, laying the laminate in the order (10) and (11) then (9) and (12). Before fitting, clean up those edges of the laminate which come into contact with the hinges, because once stuck in position, you won't be able to get at them again. Plane at an angle of 45° all the corners where 2 pieces of laminate meet to remove all sharp edges. Lip the mating edges of the box and lid with iron-on edge veneer, see page 146, using a piece of brown paper between the iron and the whitewood veneer to prevent marking and to stop glue getting on the iron sole. Trim the lipping with either a fine file or an edge trimmer.

Thoroughly clean out any sawdust from the inside of the box and lids and give them three coats of clear matt polyurethane lacquer. Allow to dry and rub down between coats. When the lacquer is dry, replace the lids permanently with 20 screws to each hinge.

Glue the 4 small rubber buffers to the top edges of the box, 2 each side, where the lids close together. These make up for the gap caused by the thickness of the hinge.

All that remains now for the completion of the box is the addition of four castors screwed to the corners of its base.

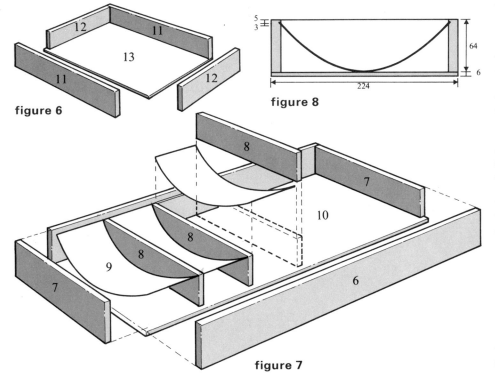

figure 6

figure 8

figure 7

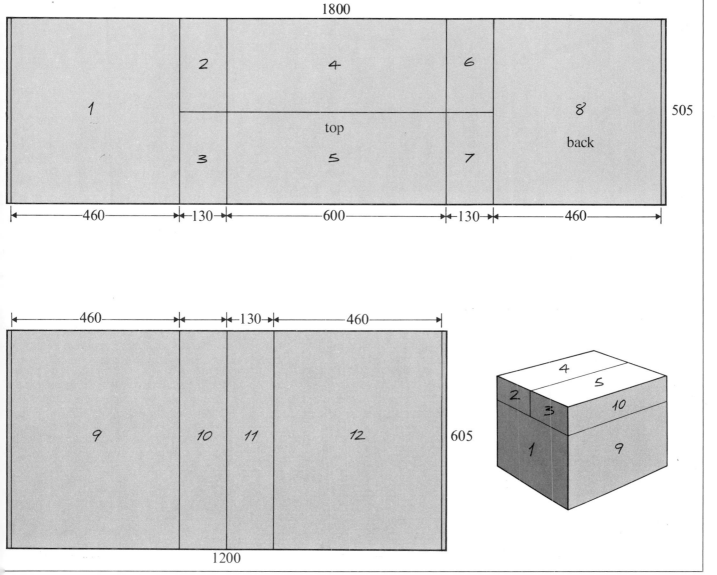

Figure 9

Drinks Cabinet

The drinks cabinet is made from a sealed box in exactly the same way as the sewing box, but with two differences: it is made of veneered chipboard instead of ply and part of the front panel of the box is cut away as shown in **figure 10**. This panel forms the false front for the glass tray, which slides out of the box on extending metal runners.

The finish of the cabinet is, as always, a matter of personal taste. We made it from mahogany veneered chipboard and painted the outside surfaces with opaque black plastic lacquer. The contrast between the reddish mahogany and the shiny black is very effective, and it is further heightened by the bright aluminium strip used along the mating edges of the lids and box.

To keep the clinking of glass to a minimum, we floored the glass tray and the bottom of the box, where the bottles are kept, with cork tiles.

Sewing Box and Drinks Cabinet

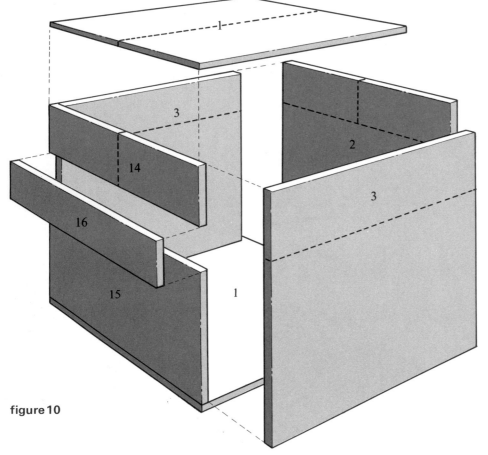

figure 10

Making Instructions

All the pieces of the carcase are cut from a 2440×1220mm veneered board as shown in **figure 3**.

The making of the basic box is exactly the same as for the sewing box except that the false drawer front (16) is omitted from the start, **figure 10**. Fit the hinges as before, but you will not need the plastic laminate packing as for the sewing box.

Measure the internal dimensions of the bottom of the box, which should be 570×470mm. Lay 4 of the 300mm square tiles together and mark out the bottom size on them then cut the tiles with a craft knife along a metal straight edge. Apply contact adhesive to both the bottom and the tiles and place the tiles carefully in position, see Contact Adhesive, page 131.

Finish the inside of the box including the cork tiles with a minimum of three coats of clear 2 part epoxy lacquer, which is resistant to water and alcohol.

The glass tray is supported on an extending metal runner on each side, **figure 12**. There are many types of runner available in DIY shops. The one illustrated in **figure 12** consists of two halves. One half is screwed to the side of the box and the other to the side of the glass tray. Each runner has a plastic wheel at one end and when in use, the tray side runner locks into and runs on the box side runner. Even at its fullest extension, the tray is held safely and there are stops on the runners to prevent them pulling out.

Screw the outside portion of the runner to the box side. The exact position will depend on what type you buy. For the runner in **figure 12**, the top edge will be about 30mm down from the edge of the box. Whatever runner you use, it should be fitted so that the glass tray runs clear of the top edge of the lower front panel (15)

Lay the inner part of the runners in position on the outer runners and measure accurately the distance between them. This will be the finished width of the glass tray and you may have to adjust the dimensions on the cutting list to go with the runners you have bought.

Since it will come in for a lot of wear, the glass tray should be made of hardwood. In our case we used utile to match the mahogany veneers.

Take one of the tray sides — part 6 — and screw it to the inner part of its runner. Pull the runner out to its fullest extent and mark with a pencil and ruler on the tray side the position of the inside front of the box as in **figure 13**. This line marks the position of the back of the tray and ensures that when the tray is fully extended it will not obstruct access to the bottles inside the cabinet.

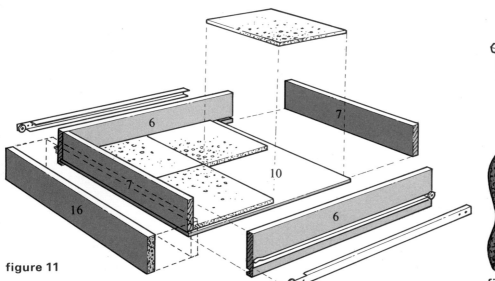

figure 11

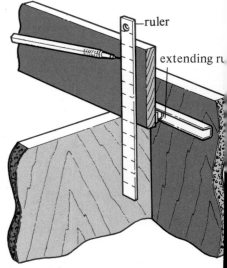

tray side fully extended

ruler

extending ru

figure 13

Sewing Box and Drinks Cabinet

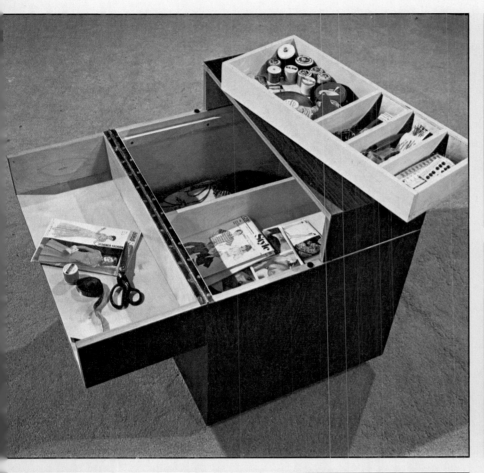

Above Left *The sewing box half-open. One of the two sliding trays has been taken out and stood on the top.*
Top Right *When closed, the sewing box is handsome but unobtrusive.*
Above Right *The drinks cabinet is a variation of the sewing box where bright aluminium strip has been used as a highlight against the black plastic lacquer.*

Left *The drinks cabinet has only one tray, which slides out on extending drawer runners. Bottles are stored in the space below.*

Wall Mounted Cabinets

Above *Nick Frewing's wall-mounted cabinets. The occasional table in the foreground is designed to match them: both pieces have the same scratch-moulded decoration (see chapter 2).*

Left *The sideboard variation uses the lower run of cabinets from the wall-mounted range, free-standing on frames built the same way as the occasional table (chapter 2).*

figure 12

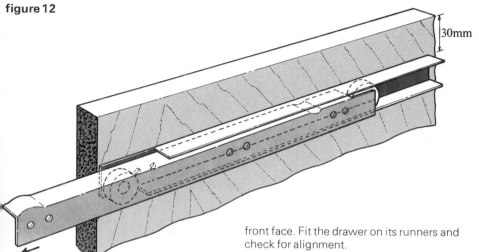

30mm

Remove the tray side from the runner. Finish the other side to the same length.

Run a 6mm groove along the inside surface of each tray side 10mm up from the bottom edge. This will receive the tray bottom (10). See Cutting Grooves, page 155. Note that there are no grooves in the tray front and back as the bottom runs underneath them, see **figure 14**.

Pin and glue the two tray sides to the front. Pin and glue in the drawer back (7) flush with the marked line and above the 6mm groove. Make sure the tray bottom is absolutely square, then run a bead of glue along its sides and slide it into position. To fix the bottom, pin up through it into the tray back and front. Cover the bottom of the tray with cork tiles as previously described for the box, using contact adhesive as before. When the glue has dried, finish the tray with a minimum of three coats of clear 2 part epoxy plastic lacquer, excepting the

front face. Fit the drawer on its runners and check for alignment.

Inspect all the surfaces of the cabinet and the false tray front (16) for any marks that may have resulted from assembly. Fill them with grain filler and rub the whole thing down with medium then fine garnet paper to give a smooth finish.

Finish the cabinet and the false tray front with black plastic lacquer. This requires no priming, but a minimum of 4 coats is needed to give a deep black lustre. Remember to rub down between coats with 'wet and dry' or silicon carbide paper. Alternatively, you can use the burnishing cream provided in the same pack as the lacquer by some manufacturers.

When the paint is thoroughly hardened, screw and glue the false tray front to the unfinished front of the glass tray. Do this with the tray closed to get an exact fit in the cabinet front.

The aluminium strip can now be attached to the mating edges of the carcase and lids and the top edge of the false tray front. Mitre the corners, see page 148, using hacksaw and file and glue in position using contact adhesive and keeping the strip flush with the inside of the cabinet and lids. After assembly, the trim can either be left bright or rubbed down with fine wire wool to produce a satin lustre finish.

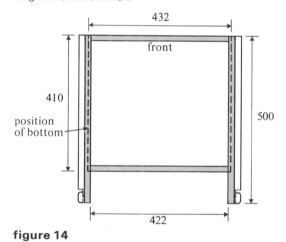

figure 14

Cutting List. See figures 10 and 11						
No.	Part	Materials	Qty	Length	Width	Thickness
1	Top and bottom	Veneered chipboard	2	600	500	15
2	Back	Veneered chipboard	1	560	500	15
3	Sides	Veneered chipboard	2	560	570	15
14	Upper front panel	Veneered chipboard	1	115	500	15
15	Lower front panel	Veneered chipboard	1	375	500	15
16	False tray front	Veneered chipboard	1	70	500	15
6	Tray sides	Hardwood	2	500	95	12
7	Tray back and front	Hardwood	2	422	78	12
10	Tray bottom	Birch plywood	1	410	432	6

Note: Remember the cutting list gives *finished* sizes only, see Buying Timber, page 109.

Other Materials

4 × 50mm twin wheeled castors

8 × 6mm cork flooring tiles 300 × 300mm

1 pair extending drawer runners 500mm long Woodfit UB335

1m bright aluminium strip 19 × 3mm

2 × 500mm lengths chrome piano hinge

20 × ½" No. 4 chrome countersunk screws for hinge

½ kilo 1¾" panel pins for box

16 × 1¼" panel pins for tray

PVA Glue

Contact adhesive

Black and clear 2 part epoxy plastic lacquer

Wood filler

WALL MOUNTED CABINETS

Nick Frewing

This handsome set of wall cabinets is intended for the dining room or lounge. The lower cabinet can be used to store cutlery and tableware, whilst the glass fronted cabinets are ideal for displaying china, books, prized possessions, etc. The top of the lower run of cabinets forms a convenient shelf for hi-fi and records.

The cabinets need not be wall-mounted. They can be stood on base frames and used as sideboards, as on page 105. They use the same scratch moulded decoration as the occasional table, on page 19, and the two items complement each other well in the same room.

Construction

All the cabinets are made in the same way and differ only in their dimensions and fittings, as shown in **figure 1**. In particular, the display cabinets and storage cabinets are closely related, differing only in size and in the material used for their sliding doors. It is these cabinets that are described in the making instructions below, whilst the china cupboard and the drawer unit are described separately.

The components of the basic cabinet are shown in the exploded diagram in **figure 2**. Each of the units is based upon the same construction technique. A track rail (9) is joined to the front edge of the top and bottom panels (1). The rails are then grooved. Next the top, bottom and side

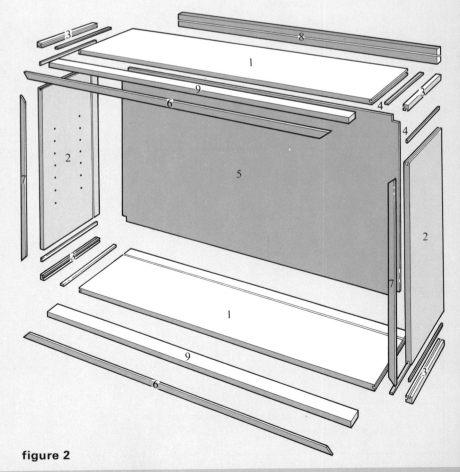

figure 2

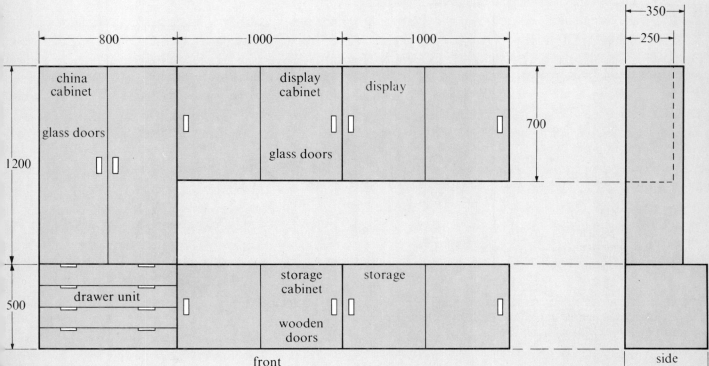

figure 1

panels (1 and 2) are joined together with separate corner pieces (3) of solid timber. The corner pieces and panels are grooved to accept plywood tongues which joint the carcase together. The back (5) plays an important role in holding the whole thing square and rigid. Each panel is grooved 25mm in from the rear edge to take the back and when in place the completed carcase is very strong. Behind the back, in the 25mm space, a diagonally-sawn hang-rail (8) is located, enabling each unit to be wall hung. Alternatively the units may be fitted with a base frame, see page 105.

If you do not wish to hang the units at all, the hang-rail need not be fitted. A further variation in this case can be to glue and screw the back into a simple rebate. If this method is adopted the back size is increased to those bracketted in the cutting list.

Each front edge is covered by a lipping which hides the raw edge of the blockboard and the corner joint. A scratch moulded detail, cut with a simply made tool, as in the table Chapter 2, offers a decorative detail outline to each cabinet.

Materials

The units illustrated are made from mahogany which has been stained and polished. A number of alternative timbers can be used including oak, teak or walnut. The limiting factor is the availability of blockboard which is face-veneered on both sides, solid timber and face-veneered (single side) plywood of the same variety.

Veneered blockboard is available to order from most hardwood timber merchants —they will also be able to supply the veneered plywood and matching solid timber. Given sufficient time, most merchants will saw and plane the solid timber to size for you. Always order in excess of the lengths shown in the cutting list to allow yourself a little extra to square off the ends as you work. The width and thickness dimensions should not be varied, however.

When ordering the hang-rail (8), ask for it to be diagonally cut before delivery. It is a simple job for a saw mill but will prove time-consuming if done at home without a power saw. See **figure 3**.

All the fittings are standard and detailed reference numbers are given in the cutting lists. Glass doors are all cut from 6mm float glass which is polished all round (P.A.R.). Order this from your local glass merchant. The handles, made from wood, are simply and effectively bonded to the glass with double-sided adhesive tape.

As befits the last project in the book, this job is more demanding than most, both in terms of skill and time. It would not be wise to attempt it without having completed at least one other project in the book first.

No.	Part	Material	Qty	Length	Width	Thickness
	Cutting List. See figure 2			**Glass-fronted Display Cabinet** $1000 \times 700 \times 250$mm		
1	Top and bottom	Veneered blockboard	2	964	221	18
2	Side	Veneered blockboard	2	664	244	18
3	Corners	Hardwood	4	250	19	19
4	Tongues	Crossgrain plywood	8	250	15	4
5	Back	Veneered plywood	1	976	676	4
6	Top and bottom lipping	Hardwood	2	1025	19	6
7	Side lipping	Hardwood	2	725	19	6
8	Hang rail	Softwood	1	964	100	25
9	Track strip	Hardwood	2	964	23	19
10	Doors	Glass	2	497	672	6
11	Handles	Hardwood	2	110	22	6
12	Shelves	Veneered blockboard	2	960	170	18
13	Shelf lipping	Hardwood	4	960	30	20

Note: Remember that the cutting list gives *finished* sizes only, see Buying Timber, page 109.
This cabinet cannot be made with a rebated back. Use with the hang rail.
The hardwood and veneered plywood must match the face veneered blockboard.

Other Materials
× 2½″ No. 12 steel countersunk woodscrews   8 × Woodfit MU412 shelf studs
× 2″ No. 12 fibre or plastic wall plugs   Double-sided adhesive tape
8 × Woodfit MU411 shelf sockets   Finishing materials (see page 158)

Wall Mounted Cabinets

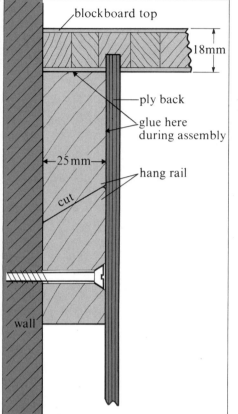

figure 3

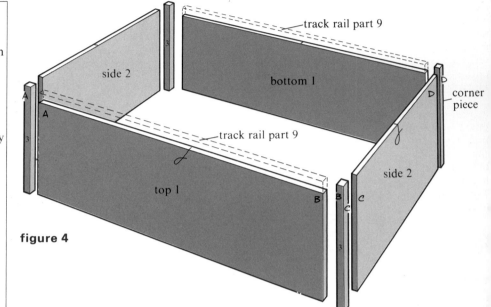

figure 4

Display and Storage Cabinet
Making Instructions

Mark out the top, bottom and side panels (1 and 2) with a knifed line and cut accurately to size. (Refer to the particular cutting list of the cabinet you wish to make). Plane the edges smooth and square — plane both sides together, then the top and bottom together to ensure that the panels of each pair are exactly the same size as one another. Cut the corner pieces (3) to length.

Stand the panels and corner pieces up on a flat surface and letter them in the order in which they are to be assembled, A-A, B-B etc. Mark the outside faces and the front edges of the panels as face side and face edge respectively, as in **figure 4**.

The next job is to cut the grooves in the corner pieces and in the ends of the top, bottom and side panels. If you are making any numbers of cabinets there will be a lot of grooves to cut and you would be well advised to use a groove cutting attachment on a power drill, particularly with the tough end grain of the blockboard panels.

The alternative is to use a plough or combination plane, see Cutting Grooves page 155. When cutting the grooves in the corner pieces, you may encounter difficulty because the side fence of the plane butts on the working surface and prevents it sitting level on the wood. To overcome this you will need to build a simple jig which allows the side fence to hang over the edge of the bench. Dimensions for the jig are given in **figure 5** and for the grooves in **figure 6**.

figure 5

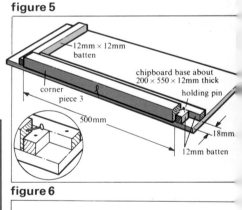

figure 6

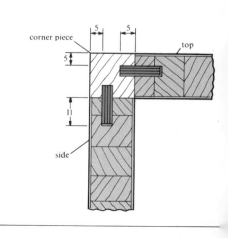

No.	Part	Material	Qty	Length	Width	Thickness
	Cutting List. See figure 2	**Storage Cabinet with Sliding Wooden Doors 1000 × 500 × 500mm**				
1	Top and bottom	Veneered blockboard	2	964	471	18
2	Sides	Veneered blockboard	2	464	494	18
3	Corners	Hardwood	4	500	19	19
4	Tongues	Crossgrain plywood	8	500	15	4
5	Back	Veneered plywood	1	976 (988)*	476 (488)*	4
6	Top and bottom lipping	Hardwood	2	1025	19	6
7	Side lipping	Hardwood	2	525	19	6
8	Hang rail	Softwood	1	964	100	25
9	Track strip	Hardwood	2	964	23	19
10	Doors	Veneered plywood	2	497	473	6
11	Handles	Hardwood	2	110	22	6
12	Shelves	Veneered blockboard	2	960	430	18
13	Shelf lipping	Hardwood	2	960	19	6

Note: Remember that the cutting list gives *finished* sizes only, see Buying Timber, page 109.
The hardwood and veneered plywood must match the veneered blockboard.
*For rebated back. See text.

Other Materials

4 × 2½″ No. 12 steel countersunk woodscrews
4 × ⅜″ No. 5 steel countersunk woodscrews
20 × Woodfit MU411 shelf sockets
8 × Woodfit MU412 shelf studs
Double-sided adhesive tape
Finishing materials (see page 158)

Note that the grooves are all cut from one width setting of the grooving plane or router—always work with the fence on the inside face of each panel and the same with the corner pieces. This simple precaution will ensure, as far as possible, that an accurate joint will result.

Cut the groove for the back (5) 25mm in from the rear edge, on the inner face of panels 1 and 2, **figure 7**. Note that if you do not wish to hang the cabinets on the wall the back need not be placed in a groove, but can be let into a simple rebate, **figure 7**. In this case the hang-rail (8) is not required. The 250mm units are not suitable for standing on bases—they will fall over.

Cut eight tongues (4) from 4mm plywood, at right angles to the grain direction **figure 8**.

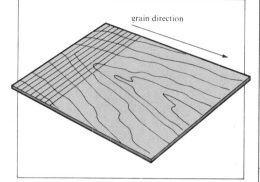

grain direction

figure 8

Cut the back (5) to size and remove a 6×6mm cut-away from each corner. If the rebated back system is adopted, cut the back to the size shown in brackets in the cutting list and do not cut the corners away.

The side panels—part 2—bear the sockets for the studs which carry the shelves. Mark out and drill the holes to the diameter and depth stated in the manufacturer's instructions. The hole centres for the 500× 500mm unit are shown in **figure 9** and for the 700×250mm unit in **figure 10**.

Note that the top and bottom panels of the cabinets are narrower than the side panels by 23mm. This is to make room for the track strips which carry the doors. Bond one track strip—part 9—to the front of the top and bottom respectively, using a

figure 7

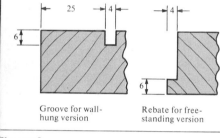

25 4   4

6

6

Groove for wall-hung version | Rebate for free-standing version

figure 9

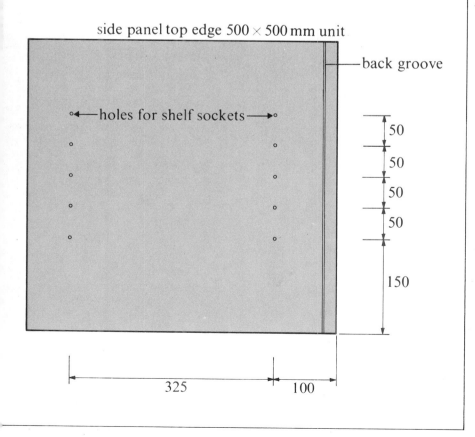

side panel top edge 500 × 500 mm unit

back groove

holes for shelf sockets

50
50
50
50
150

325   100

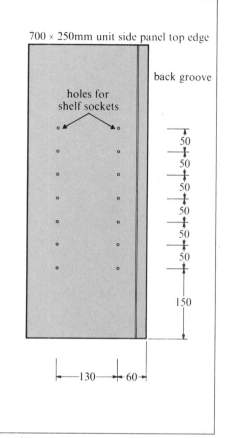

700 × 250mm unit side panel top edge

back groove

holes for shelf sockets

50
50
50
50
50
50

150

130   60

figure 10

glued rub joint, see page 148. Cramp securely in place with a softening batten, see page 28.

The track strip is 19mm thick—just 1mm thicker than the veneered blockboard of the top and bottom. When the glue is dry, remove from cramps and plane it flush with the blockboard. But be careful, using a very sharp plane with a very fine setting, or it will tear the veneer. Trim the ends flush with the panel ends.

You still need to cut the grooves in the track strips and this is best done after the track strip is glued to the top and bottom, as the pressure of the cramps during gluing may crush a section with grooves in it. The dimensions of the grooves are given in **figure 11**. Note that they are deeper in the top panel than the bottom. Do not extend the grooves cut in the ends of the top and bottom across the ends of the track strips.

Assembly of carcase

Assemble the carcase dry, that is without glue, complete with corner pieces and tongues in their lettered order. Join the bottom to its corner pieces using the plywood tongues, add the sides, slide the back into position (not if it is rebated) and then add the top and remaining corners.

Cramp up, using softening strips, and add the back at this stage if it is set into a rebate.

Wall Mounted Cabinets

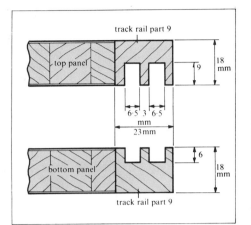

figure 11

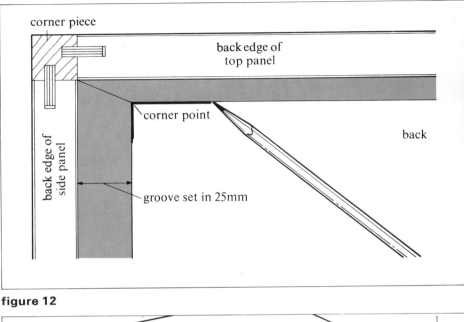

figure 12

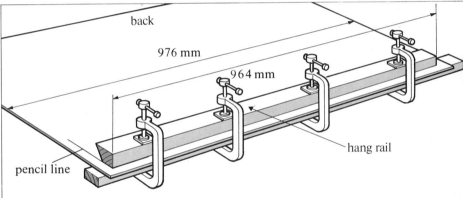

figure 13

Check the carcase for square using a diagonal measuring stick, page 145, and sight across opposite edges to see that they are parallel. Make any adjustments at this stage. Unless the carcase goes together square, the doors will not fit correctly.

If the carcase is to be wall hung, while it is still in cramps, and after it has been corrected and is square, draw a pencil line along the back of the back panel where it sits into the groove in the underside of the top. Mark the top corner points as well. See **figure 12**.

Remove the cramps — do not alter their setting, as this will help to speed up the final gluing operation. Dismantle the carcase carefully and keep the parts in lettered order for final assembly.

Cut the hang rail (8) sections to length. Glue and G cramp the top piece to the back face of the back panel (5), carefully lining it up with the pencil line and corner points. Wipe away all surplus glue, **figure 13**. Remove cramps when dry.

Rub down all the internal faces of panels 1 and 2 and the inside of the back (5) with fine abrasive paper on a cork block.

Finally, assemble the carcase carefully, applying adhesive to all grooves and tongues and the top edge of the hang-rail (8). Help at this stage is advisable. Check at each assembly stage that the parts are going together in their lettered order. Remember that the grooved-in back is fitted before the top panel is positioned. Cramp up as before and check finally for square — follow the same procedure as before. Apply G cramps to grip the hang-rail firmly to the underside of the top. Wipe off all traces of excess adhesive with a damp cloth. Glue and screw the rebated back into place if applicable.

When fully set, remove the cramps and trim off the surplus from the ends of the tongues and corner pieces with a saw.

Plane the front and rear edges flat and flush. Plane the corner pieces flush with the veneered surfaces of the panels, again using a very sharp plane finely set.

With hacksaw and flat and round files, shape one corner of a cabinet scraper as

shown on page 21 (Occasional Table). Cut the bead detail as shown there along one face edge of each piece of lipping (6 and 7), **figure 14**.

Cut mitred corners at 45° in a mitre block (page 148) on both ends of top and bottom lipping (6), to fit exactly between the corners of the carcase. The beaded edge is next to the inner faces of the cabinet. Glue and cramp in place with sash cramps and softening battens, page 128, to distribute the cramp load evenly along the bead length. Wipe off all traces of excess glue, especially at the mitred ends. Remove cramps when dry.

Clean the edge of the beading down flush with inner and outer faces of the panels with a sharp plane and file.

figure 14

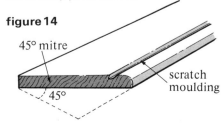

Cut mitred and matching ends to each side lipping (7) to give an exact fit between the ends of the top and bottom beads. A block plane or file can be used to make minor adjustments if necessary. When a perfect fit has been achieved, glue and cramp these in position. On this occasion place a small piece of waxed paper over the mitred joint and under the softening strip — this will prevent excess glue from the joint sticking the softening strips to the job. Wipe off surplus glue as before. Trim flush with panels when dry.

Final cleaning up

Clean up all the external surfaces to a smooth finish with fine abrasive paper supported on a cork sanding block. The inside may need minor attention in spite of being done earlier — the damp rag used to remove the surplus glue may have raised the grain slightly. The smoother the surface achieved at this stage the better the final surface after polishing or varnishing.

Take particular care to follow the direction of the grain at this stage. It is inevitable that when cleaning up the top and side panels, some overrun across the grain of the corner pieces will occur. Don't worry—if fine paper is being used the scratches will be shallow enough to remove with a few passes of the abrasive paper, still on the cork block, along the grain of each corner piece. This completes the basic carcase.

Sliding Doors

Check the height of the doors (see under 'width' in cutting list) against the carcase before cutting the wooden ones or ordering the glass. The height of the doors is measured from the bottom of the bottom panel groove to the underside of the top panel (not into the groove). Add 3mm to this dimension. That is the height of each door, **figure 15**.

Smooth off top and bottom edges of the plywood doors. Plane the upright edges (i.e. those that do not go into the grooves) and cover them with iron-on edge veneer to match the face veneer.

Clean up with fine abrasive paper.

The doors are fitted in position by lifting the top edge into the full depth of the top groove. The bottom is then swung into the corresponding bottom groove and the door is dropped into place. After staining and polishing, lubricate the doors and track by rubbing with wax candle.

When staining or polishing wooden plywood doors it is essential to treat back and front in the same way — stain both sides and polish both sides. This reduces the chances of the door twisting.

figure 15

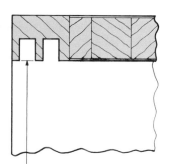

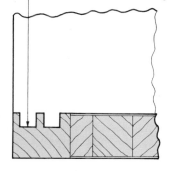

this height + 3mm = door height

Handles

The tool used for cutting the bead detail on the lipping is also used in the making of the 6mm thick handles for sliding doors, **figure 16**. A bit of cheating goes on here as the scratch tool will not cut end grain easily.

Begin with a strip of handle section in one length, long enough to cut into the number of handles you require later. Scratch mould the two top corners throughout the length of the piece. Then cut each handle 110mm long and clean up and square the ends carefully. Copy the scratch moulded detail across the end grain by making an initial saw

figure 16

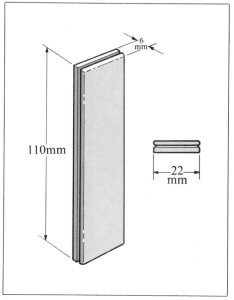

cut to join the Vs at the top of each side bead — the cut needs to be about 1½mm deep. Then cut the rounded shape with chisel and file. Finally clean up with fine abrasive paper. Finish them to match the carcase. Screw and glue the handles to the plywood doors. Stick the handles to glass doors with double-sided adhesive tape. Position them centrally in the height of each door and 25mm in from the closing edge.

Shelves

Shelves to take medium loads are adequately made from veneered blockboard with a 6×19mm lipping (detail of edge **figure 17**). These have been included in

figure 17

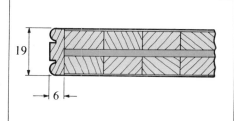

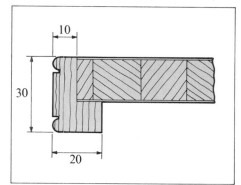

figure 18

the cutting lists of the 500×500mm unit. Where heavy loads — rows of books or magazines—are to be held it is advisable to increase the strength of the shelf by using heavier lipped edges on both edges of the shelf (detail of edge **figure 18**). These have been included in the cutting list for the 700×250mm unit.

China Cupboard

See **figure 19** overleaf.

The construction of the carcase is exactly the same as for the sliding door units, except that extra pieces of softwood 100×21×21mm are rub glued between the back and sides to strengthen the back as shown in **figure 20**. No top and bottom track rails are required.

A number of shelves can be fitted into this cupboard and they are of the medium load variety with a 6×19mm hardwood lipping — **figure 17**. They do, however, have a different shelf fixing—the so-called magic wires. See Tools Section, page 140. The wires, which have 90° bent ends, plug into the matching hole pairs in the cupboard sides. A groove 4mm wide and 9mm deep is required in the centre of each shelf end to slide over the projecting wire 'loop'. Groove the ends before lipping so that it does not show at the front.

The position for the 3mm dia. drill holes 50mm apart are shown in **figure 20**.

The doors are made of 6mm float glass 1160×378mm. Check that this size allows 2mm clearance all around the inside of the cupboard. The doors should be obtained from your glass merchant exactly to size (with that essential clearance) and polished all round. The hardwood handles are scratch moulded in the same way as for the sliding door cabinets and are fixed to the glass with double-sided adhesive tape.

There is no difficulty in fitting the glass doors, providing you have built the cabinet square. Otherwise they will not fit at all, or at best swing open. There is no need for door catches as the hinge we recommend usually hold the doors closed without further assistance.

See page 140 (Hinges) for fitting instructions.

Wall Mounted Cabinets

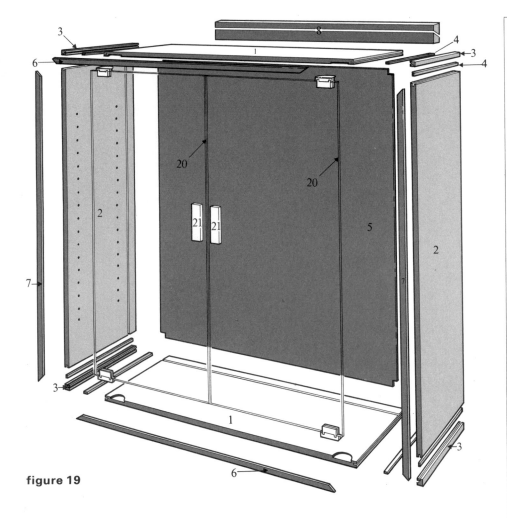

figure 19

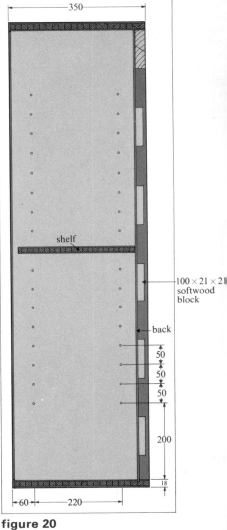

figure 20

Drawer Unit

The carcase is made in exactly the same way as the sliding door cabinets, except that there is no track strip to take the doors. Complete and finish this as before, then move on to make the drawers. This should be done with care to ensure a good fit.

Measure the inside width and height of the complete carcase. If everything has gone together perfectly it will measure 764 × 464mm. Drawer fronts to fit this size need to be planed 760mm long (allowing for a 2mm gap between each end and the carcase sides) and 113mm wide (allowing approximately 2mm gap at top and bottom and 3mm between each drawer).

If the internal cabinet sizes vary from the sizes above, adjust the drawer front sizes to compensate. Leave the gap sizes as they are. Plane the ends square and mark the face sides and edges.

Cut the drawer sides to length and plane them square at the ends. Do this in pairs so that they are both exactly the same length. Stand the front (14) and two sides (15) of each drawer together in order of eventual assembly, face-edge down and

Cutting List. See figure 19		Vertical cabinet with hinged glass doors 1200 × 800 × 350mm				
No.	Part	Material	Qty	Length	Width	Thickness
1	Top and bottom	Veneered blockboard	2	764	344	18
2	Sides	Veneered blockboard	2	1164	344	18
3	Corners	Hardwood	4	350	19	19
4	Tongues	Crossgrain plywood	8	350	15	6
5	Back	Veneered plywood	1	1176(1188)*	776(788)*	4
6	Top and bottom lipping	Hardwood	2	825	19	6
7	Side lipping	Hardwood	2	1225	19	6
8	Hang rail	Softwood	1	764	100	25
12	Shelves	Veneered blockboard	2	760	305	18
13	Shelf lipping	Hardwood	2	760	19	6
20	Doors	Float glass P.A.R.	2	1160	378	6
21	Handles	Hardwood	2	110	22	10

Note: Remember that the cutting list gives *finished* sizes only, see Buying Timber, page 109.

The hardwood and veneered plywood must match the veneered blockboard.
*Sizes for rebated back. See text.

Other Materials
4 × 2½″ No. 12 steel countersunk woodscrews
4 × Woodfit ME922 magic wires
2 prs. Woodfit HH368 glass door hinges

face-side out. Letter the corners in sequence, **figure 22** overleaf. If you are making all the drawers together, as is the usual case, the lettered joints should also vary from drawer to drawer so that the components from one do not get mixed with another. Allocate letters A–D for drawer one and E–H for the next, and so on.

Cut the groove to take the thickness of the drawer bottom in the bottom of each side (15) and front (14) 12mm up from the inside edge (opposite face to the face-side mark) and 6mm deep, **figure 23**.

Cut a lap joint to take the thickness of the drawer sides on the inside face of each drawer front leaving a 6mm thick lap, **figure 24**. Also cut the 80×12mm recesses for the drawer handles, **figure 22** overleaf.

Cut drawer runner grooves centrally in each outside face of the drawer side (the one with the face-side mark) 7mm deep and 15mm wide, **figure 23**.

Cut all the drawer backs to size and plane them square on the ends.

The depth of the backs is equal to the distance between the top edge of the drawer bottom and the topmost edge of the drawer side. Subtracted from this is the 4mm clearance given which helps to prevent things in the drawer becoming jammed, **figure 25**.

The back fits into the sides of the drawer with housing joints, see page 148. Reference to **figure 26** will show that the length of the back is made up of the distance

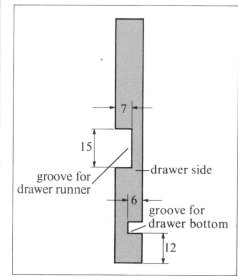

figure 23

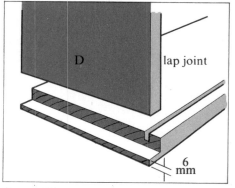

figure 24

figure 25

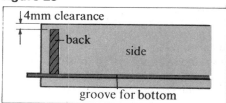

figure 21

No.	Part	Material	Qty	Length	Width	Thickness
1	Top and bottom	Veneered blockboard	2	764	494	18
2	Sides	Veneered blockboard	2	464	494	18
3	Corners	Hardwood	4	500	19	19
4	Tongues	Crossgrain plywood	8	500	15	6
5	Back	Plywood	1	776(788)*	476(488)*	4
6	Top and bottom lipping	Hardwood	2	825	19	6
7	Side lipping	Hardwood	2	525	19	6
8	Hang rail	Softwood	1	764	100	25
14	Drawer fronts	Hardwood	4	760	113	18
15	Drawer sides	Hardwood	8	460	113	12
16	Drawer backs	Hardwood	4	744	91	12
17	Drawer bottoms	Plywood	4	748	460(485)*	4
18	Drawer runners	Hardwood	8	465(490)*	15	8
19	Drawer handles	Hardwood	8	80	38	12

Cutting List. See figures 21 and 22 overleaf. **Drawer unit 800 × 500 × 500mm**

Note: Remember that the cutting list gives *finished* sizes only, see Buying Timber, page 109.

The hardwood for parts 15, 16 and 18 does not have to match the face veneer of the blockboard, since it is not normally seen.

*Sizes for rebated back. See text.

Other Materials

× 2½″ No. 12 countersunk steel woodscrews

2 × 1″ No. 8 countersunk steel woodscrews

Wall Mounted Cabinets

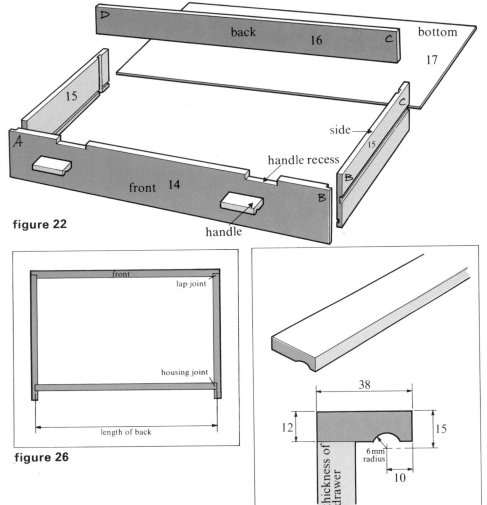

figure 22

figure 26

figure 27

bottoms before pinning in position into the bottom edge of the drawer backs.

Clean up all external edges with a sharp plane to flush them off. Clean up all external faces with fine abrasive paper. You will now need to make the drawer handles, **figure 27**.

Drawer Handles

Cut one strip of timber 38mm wide and 12mm thick which is long enough to produce all the handles (19).

Hollow out the finger grip on one face with a shaped grooving cutter to the dimensions in **figure 27**.

Mark with a cut-line the lengths of each handle, cut and clean up the ends.

When fitting into the drawer fronts, number each handle and mark its exact length where it is to be fitted. This will ensure the best fit in each case.

Glue and cramp (using softening) the handles into their respective positions in the drawer fronts. Ensure that the back edges are flush. Remove surplus adhesive.

Fitting the Drawers

Cut the drawer runners (18) to size and check that the lengths slide freely into the drawer side runner grooves.

Drill and countersink each runner in four equally spaced places to take 1" × No. 8 countersunk wood screws. Lift the drawers into the carcase with a 2mm spacer at the bottom, then a drawer, then a 3mm spacer followed by another drawer, and another 3mm spacer and so on, **figure 28**.

between the shoulders of the lap joints at the front of the drawer plus the depth of the two housing joints. The length of 744mm on the cutting list allows for housing joints 4mm deep, but it is wise to measure your own drawer for small variations which might drive it out of square. The width of the housing is the same as the thickness of the backs — 12mm. Note that they must be cut with a chisel and saw rather than a plough plane because they run across the grain.

Cut out the housing joints, number them ready for assembly and clean up all internal faces.

Cramp together dry, in numbered order and check that sides and front and back are parallel. Take apart, glue and pin together, checking as you assemble that the bottom grooves line up and that the back (16) lines up at its bottom with the top edge of the grooves in either side.

Cramp together and check for square using diagonal measuring rods. Leave to dry but wipe off all surplus glue.

Cut the bottom 'square' to fit snugly into the grooves in the drawer sides and front. The bottom should extend beyond the extremities of the drawer back. Cut bottoms to the bracketed length if a rebated-in back has been fitted to the carcase. Clean up the

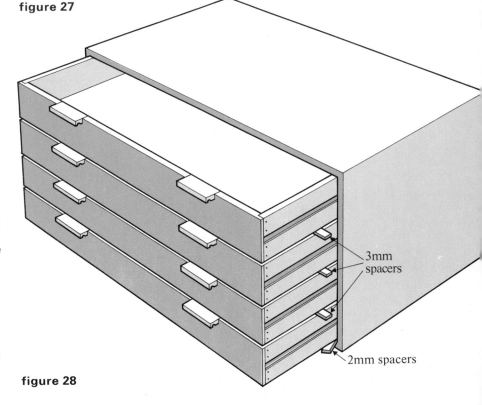

figure 28

Mark the point at which the top of each runner groove lines up with the cabinet on both sides.

Remove the drawers. Square lines across the inside of each side from the marks just made, checking as you mark that those lines are parallel with the cabinet bottom.

Fix one drawer runner at a time (with the front and back screws only) accurately beneath and touching each line and 6mm in from the front edge of the cabinet.

Test by sliding the drawers in place. Adjust the runners if necessary to prevent jamming. When running freely fix the remaining screws. Lubricate with wax candle.

Plane off the surplus length of the drawer bottoms, to adjust the front alignment of the drawers when closed.

The drawer unit is now ready for staining and finishing. See page 158.

Sideboard Variation

See colour photograph, page 94.

You can, if you prefer, arrange your cabinets as a run of low-level sideboards by standing them on base frames. The 250mm deep glass display cabinet is not suitable for this purpose, as it is unstable when free-standing.

Base frames for floor standing units are constructed in exactly the same way and with the same sections as the occasional table on page 19.

Each base frame is screwed through counterbored holes in the frame into the cabinet base. The front edge and sides are set in by 5mm and the depth of the frame allows it to stand clear of most skirting boards whilst the back of the cabinet is against the wall.

The overall base dimensions for the cabinets are as follows:

Sliding door unit	$1000 \times 500 \times 500$	
Base size	$990 \times 465 \times 250$ high	
Drawer unit	$800 \times 500 \times 500$	
Base size	$790 \times 465 \times 250$ high	
China cupboard	$1200 \times 800 \times 350$	
Base size	$790 \times 315 \times 250$ high	

As with all shallow and tall cabinets the glass-doored 1200mm high china cupboard may be unstable on uneven floors whilst empty and with the doors open. Care should be taken. For complete safety use the age-old method of fixing the top of the cupboard through its back to the wall.

TIMBER, TOOLS and TECHNIQUES

Nick Frewing

TIMBER SECTION

Types of Timber

Timber can very generally be divided into *softwoods*, which come from evergreen coniferous trees, and *hardwoods*, which come from deciduous trees. For the most part, this separation works reasonably well, the hardwoods having a tougher, closer grained consistency, but there are one or two surprises—balsa wood, for example, is classified as a hardwood because the tree drops its leaves in winter!

Softwoods

The most widely-used softwood in the United Kingdom is *European redwood*, also known as *deal* or *pine*. It dries more quickly than hardwoods and when dry works easily to a fine finish. Most of the finest wood comes from the huge forests of the Baltic and these imported boards may frequently be 5 or 6 metres long and 225mm wide with scarcely a knot showing. Unfortunately, the more commonly available grades have knots occuring regularly.

European redwood and whitewood is easily obtainable in an extensive range of sawn and planed stock sizes. In addition there are many moulded sections, such as tongued and grooved boards, tongue groove and 'V' jointed, quadrant/ quarter round and many specials for the building industry, for example skirtings, architraves, handrails and sash mouldings of various types.

Hardwoods

Hardwoods come in a bewildering range of exotic varieties, both home-grown and imported, but the great majority of them are used only by specialist furniture makers. For all practical purposes, we can confine ourselves to five main species— teak, mahogany, oak, elm and beech.

Teak is an expensive wood in its solid state. Its colour and grain vary considerably from piece to piece and when freshly sawn, the interior is often much paler than the the surrounding wood. However, it darkens quickly when exposed to light.

Teak saws and planes surprisingly easily, but it does require sharp tools because its sandy texture dulls edges quickly. The wood is rather oily, and because of this abrasive papers become clogged with dust, which must be tapped or shaken free from time to time. Because of the oily surface, teak is sometimes difficult to bond. Wherever possible use a formaldehyde-type glue and wipe the surface to be bonded with methylated spirit just before applying the glue. Make sure that the bonding surfaces are dust-free. Another consequence of the oiliness of the wood is that teak will not stain effectively.

Teak veneered boards are easily obtainable in a range of standard sizes. Most are 16mm thick and have a chipboard core. You may buy them with either single or double faces of teak; the single variety is usually backed with a commercial grade of mahogany.

Mahogany is a portmanteau word: there are hundreds of mahoganies. They are imported from South America and Africa and rejoice in names like utile, gaboon and sapele. Each has its own individuality with regard to texture, colour, weight and strength. Some mahoganies have a wild grain and are very difficult to plane by hand, whilst others are surprisingly mild and easy to work, indeed most of the readily obtainable mahoganies are relatively soft and some care is needed to prevent accidental damage to parts that have been planed to size. As hardwood go, some mahoganies are almost the most expensive and others are the cheapest, so it is worth discussing the choice of timber with your local merchant.

Oak. A number of oaks, usually known by their country of origin, are available in Britain, for example American oak, English oak and Japanese oak. English oaks provide a variety of colours, hardnesses and grain effects and their wood is usually heavier in weight than imported varieties. The most readily available imported oak is the Japanese. It is much lighter, usually easier to work, less strong and finer in grain than the English variety.

Timber Section

Much of the character of oak comes from the conditions of its growth. In woodlands it grows tall quickly, with few branches lower down. This produces timber which is straight and even in texture. The furniture industry and veneer makers purchase most of this. Oaks grown in hedgerows, on the other hand, have a tougher life, and are stunted in comparison to the woodland oaks. Their timber is harder, less regular and often heavier. In the past they were used for cart and boat building.

Users of oak will find that the timber stains purple in contact with hot hands. The stain can be removed from the wood with abrasive paper, but it may take some time to wash from fingers.

Elm was until recently one of the most common trees in this country. It has been used for centuries by wheelwrights, cartwrights, chair makers and coffin makers. The grain is usually fairly wild and requires care and time to achieve a good finish. It is extremely tough. During the drying process it has a tendency to split along its irregular grain.

Home-grown elm is available from smaller merchants who specialise in home-grown hardwood. They usually have a sawmill and convert the timber from the log themselves. Japanese elm is less wild in grain and is far easier to handle. It is kiln dried before export and, unlike English elm, is square-edged into standard width boards. Because of this, there is less waste, but the cost is much higher.

Beech is hard, relatively cheap, strong and has a finely-patterned grain. Although we grow a certain amount in this country, we rely on substantial imports from Europe, and it is readily available from most hardwood timber merchants.

Because of its characteristics, beech is used extensively in furniture making and is an ideal wood for chair frames. It is also a favourite material for making wooden toys. Its light colour and delicate grain mean that it is not the most dramatic of woods, but it takes coloured wood stain very well, so a wide variety of appearances is possible. Beech does not last long outdoors because it is particularly susceptible to fungal attack.

Figure 1. Basic sizes of sawn softwood (cross-sectional sizes)

Thickness	Width								
	75	100	125	150	175	200	225	250	300
16	●	●	●	●					
19	●	●	●	●					
22	●	●	●	●					
25	●	●	●	●		●	●	●	●
32	●	●	●	●	●	●	●	●	●
36	●	●	●	●					
38	●	●	●	●		●	●		
44	●	●	●	●		●		●	●
50	●	●	●	●		●	●	●	●
63		●	●	●		●	●	●	●
75		●	●		●	●		●	●
100		●		●		●		●	●
150			●			●			●
200						●			
250								●	
300									●

NOTE: The smaller sizes contained within the broken lines are normally but not exclusively of European origin. The larger sizes outside the dotted lines are normally but not exclusively of North and South American origin.

108

Buying Timber

In April 1970 the timber trades adopted metric measure as their standard and since then all timber has been cut to millimetre sizes. See **figure 1**. Most are roughly equivalent to the old Imperial dimensions, but do not be tempted to try to convert back. Always work in metric sizes to avoid confusion.

If you have not bought timber before, it is as well to be quite clear about the sizes in which timber is sold. All solid timber sizes relate to the planks when they have been sawn from the log. This is known as the *nominal size.* Planing down sawn wood at home involves a great deal of labour and it is very difficult to keep the dimensions totally accurate, so you will almost certainly buy wood which has been *Planed All Round* in a machine, when it is known as P.A.R. During planing the sawn wood will lose about 2mm from each side, so a piece of wood with a nominal size of, say 25 × 100mm will measure approximately 21 × 96mm PAR.

When you refer to the cutting lists for the projects in this book, you will note that they give the *finished P.A.R. sizes* required for the piece of furniture in question. As far as possible, these relate to one of the standard nominal sizes in **figure 1**, and you can check this by adding 4mm to the width and to the thickness. Do not worry, however, if some of the measurements do not add up to a standard size. On nearly every job some non-standard piece will be required. In these cases, the pieces will have to be cut from standard boards which are the nearest in size. From time to time you will also see the letters EX written by a dimension in the cutting lists. This only occurs with curved or slanted pieces and gives the size of the board from which the curved piece must be cut.

The standard sizes (width and thickness) of softwoods are shown in **figure 1**. Standard *lengths* of timber begin at 1·8 metres and then occur at 300mm intervals— 2·1m, 2·4m and so on. Hardwood sizes follow the same pattern, but many boards are not square sawn at the edges, following as they do the natural waney edge of the board as it is cut from the tree (see Timber Faults below). In these cases, the width of the timber does not, of course, follow any standard. Remember if buying waney-edged hardwood that the sapwood has to be removed and due allowance for this waste has to be made.

Inspect your timber at the yard before purchase and reject any boards that are frankly damaged. Damage apart, you may as well face the fact that all timber has natural faults and that you will have to accept some waste and allow for it in your calculations. Be particularly careful to allow for end shakes in boards. Generally the timber merchant will supply you with a set of boards from which you can cut the pieces you require, but some yards will cut all the parts to size for a small extra cost. If you elect to do this, make sure the supplier knows that the cutting list contains finished sizes and ask for the lengths to be left longer than quoted, so that you have some waste to play with in joining pieces together. If your project involves veneered boards, make sure that the veneers and the solid timber match each other.

Distribution and sales of timber are divided into a number of outlets. At the specialist end are veneer suppliers and rare hardwood importers. Of more immediate interest to the home furniture maker are the hardwood and softwood merchants and the DIY centres.

Hardwood Merchants sometimes specialise in either imported or home-grown woods and it is to the latter that you may have to refer if you are making the elm dining set on page 51.

Softwood Merchants sell the bulk of their stock to the building industry. They usually carry a wide range of standard sections in both the sawn and the planed state. They also stock a wide variety of sheet materials including hardboard, plywood, chipboard and blockboard. Some of these merchants limit small sales to particular times of the week, Saturday mornings being the most common. Many merchants now have special DIY departments which offer

Timber Section

excellent service in a wide range of materials. A limited range of solid hardwoods is usually available to order from softwood merchants, as are veneered boards.

DIY Centres are set up to cope with the various demands of the amateur and hold stocks of a wide variety of materials in several sizes. They, unlike many trade merchants, will cut to order and will frequently be able to offer useful advice on supplies and alternatives. From these centres you can now obtain veneered chipboard panels, lip edging, melamine coated sheet and edging, hardboard, blockboard, chipboard and a wide variety of solid timber mouldings. The mouldings are usually cut from *ramin* a fine-grained hardwood which is normally dry and reliable. PAR softwood is frequently stocked in a number of sizes.

Large veneered blockboard or chipboard sheets will usually have to be ordered by the DIY centre and if they are not stock items, it is advisable to shop around for a quotation. Establish at the same time whether the shop can supply matching hardwood. If not, you may have to go to a hardwood specialist.

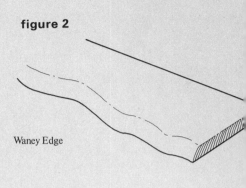

figure 2

Waney Edge

Faults in Timber

Before you purchase timber, it is worth inspecting each board for faults. This will save a journey back to the yard with the possibility of an argument or, worst of all, having to stop in the middle of the job because one of the components is unsatisfactory.

Warping
Twisting or bending due to inadequate storage and drying out. The board may be bent lengthwise or along its width. Check the board by laying it on a flat surface to see if it rocks and by sighting down the length of the board from one end.

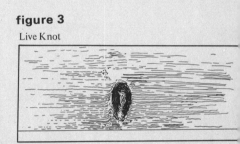

figure 3

Live Knot

Waney Edge See **figure 2**
The natural edge of the board where it meets the sapwood beneath the bark. It makes no difference to the quality of softwood, but it does interfere with the normal square sawn edge. In the majority of hardwoods, however, all waney edges and the adjoining sapwood are removed, because this part of the timber is inferior to the heartwood.

Live Knot See **figure 3**
As the name implies, a live knot is one which is integrated into the substance of the surrounding timber. A live knot is only a problem in softwood where it is very large and there is a risk of it cracking. Large live knots are fairly common in some hardwoods. Since they frequently star-crack and can be very difficult to plane and finish, they are best avoided. Small bunches of fine knots in timbers like oak and yew are very decorative and are sought after in some cases.

figure 4

Dead Knot

Dead Knot See **figure 4**
Commonly found in softwoods, these knots have black rings round them. They may be loose, or will become loose as the surrounding wood dries out, so avoid them if possible. Where dead knots cannot be cut away in the waste, it is possible to cut them out locally and then to let in a patch of matching timber, but this is rather a lengthy job.

End Shake

figure 5

End Shakes and Heart Shakes See **figures 5** and **6**
Shakes are cracks. They are commonly found in the ends of boards because the end dries out faster than any other part. The wood farther into the board is damper than at the end and shrinks at a slower rate. The resulting tug-of-war causes a crack or cracks to form, **figure 5**.

Heart shakes—**figure 6**—occur because of differing rates of shrinkage at the centre of boards which have been cut across the heart of the tree. They are usually accompanied by dishing of the board.

Our Renovation Project

Above Left *The oval dining table bought for £52 at auction.*
Above *One of six dilapidated chairs bought in a second-hand shop for £5 each. The brown varnish has been rubbed away on part of the right front leg to show the original gold paint.*
Left *Detail of the top surface of the table. The cracking and scratching of the lacquer is very evident, but there is an attractively-grained veneer below.*

Left *The edge of the table. The ugly brass decorations on the side of the top and on the legs can be seen. The cheap gold plastic trim is falling away from the bottom edge.*

Our Renovation Project

Above Left *The renovated dining set. Note the black lacquer on the side of the table top and on its legs, and the deep sheen on the table surface, reflecting the table-ware.*
Above *The finished chair. The frame has been painted with black plastic lacquer and the cane seat has been replaced with an upholstered velour pad.*

Left *The garden table we made from an old sewing machine. The underframe of the sewing machine, now painted white, is used to support the tiled top. Unfortunately, you have to buy the chairs*

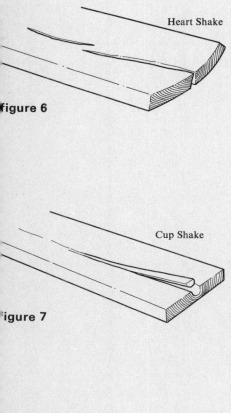

Heart Shake

figure 6

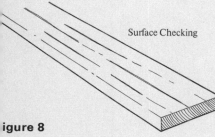

Cup Shake

figure 7

Cup Shakes See **figure 7**

Cup shakes are most commonly found in softwood, where a board contains part of the centre rings of the heart. Splitting takes place along the line of the rings and a central piece may separate out completely. The centre has to be rejected.

Surface Checking See **figure 8**

A series of fine cracks on the surface of timber and on blockboard. On solid timber this problem occurs where the wood has been subject to rapid surface drying—so fast in fact that the centre of the wood has not varied in its moisture content whilst the outside has become very dry. There is no remedy once it has happened. If the checks are wide they will be deep and the wood is useless for furniture. On sawn timber, fine surface checks are frequently very shallow and will be cut out when the wood is planed.

Surface checking frequently occurs on blockboard when it has been used indoors and after drying out. It is often not seen until the surface has been polished or painted for some time. The cause is the pull of the top veneer reacting against that of the core material, which runs in the opposite direction and is bonded to it.

Storing Timber

If there is one maxim that every home furniture maker should have pinned to his workshop wall, it is USE DRY WOOD. Wood which is too damp will not plane without tearing and will clog abrasive paper. In extreme cases, adhesives will not set. Worse, if you construct a piece of furniture from wood which has not properly dried out, it will shrink and warp, either during the making or after the piece has been completed. In furniture which requires a square frame, such as a table or chair, the warping may mean that the piece will never stand level again.

The story starts back at the timber yard. A tree which has just been felled is a living thing and it is full of water—in fact it is wringing wet. After the timber has been sawn into boards, it is stacked outdoors but under cover with a free circulation of air between the boards and left until it is *air dry*, that is about 17% moisture content by weight. This is roughly the condition of the wood when it is sold by timber merchants. Although thoroughly suitable for outdoor work and for building projects, it is still too wet for furniture making.

The moisture content of timber which is to be used in a warm, dry house, usually with central heating, should be about 10–12%. The simplest way to achieve this is to buy the wood some weeks, or even months, before you intend to use it. Store it in the house in an area which is heated—but not next to the boiler—so that it can acclimatise gently. The best way to stack the timber is *in stick*, that is with sticks of constant section—say 18mm square—between each board, as shown in **figure 9**.

This allows air to circulate between the boards, and placing the boards one over another reduces the chances of their twisting as they dry out. If you have weights available, add them to the top of the pile to help the top boards. Keep all the sticks above one another and keep the weights over the line of the sticks. Good ventilation will help to speed up the drying.

If you cannot plan far enough ahead to buy the wood several weeks ahead of using it, buy it as early as possible. Even a couple of weeks makes a considerable difference. If you are making the furniture in an outside workshop which is normally left unheated, bring the timber back into the house when you are not working on it, otherwise the moisture content may rise again.

Many of the imported hardwoods and some softwoods are *kiln dried*, which reduces the moisture content to about the indoor level. The timber is stacked in great sheds or kilns and warm air is circulated around it by large electric fans. Provided that kiln dried timber has not been stored outside for long periods after drying, it will usually be ready for immediate use. At worst, it will require less time to dry out indoors.

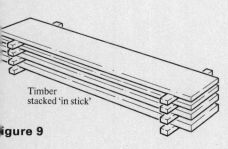

Surface Checking

figure 8

Timber stacked 'in stick'

figure 9

Timber Section

All sheet materials, including hardboard, plywood, chipboard and blockboard
are dry at the time of manufacture and will acclimatise quickly indoors, providing
that they have not been left in an outside store for the long winter months. Avoid
buying boards which have the tell-tale signs of water staining on them if you are
making something which matters.

Sheet materials are best stored flat. If this is not possible, stack them vertically on
edge. Avoid leaning them at an angle to the wall, as this will invite them to bend.

Sheet Materials

Plywood

Plywood is made by sticking a number of veneers, or plys, together under pressure
in a machine. The top and bottom veneers of a sheet of plywood run along its
length; the centre and alternate veneers, if any, run from side to side. The number
of veneers is always uneven, from three upwards, the commonest being five,
seven and nine ply. The number of veneers does not necessarily decide the
thickness of the plywood, since the veneers themselves may be thick or thin.

The grades of plywood vary from boards which are perfect on both sides, to
the lowest grades, used by the packing trades. There are also plywoods which are
made for exterior use, such as shuttering. Plywood is generally more expensive
than hardboard, chipboard or blockboard. It can also be obtained face veneered
with timber or melamine. Many merchants and DIY Centres stock a limited range
of each, or can supply to order.

The commonly available thicknesses of plywood are 3, 4, 6, 9, 12 and 18mm,
although others are made. If you are making something where the thickness has
to be exact, always check it before purchase, as minor variations are common.

Many different sheet sizes of plywood are available. The largest standard
sheets are 1220×2440mm. Derivative cut sizes are therefore about 1220×
1220mm and 610×1220mm. Another standard size for thinner sheet plywood is
1525×1525mm.

Chipboard

Made from chips of softwood which are layered and bonded together under
pressure, this versatile material is made in a number of grades to suit special
requirements. The general purpose quality is the one most generally available and
is quite suitable for all indoor work. A tougher quality is made for flooring and
other grades are made specially for outdoor work in roofing and shuttering.

Most DIY centres stock chipboard in a variety of finishes. The standard sheet
is sanded on both faces and bears no veneers: it can also be obtained primed and
filled on both faces, ready for painting. There are several well-known commercial
brands of chipboard decorated with timber veneers. These may have only one face
veneered in a selected hardwood or softwood, or both. Where only one face is
special, the other will have a balancing veneer to keep the board flat—usually an
African timber resembling mahogany. Since all wood veneers vary from batch to
batch, buy all the face veneered panels you require at the same time. In this way,
you can select and compare them easily.

Melamine covered chipboard comes in two varieties—one where a thin coat of
melamine, commonly coloured white or brown, has been applied in a machine and
another which is covered with a more substantial melamine veneer, made
especially for worktops. Wherever possible, get your melamine covered board
cut to exact size by the supplier—he will probably have a tungsten-tipped saw
designed for the purpose.

Standard full size sheets of chipboard measure 2440×1220mm and are
readily available in 9, 12, 15 and 18mm thicknesses. Standard melamine coated
and timber veneered panels are supplied in the 15mm thickness, which when the
coating or veneers is added goes up to about 16mm.

Lengths		Widths
915mm (36")		150mm (6")
1220mm (48")		230mm (9")
1525mm (60")	×	300mm (12")
1820mm (72")		380mm (15")
2440mm (96")		457mm (18")
		530mm (21")
		610mm (24")

Standard sizes for veneered and coated chipboard.

Melamine coated and timber veneered chipboard panels are generally available in the sizes listed alongside, although some variation occurs between makes. Most of these panels have veneered edges, so check to see that these are not damaged, or that the damaged pieces will be cut away when you trim the panel to your size. The metric sizes in the table are all derivatives of the 2440×1220mm standard sheet. The Imperial equivalents, although still often quoted, are not always accurate and should not be used.

Blockboard See **figure 10**

Basically, blockboard consists of a series of rectangular timber battens bonded side-to-side along the length of the board. On either face of this central core, and at right angles to it, is laid a sheet of constructional veneer about 1·5mm thick. For this reason, blockboard resists bending more in its length than in its width, so when cutting components for furniture, try to cut the length of the pieces in line with the core, that is across the grain of the constructional veneer.

The larger suppliers sometimes carry stocks of face-veneered blockboard, although it will usually be more expensive than the same veneer on chipboard. The veneers will be limited to those in popular demand—probably oak, mahogany and teak—but others are available. The face veneer is applied on top of the constructional veneer and its grain runs counter to it, that is in line with the core.

As a rule, it is better to lip edge blockboard, rather than using an iron-on veneer. The reason is that all blockboard edges contain end grain, either the end grain of the constructional veneer or the end grain of the core. If you are using face veneered blockboard, make sure the supplier can provide matching hardwood strips for edging. The cutting lists give the sizes of hardwood edgings and sections required.

Blockboard is commonly supplied in 12, 16 and 18mm thicknesses and standard sheet sizes of 1220×2440mm, although other thicknesses and sheet sizes are made. Most suppliers will cut to other sizes given time. There is usually a surcharge for cutting, or alternatively the price charged per sheet is greater.

figure 10

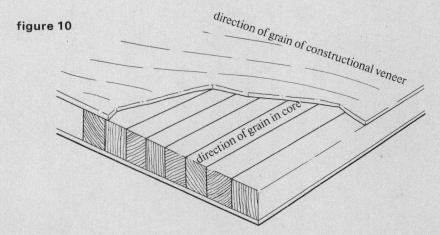

Hardboard

This is a thin, hard sheet material, brown in colour, made from wood fibres subjected to high pressures. The standard sheet is shiny on one side and dull on the other, although double sided hardboard is available in two thicknesses. The standard sheet measures 1220×2440mm and has a thickness of about 3·4mm. Most suppliers have smaller boards derived from the standard sheet. Sizes are usually 1220×1220mm, 1220×1830mm, 1220×610mm and 610×610mm. Patterned hardboards, such as pegboard and reeded hardboard, are available from most suppliers. Sheet sizes and thicknesses are the same.

Working Safely

There is no denying that the workshop can be a dangerous place and that many unnecessary accidents happen every year. But the truth is that the vast majority of these accidents could be avoided if the people using the tools observed a few common sense precautions. Here is a list of basic rules for using tools in the workshop. Make sure you keep to them and there is no reason why anything should go wrong.

1. Never allow young children access to tools with cutting edges. Keep everything, including materials, out of their reach.
2. Never leave any tool lying about—especially not on top of a pair of steps nor inside partially finished furniture.
3. Always unplug power tools and wander leads immediately after use.
4. Never tape or wedge switches or on-off devices, on power tools or machines.
5. Never alter settings or change cutters on any power tool or machine without first disconnecting it from the mains.
6. Never leave any power tool until it has become stationary.
7. Never remove guards from tools.
8. Inspect electric cables and leads on power tools regularly, to ensure that they are in first class condition. Replace worn cables and broken plugs immediately. Do not use power tools with loose or frayed cable connections.
9. Remove loose clothing, such as ties, before using power tools and keep long hair tied up, or within a hat.
10. Wear a filter mask when using machine sanders. These are readily available at most chemists and nearly all DIY stores.
11. Never use blunt cutting tools—these cause more accidents than sharp ones.
12. Don't use saw blades or files without handles.
13. Dust, shavings and offcuts are dangerous and are a greater fire hazard than uncut materials. Always clear up as you work.
14. Never work in an area with an open fire or any heating appliance which has a glowing heater element.
15. Never use any inflammable or noxious substance without obeying the manufacturer's instructions in full.
16. Pay particular attention to petroleum, cellulose and polyurethane-based substances. These must be used only in very well-ventilated areas, where there is no flame or naked light. Replace the lids of the containers of these substances immediately after pouring. If you happen to be using them in a kitchen or in a room with a gas fire, extinguish all pilot lights before you start.
17. When drilling walls, check that there are no water or gas pipes, and no electric cables, near to the drilling point.

A Basic Tool Kit

Our basic tool kit is primarily intended for home furniture makers who are starting from scratch, but readers who have gradually accumulated tools over the years may find one or two useful suggestions for additions to their collection. The kit has been selected for its versatility in general use all over the house, as well as for its immediate application in making the furniture in this book. Some additional tools will be required for some of the projects, but if you do not wish to buy them, they can usually be hired over a weekend.

Always buy tools from reputable suppliers, preferably specialists, and buy the best possible ones you can afford. Although they cost a little more, high quality tools do their job better and, since they will last a lifetime, they can justifiably be considered as an investment.

Keep your tools sharp, store them in a dry atmosphere and don't lend them to anyone. These three rules are those of all good craftsmen. They keep their tools sharp so that they are always ready for use, they keep them dry because rust ruins tools rapidly and they don't lend them so that they always have their tools to hand when they are needed. Of course the no-lending rule works in reverse too—if you don't borrow, you can never be accused of misusing or failing to return tools.

Collecting tools can become a life-long occupation. Once you have the basic kit, the occasional purchase or birthday gift can establish a substantial stock within a surprisingly short time. Occasionally you may get the opportunity to buy tools from a craftsman who is retiring. Some good tools also turn up in second-hand shops, so keep an eye out for them. Do not be tempted into buying second-hand power tools unless they are covered by a guarantee.

In compiling the basic kit, we have assumed that most people will have, or are seriously contemplating the purchase of, a portable electric drill. These tools are well worth their cost, which will be repaid many times over in time saved, accuracy and versatility. Those who are about to buy a drill should turn to 'Drills and Drilling' on page 123, where the types of drill and their various accessories are discussed.

Here, then, is our basic tool kit:

1 A bench or rigid worktop with vice, or a Workmate.
2 A portable electric drill.
3 A set of twist drills, H.S.S. 1—6mm by 0·5mm intervals.
4 A 16oz. claw hammer.
5 A pin hammer.
6 A panel saw or circular saw.
7 A set of three bevelled edge chisels, 18mm ($\frac{3}{4}$"), 12mm ($\frac{1}{2}$") and 6mm ($\frac{1}{4}$").
8 One 200mm (approx.) try square.
9 A smoothing plane.
10 A marking gauge.
11 A marking knife.
12 A tenon saw.
13 A 2 or 3 metre steel tape measure.
14 A cork sanding block.
15 A pair of 150mm pliers.
16 A combination oilstone.
17 An oil can.
18 Two 150mm G cramps.
19 A 600mm flat steel rule (to double as a straightedge).
20 A countersink.

One of the most important items on the list is the workbench. A Workmate is an ideal starter bench, in that it will hold work steady between the jaws of its top, or alternatively work can be held across its top with the aid of cramps. For large sheet work, a supporting trestle table of the same height as the Workmate is required. If you have a garage or workshop, you may have sufficient room to make a folding workbench which hinges from the wall. Benches of this type fold up out of the way when not required and gain a great deal of stability from the wall to which they are attached. Free-standing benches can be made from a number of materials, such as slotted metal angle iron for the underframe, with a double thickness of blockboard or chipboard for the top.

Alternatively, professionally-made benches are readily available through specialist tool or timber suppliers. There are many patterns, mostly fitted with vices. All of them are relatively expensive, but with care will last for fifty years or more.

If, for reasons of cost or space, you are forced into using the kitchen table, it is well worth making a protective false top to fit over it, as shown in **figure 11**. This can be made from blockboard or chipboard, with a lip edging screwed and glued on to each side, so that it is flush with the top and extends down to finish flush with the underside of the table top. A cramp-on vice can then be fitted temporarily

Tools Section

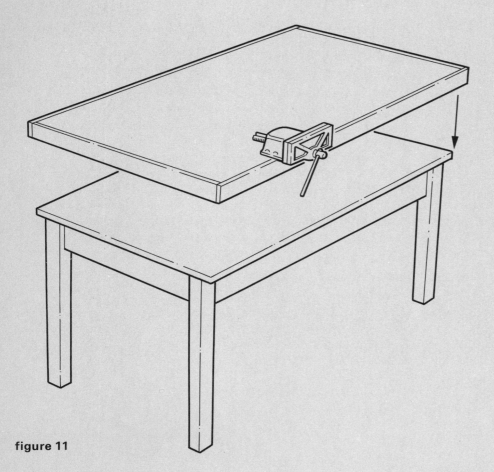

figure 11

in place when required. Use a piece of plywood over the cramp head to protect the underside of the table. Get the largest vice you can: the bigger the surface area it grips the better, and the wider the jaws open, the greater the variety of objects the vice will hold.

Saws and Sawing
Saws for Straight Cutting
The two most useful hand saws are the *panel saw*, which can be used with or across the grain, and the *tenon saw*, which is made for cutting small sections and for jointing. Both saws can, and should, be sharpened and set regularly.

figure 12

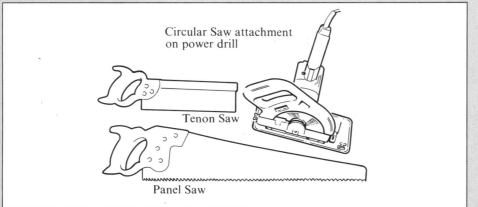

Circular Saw attachment on power drill

Tenon Saw

Panel Saw

The set of a saw refers to the sideways angle of the teeth. The fewer teeth a saw has, the greater the set. It therefore follows that the panel saw with about 6 points (teeth) to the inch (not yet metricated) is set more obviously and cuts a wider slot than the finer 10 point tenon saw.

In use, saws should be gripped positively but not hard and should be drawn through each stroke steadily without being forced. Some pressure on the forward stroke is required. Always make use of the full cutting length of the blade.

Wherever possible, grip work in a vice or with cramps. On large sawing jobs, support the work on trestles so that both the piece required and that being sawn off are held up until the sawcut is complete. Failure to do this will result in splitting.

When sawing, *always cut on the waste side of the marking line* and allow sufficient waste to be left for final trueing up of the edge with a plane. To prevent veneers lifting and cross grain from tearing, mark out with a knife cut (See. Measuring and Marking Out. page 142).

Circular saw attachments on electric power drills can reduce sawing time substantially. When set correctly and with the use of sharp blades of the correct tooth pattern, very accurate work is possible. The importance of sharp saws of the correct tooth pattern cannot be over-emphasised. When both these factors are correct, the cut will be fast and clean and the motor will not sound laboured. However, because the saw diameter is small and the motor low-powered, everything has to be kept in first class order to run effectively. Read the manufacturers' instructions on the assembly of these attachments carefully and keep them handy for further reference. Always disconnect the power unit from the mains when stopping work, modifying the settings or changing blades.

Among the range of blades available for these saws are *cross cut* (fine tooth), *combination* (middle tooth size) for cross cut and cutting with the grain, and *rip*, which is for cutting along the grain only. For cutting melamine coated surfaces there is a blade which has tungsten teeth designed especially to withstand the heavy demands of this very hard surface. All these blades can be mechanically re-sharpened by specialists. Refer to your tool supplier.

Portable electric saws, which are self-contained units, are made in a number of sizes. In each case, the saw diameter is matched correctly to the motor size. These tools are more efficient than the attachment type because, among other things, the power units do not have to perform more than one function and the speed is fixed at the correct one for sawing.

Saws for Curve Cutting

Many saws are made for cutting curves. They include the fret saw, keyhole saw, bow saw, coping saw and jig saw.

figure 13

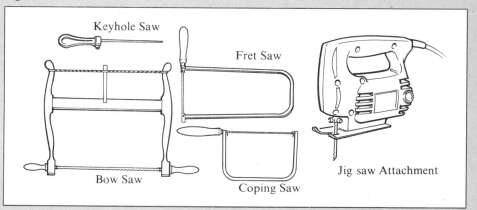

Keyhole Saw

Fret Saw

Bow Saw

Coping Saw

Jig saw Attachment

Tools Section

The Fret Saw is suitable for sawing thin materials such as plywood and hardboard. This saw's association with decorative work is largely due to its ability to cut very tight curves and to the fineness of its cut, both attributable to the very fine blade it uses. It is not robust enough to be included in the list of general woodworking tools.

The Keyhole Saw comprises a thin tapering blade of about 300mm in length. The teeth are relatively coarse to enable it to cut through timber of door thickness. Traditionally, this saw was used to cut keyholes and letter boxes. The blade is held in a hollow clamping handle at one end only. If forced, the blades bend rather easily but can be straightened out without too much trouble. This tool is about the only hand saw which is capable of cutting corners or curves in panels where their extreme edge is more than about 150mm from the nearest edge.

A small hole is drilled at a convenient place in the waste material next to the line of cut for the saw to enter and begin its cut, as shown in **figure 14**. When buying keyhole blades check to see that they are sharp—quite a number are not.

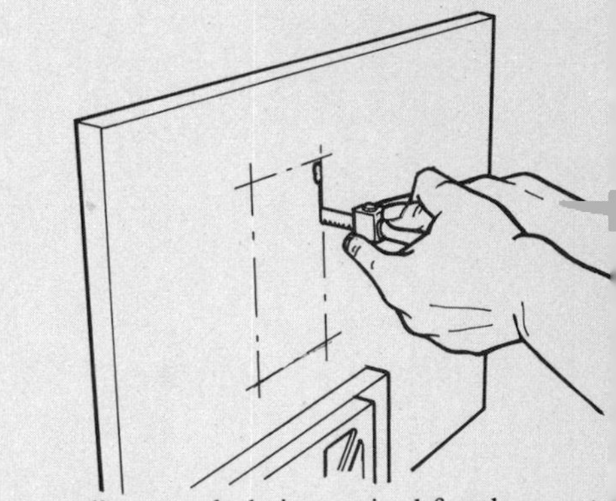

The Bow Saw is a traditional saw with a substantial blade. Its main function is to saw curves in fairly thick timber. The blade can be tilted relative to the frame, which allows the saw to cut curved detail down the edge of boards. A saw of this type would have been used to cut the decorative boards often found at the top and bottom fronts of dressers.

The Coping Saw is a lightweight, steel-framed equivalent of the bow saw. The blade can be set at any angle relative to the frame. It is capable of cutting comfortably through wood up to about 20mm in thickness. If care and time is taken, thicker work can be done. The limits of its abilities are confined by the distance from blade to frame, but it is nevertheless a very useful tool to have. The blade has a pin set in either end which locates into matching slots at the front and handle ends of the frame. It is tensioned by tightening the threaded handle.

Figure 15 shows the coping saw in action. Note how the high arch of the frame allows the saw blade to move into the wood. When the saw is used to cut internal shapes, a starter hole is drilled in the waste area adjacent to the cut line, much as for the keyhole saw, **figure 14**. The blade is released from the frame, passed through the hole and re-engaged with the frame and tensioned. Blades are replaced when blunt. Care has to be taken in use or the blade will jam and snap.

Jig saw Attachments are available for a number of makes of electric drill. Self-powered jig saws are also available. In either case, jig saws are faster and more accurate than hand tools. Like the keyhole and coping saws, a starter hole is normally required for the blade to enter enclosed cut-outs. There is no restriction on the placing of cut-outs in boards since there is no frame on a jig saw. Jig saws can also be used for straight cuts, but to achieve the best results it is advisable to run the edge of the cutter plate along a guiding straight edge. Blades with differing tooth patterns for metals, plastics and wood mean that the jig saw can be used for a greater number of jobs. The blades are expensive to replace, so care in use is essential.

A small starter hole is required for the saw to
Position it in the area of waste next to the cut

figure 14

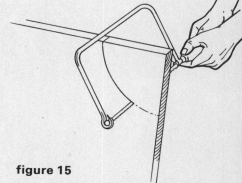

figure 15

Planes and Planing

There are many types of plane and most are made in more than one width. Three common ones are illustrated in **figure 16**.

The Smoothing Plane is included in the basic tool kit because it can be used for so many purposes. It is suitable for all normal planing jobs including the trueing up of end grain of solid timber and sheet materials. It is fairly short, which limits its usefulness in getting long boards flat, but this can be overcome with the use of a straightedge to check the work at regular intervals. It is made in two widths: the 55mm blade version is the best general purpose size.

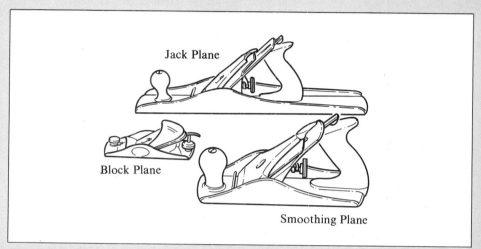

figure 16

The Block Plane is the cheapest because of its size. It has a shallower cutting angle which suits it particularly well to planing end grain on small sections. It is not suited to planing flat, wide surfaces. Adjustable front types are more versatile than those which do not have them.

The Jack Plane has the advantage of length and weight, making it an ideal tool for planing long lengths accurately. It is too large to use on small sections—especially end grain. This is a tool for the more experienced maker.

The parts of a plane are shown in **figure 17**. The *blade* is held in place by a *wedge iron* and a *cap iron*. The leading edge of the cap iron is set about 1·5mm behind the sharpened edge of the blade. The large headed cap iron and blade are gripped firmly together with a well fitting screw. This must be done up tightly with a large screwdriver. The *knurled knob* controls how far the blade sticks out of its slot, and hence the depth of cut of the plane. The *adjustment lever* is used to check the alignment of the blade in its slot, so that it does not tilt down more to one side than the other. Blades must be kept sharp at all times, see Keeping Tools Sharp, page 136.

When storing the plane after use, either retract the blade or stand the plane on its side to protect the cutting edge. Do not allow the body of the plane to become rusty. Keep it in a dry place and if you do not intend using it for some time, wipe it over with an oily rag before putting it away.

figure 17

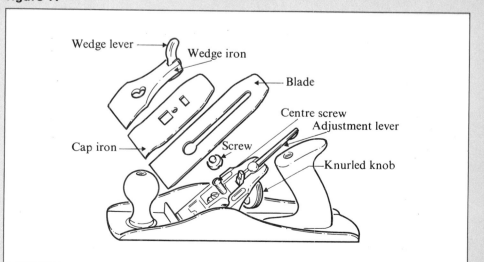

Tools Section

All the parts of the plane can be bought separately, including the body casting. All but the blades will usually have to be ordered, so be prepared for an inevitable delay. Blades should be renewed when grinding and honing have worn them down to within about 6—8mm of the hole at the base of the slot.

Occasionally, when planing some timbers, resin and dust may build up on the bottom of the plane. This can be easily cleaned off with white spirit. Avoid scraping it off as you may unintentionally score the ground surface.

Using a Plane

If the blade is advanced too much it will jam into the wood and no amount of effort will shift the plane. You will learn how much can be taken off a piece of wood in a single pass and how this varies between soft and hard woods. The temptation is to make heavy cuts, but it is easier to take off less at a time. As you approach the final size of the wood you are planing, fine down the cut and this will give a smoother finish, especially if you retouch the blade on a fine oilstone.

You will find that it makes planing a bit easier if you rub a candle over the sole of the plane occasionally. Do not do this when finally finishing off, because there is a chance that some wax may find its way on to the surface of the wood. Candlewax will reject stain and varnishes.

Work which is to be planed must be held firmly, so that your hands are free to hold and control the plane. A vice and a steady worktop are essential to support the work and to resist the considerable thrust of the plane as it cuts.

Always use the plane with both hands. Hold it firmly and guide it in even strokes over the whole length of the surface. Draw the plane back over the work until the blade is behind the wood before making the next pass. Take your time.

In a sudden burst of speed you may well pull the plane back off the work, drop it slightly and then crash your hand into the end of the wood. Pace yourself evenly and you will be able to plane all day, without accident or undue fatigue.

Always plane with the grain to achieve the best finish. The grain pattern on the edge of a piece of timber will usually give an indication as to which way it is lying. The grain lines seldom follow a direct path along the length of a board. They usually rise from one edge to the other and you need to plane in the direction of that rise. It follows that when planing the opposite side the grain direction will be running the other way, and planing must follow suit.

If, when planing, the grain tears and does not cut properly, there are three possible causes: you are planing against the grain, the plane cutter is blunt or the wood is too wet to work. Some timbers have patches of wild grain in them which will not plane in either length direction and finish smoothly. If you hit that problem and are sure that none of the three faults apply, try planing diagonally across the area with a finely set, very sharp plane. This is often successful but it will mean that more work may be called for in the final stages of cleaning up with abrasive paper.

When planing to size it is necessary to establish two adjacent sides as flat and square to one another before any attempt is made to plane to thickness and width. Refer to Measuring and Marking Out, page 142. A *marking gauge*, page 135, is used to mark width and thickness lines. The spur of the gauge makes an indented V in the timber. As the final shavings are removed the V can be seen as a slightly ragged edge. If it appears on one side before the other, it is a positive indication that you are planing at an angle. This can be corrected by shifting the plane over so that it cuts on the high side of the timber only until an even thickness or width results.

Planing End Grain

As far as ends are concerned, it is best to regard a plane as a finishing tool only. A very sharp blade is needed and you should take only fine cuts. If a lot of waste has to be removed, do it with a saw first. Accuracy in saw cutting also reduces the amount of planing work to be done.

Plane end grain and the edges of sheet material from end to centre, then reverse the work and repeat the operation. Note the position of fingers running along the edge under the plane.

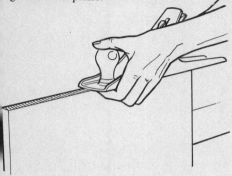

figure 18

figure 19

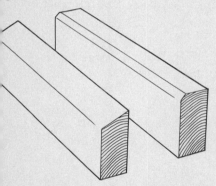

Left: a bevel. Right: a chamfer. Both cut with a plane. If they are required on a curved edge they are cut with a spokeshave or file.

In all cases of marking out end grain, use a marking knife, so that the edge fibres are severed, and the chance of them splitting out is reduced. It is equally important that the plane is used exactly down to the line and not beyond it. Like the gauge line, the knife cut can be easily seen as the plane reveals it.

The other danger of splitting out occurs at the corners of the end grain. To avoid this, plane from the corner to the centre only, then reverse the work and repeat the cut from the other side. Keep the plane in line with the thickness of boards at all times. See **figure 18**. When planing edges, rocking of the plane must be avoided if a flat surface is to be achieved. Start by holding the plane on the edge of the board and lift the plane from side to side to feel when it is firmly bedded. Have a good look at the plane and see if it is square to the faces. If it is, grip the plane handle firmly and lock your wrist so that the plane won't tip. Place the other hand over the front of the plane as in **figure 18** with fingers extended beneath the sole of the plane to act as a guide against the face of the board. Make two or three passes over the edge, maintaining that hold. Those few cuts should have established a flat which is easier to plane from. Continue planing using the same grip until down to the required level. If the work is out of square initially, use the same grip, but let the plane lie at the angle of the end and then tip it up until the plane is square. Hold the plane square and make a number of cuts until a flat is established. Check with a try square and adjust the angle with further cuts until it is true.

Chamfers and Bevels

A chamfer is an angled corner, whereas a bevel is an angled edge. See **figure 19**. On straight work, both are cut with a plane. On shaped sections, they have to be cut with spokeshaves or files. For straight cuts, you can again use the process of tipping the plane to the required angle, locking the wrist and using the fingers of the forward hand as a guide. A sliding bevel can be used to check the accuracy of the shape relative to a face side or edge. See page 135.

The use of either marking or cutting gauges for marking out chamfers and bevels is not advisable because both leave indented lines which would remain in the finished piece. The best way is to pencil mark the extremes of the bevel or chamfer on the relevant edges, using a straightedge between measured points. The accuracy of the angle can then be set precisely with a sliding bevel.

Drills and Drilling

Nearly all the projects in this book require the use of a portable electric drill at some stage, so if you do not already own one, a drill should be near the top of your shopping list. There are three important factors in selecting a portable electric drill. These are its power, the number of speeds it has and the capacity of its chuck.

Power Although most electric drills look about the same size, there is quite a range in their power output. Since most of them are worked heavily for their size, go for the highest power rating you can. There is a proviso here, in that if you wish to take advantage of the numerous accessories available, you must not choose one of the heavy-duty industrial drills, which are usually too large to fit many of the DIY attachments. 450/500 watts is about as high as you will be able to go.

Speeds Ideally, each operation of drilling, sawing and sanding should be done with a specially made, separately powered tool, because each of these operations requires its own range of speeds. With an electric drill as the power unit for a range of accessories, compromises have to be accepted. It is essential, therefore, to have as much flexibility as possible. Four speeds are best; two are better than one.

Chuck size The smallest acceptable chuck is 10mm ($\frac{3}{8}$"). The higher powered drills have a 13mm ($\frac{1}{2}$") capacity, which is obviously more versatile.

Tools Section

Attachments The makers of electric drills now market a very large variety of accessories which can be attached to the drill. Those that are useful in simple furniture making are mentioned in the appropriate section, for example jig saw attachments under 'Saws and Sawing' and so on.

Using the Electric Drill

The electric drill can either be used freehand or in a drill stand. When working freehand, a side handle, which is supplied with some makes and is available as an extra with others, is a particularly useful accessory. See **figure 20**. The grip it offers enables the operator to steady the drill and to hold it firmly on course.

Drilling, using a wooden jig to keep holes centrally in pieces being drilled. Note the depth stop on the pillar and the piece of waste beneath the work.

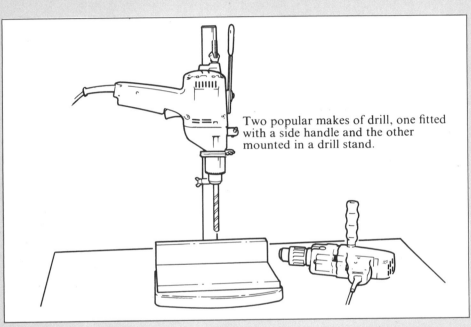

Two popular makes of drill, one fitted with a side handle and the other mounted in a drill stand.

figure 20

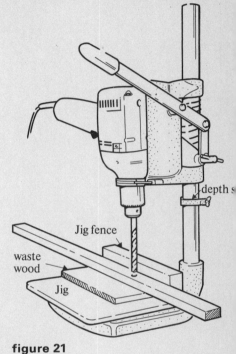

depth s

Jig fence

waste
wood

Jig

figure 21

Drill stands are essential for accuracy and squareness. All stands have a lever arm action and depth stops which allow drilling depths to be made within minute tolerances. In **figure 21** a simple block has been secured to the drill stand table. This device, known as a jig, ensures that every hole drilled in pieces of wood pressed against it will be exactly the same distance from the edge. A jig similar to this was used for the wall-hung shelving system on page 13. If holes are required at an angle other than 90°, a wedge-shaped base block can be made, to sit between the work and the drill table.

When drilling through a piece of wood, a piece of flat waste material is placed over the drill stand table. This has two uses: firstly it prevents the drill and the stand coming into contact, and secondly it ensures clean drilling on the underside of the piece of wood you are working on. After each hole is drilled, the waste is moved along, so that there is always a clean surface beneath the drill. With practice you will find that this simple tip will prevent breakthrough on the underside of any hole.

Hand Tools for Drilling

There are two of these, as shown in **figure 22**, the *swingbrace*, or brace and bit, and the *wheelbrace* or hand drill. Neither of them is necessary for the beginner who possesses an electric drill, because for most purposes there is a sufficiently wide range of bits to fit the electric drill.

The wheelbrace will only take twist drills up to 6mm diameter, and is therefore confined to drilling small holes and countersinking. Some bits larger in diameter than 6mm are made with 6mm shanks, but the amount of effort required to cut with them is frequently too much for the tool.

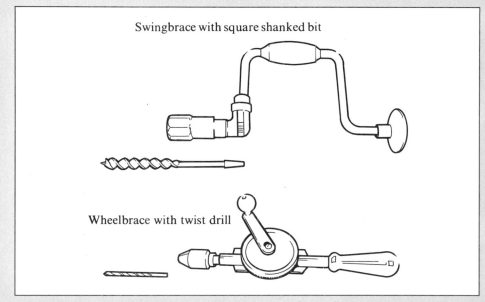

figure 22

Swingbraces are made with or without a ratchet. The ratchet variety costs more, but its use in confined spaces more than repays the extra outlay. The swingbrace will only take square shanked bits. There is a great variety of these—see below.

Drills and Bits
Electric drills take round-shanked drill bits only, the commonest example of which is the *twist drill* shown with the wheelbrace in **figure 22**. Twist drills can be bought individually or in sets and they can be re-sharpened. *Flat bits* are also made for electric drills and are sold in a range of sizes at most DIY centres.

Figure 23 shows a range of square shanked bits suitable for the swingbrace. The *Jennings pattern* is the most commonly used because its close spiral keeps the hole straight, and closely related to it is the *solid centre bit* which drills faster but does not keep so straight. The *expansive bit* has an adjustable cutter on the end so that it can make holes of different sizes. The most commonly used pattern is the *centre bit*, although it tends to wander on deep holes.

Two other essential bits are the *countersink bit* and the *dowel bit*, whose centre point reduces the chance of the drill wandering away from the critical centre mark during dowel jointing, see page 150. Although not strictly bits, it is appropriate here to mention *hole saws* with round shanks. These are very good tools for cutting large holes in materials up to about 10mm in thickness, using an electric drill at low speed.

Figure 23

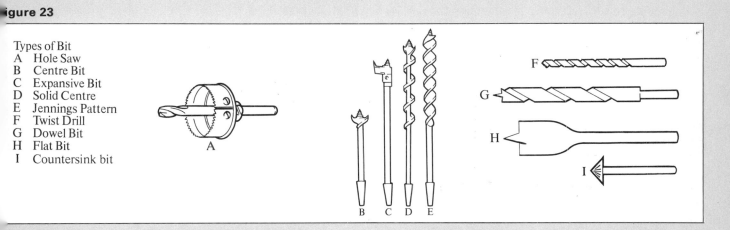

Types of Bit
A   Hole Saw
B   Centre Bit
C   Expansive Bit
D   Solid Centre
E   Jennings Pattern
F   Twist Drill
G   Dowel Bit
H   Flat Bit
I   Countersink bit

Tools Section

Metrication has not completely taken over in the world of drills and bits. Twist drills are sold either in metric sizes or in Imperial: both are necessary because of high accuracy requirements in engineering. Woodbits are still basically thought of in Imperial. Although they are frequently labelled in both systems, the metric sizes are clearly a conversion from the Imperial, for example $\frac{1}{4}$"/6·3mm.

Use of Drill Bits

Any drill thrust straight through a piece of timber will cause the wood at the far side to break out. There are a number of ways of overcoming this problem.

When using twist drills in either a freehand electric drill or a wheelbrace, cramp a piece of flat waste timber to the back of the piece being drilled. On drill stands, place a piece of waste between the piece you are working on and the drill stand base. The same technique is used for hole saws and flat bits.

With centre and Jennings pattern woodbits, the technique is to drill through from the face side until the point just appears. Withdraw the bit, turn the work over, insert the point of the bit into the hole just made and drill until the full-size holes meet.

When drilling into metal or plastic, always use a centre punch to indent the centre of the hole before beginning to drill. This will prevent the drill from wandering off course as it starts. Small holes up to about 3mm can be drilled in one go, but larger holes are best drilled in stages, beginning with a small size and increasing by stages up to the required diameter. Always secure small pieces of metal with cramps before drilling them. If you do not, the work may spin through your fingers without warning and this is obviously a cause of accidents. With large bits, always use the lower speeds.

For drilling into walls, it is necessary to use special *masonry bits* with tungsten carbide tips on the slow speed of the drill. Use the drill with the side handle to ensure good control and get somebody to sight the drill to make sure that it keeps at 90° to the wall. Keep the pressure relatively high, as this minimises the wear on the hardened tip and do not swing the drill to change direction once the tip is in hard material. In old walls there are sometimes chips of granite which even the masonry bit cannot penetrate, and the drill will probably skid off to one side. The only solution is to dig the granite chip out of the wall and fill the hole with filling compound.

Again with safety in mind, make sure there are no hidden pipes or electrical wiring before drilling into walls.

Countersinking and Counterboring

Countersinking is the widening of the top of a screw clearance hole, so that a countersunk screw will lie flush with the wood. This technique is used constantly in the projects in this book, for example in making up the square frames for the wardrobe range in Chapter 4, see **figure 24**.

A countersink bit is used and this is best mounted in a wheelbrace or in an electric drill on a stand, because control of the speed and depth of cut is essential. Using an electric drill freehand often leads to the bit snatching and cutting far deeper than intended and the resulting screw fixings can look very untidy.

Counterboring is the drilling of a hole so that the head of the screw sinks down below the surface of the wood, as shown in **figure 25**. It eliminates the need to use long unwieldy screws. We used the technique to fix the table top to its under frame in Chapter 2 and the underframes to the sideboard cabinets in Chapter 10. It is important to calculate carefully the depth of the counterbore, or the tip of the screw may break out on the opposite surface, quite a problem if that surface happens to be a table top.

When using woodbits, always drill the counterbore before the clearance hole. The lead screw of the woodbit will have nothing to bite on if the clearance hole has already been cut. This difficulty does not occur with twist drills.

The counterbored holes should be marginally larger than the diameter of the

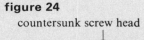

figure 24

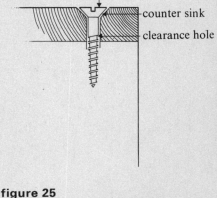
countersunk screw head — counter sink — clearance hole

figure 25

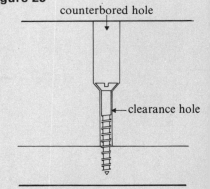
counterbored hole — clearance hole

screw head. Screw head diameters, together with the appropriate clearance holes, may be found in the table in the section on screws, page 138. You may use either round headed or countersunk screws, but if using countersunk screws, reduce the depth of the counterbore slightly to allow for the screw head to sink a little as it is tightened.

Counterbored holes may be plugged with small pieces of dowel. Alternatively you can buy plug cutters, which look like hollow drills. They come in a limited range of sizes, so be sure that the counterbored hole size matches.

It is best to use a drill stand when counterboring. This will ensure that the holes are at right angles to the surface, whilst the use of the depth stop makes certain that they are of the right depth. The need to drill holes to a fixed depth occurs frequently in wood working. The best plan is to use the drill stand wherever possible, but there are several other ways as well:

1 Wrap a length of adhesive tape around the drill to mark the position at which drilling must stop.
2 Some drills, dowel bits in particular, are supplied with tight-fitting rubber bands. These bands can be moved up and down the length of the drill to indicate the depth of cut required.
3 Purchase one of the screw-on depth gauges which are available from tool specialists.
4 Drill a hole through a piece of timber, then slide the piece of timber up till it touches the chuck. Measure the depth of cut required from the tip of the drill back on to the piece of timber. Remove the timber, saw it to the correct length, then slide it back over the drill. When the job is complete, keep the piece of timber handy, then you can cut it to a new drill depth for a future job.

Cramps and Cramping

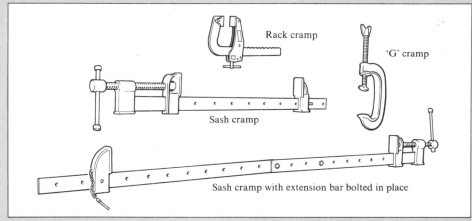

Rack cramp

'G' cramp

Sash cramp

Sash cramp with extension bar bolted in place

figure 26

There are two types of cramps, those for gripping over relatively small distances—the 'G' and 'rack' types—and those for gripping long sections, which are called sash cramps. See **figure 26**. The usable length of sash cramps can be increased by bolting extension bars to them.

Each type of cramp is available in a range of sizes. G or rack cramps with an opening of about 150mm are very useful to have initially. They will close fully (something which not all the larger sizes of G cramp do) and are capable of holding a sufficiently large section to cover most jobs. Cramps of this size are mainly used to hold the width and thickness of things.

Sash cramps (their name comes from their use in the making of window sashes) are designed to hold long work such as cabinet sides, doors, etc. Sets of sash cramp heads are available which can be fitted to hardwood bars. Although these are not as robust as professional cramps, they are a cheap alternative and are reasonably effective.

Tools Section

How Cramps Operate

'G' cramps are adjusted to the opening required by means of a wing nut or tommy bar situated at the top of the threaded steel section.

Rack cramps have two variables. Rapid approximate adjustment is made by sliding the movable head along until it engages in the appropriate notch in the arm of the cramp. Final adjustment is made by turning the tommy bar. High pressures are achievable.

Sash cramps of the traditional size illustrated are made with two types of bar—rectangular or 'T' section. The 'T' bars are designed to offer greater resistance to bending stresses and come into their own at cramp lengths of 1220mm and above.

Each sash cramp has one moveable shoe (jaw) which will slide along the whole length of the cramp. Its movement is restricted by the insertion of a steel pin through one of the holes in the bar. Final adjustment and tightening is achieved by turning the tommy bar at the fixed shoe end.

Sash cramps can be extended by bolting on extension bars of the same section as the parent cramp. Alternatively, two cramps with their free shoes removed can be bolted together through the pin holes to give additional length.

The cost of sash cramps is considerable and unless you are likely to make things often you may find that hiring them is much more acceptable. If you do think of buying sash cramps, two 1220mm in length will be a useful starter set.

The wing nut or tommy bar fitted to each cramp is designed to be done up by hand. Never use additional levers or pliers to get more leverage, as this will bend or shatter the cramp.

Softening

Because the jaws or shoes of cramps are applying a very hard grip, they will invariably mark the wood they are holding at the points of contact. To overcome this, and to spread the load along the length of whatever is being held, use pieces of plywood or solid timber between the work and the cramps. These are known as softening pieces. A worthwhile tip is to run a candle over all the faces of softening strips before they are used. This thin layer of wax prevents them from bonding to any spare adhesive which may exude from joints during cramping. Keep all softening pieces parallel in thickness or they will tend to throw or force the cramp away from its intended position.

Cramping and Gluing Methods

As a rule never tighten cramps more than is required to push joints together and hold them there. If, with reasonable tightening, the work does not go together properly, there is usually something wrong with the connecting surfaces and this must be corrected. This is one of the reasons for suggesting that all work should be assembled and cramped up without glue in the first instance. The second reason for this trial run is to test the effective placing of the cramps and their softening pieces so that they are all set at the correct sizes and ready to go back in place as rapidly as possible after the glue is applied.

At the time of finally assembling a piece of furniture, you must be free of interruption, have a damp rag to wipe off all excess glue and have try squares and diagonal rods at hand. (See Keeping Square, page 145). On large jobs, a second pair of hands is necessary. Adhesives go off quickly and time is at a premium. Once the glue is set, there is little chance of getting a job apart again.

Whenever possible, take gluing and cramping by stages. For example, when gluing a number of narrow boards together to make one wide one, glue two boards together, allow them to dry and then add another. If there are five boards in all, glue two pairs together separately and then glue in the centre board. This will avoid the nearly impossible task of trying to get four slippery joints to line up while trying to adjust the pressures of the cramps.

When lip-edging four sides of a panel, glue two opposite sides and when they are dry, add the others. On underframes, such as those for the occasional tables in

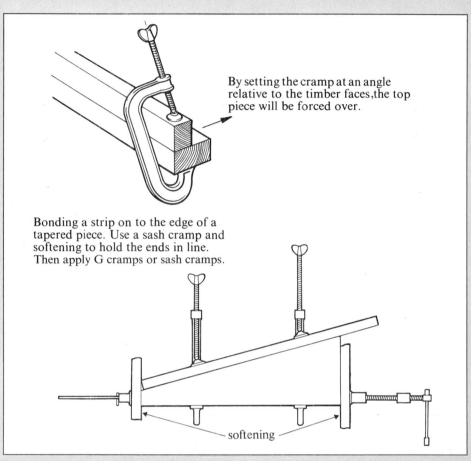

By setting the cramp at an angle relative to the timber faces, the top piece will be forced over.

Bonding a strip on to the edge of a tapered piece. Use a sash cramp and softening to hold the ends in line. Then apply G cramps or sash cramps.

softening

figure 27

Chapter 2, glue up opposite side frames first and then glue the two frames to their joining side rails. With less to glue up at each stage, there is more time to spend aligning cramps and testing for square.

Cramps in Use

Short cramps (or long cramps used over short distances) seldom create problems in terms of distorting the work or themselves, but glue-line slipping does occur, so watch out for it and don't leave anything to dry without checking that it is stable.

The slipping of parts after gluing and during cramping occurs when pieces of wood are being glued together without formal joints. The table leg in Chapter 2 is typical. Here two pieces are glued together to form a right angle as in **figure 3** of Chapter 2, page 20.

As each cramp is applied to the two parts, the pressure will cause them to move. Theoretically, if all the cramps are exactly true and are positioned perfectly at right angles to the work and exactly in line with the centre of the smaller section, nothing will move—but it does. The parts will slide sideways, lengthwise or on the skew. To reduce the movement to a controllable level, place all cramps with a light grip and tighten them evenly, adjusting the pieces being held as necessary. You may have to shift the cramps slightly if movement does not stop.

Where more than two cramps are in use, alternate them on left and right sides wherever possible. This helps to keep an even balance.

Above in **figure 27** we show how cramps can be used to force work in one direction or another.

Sash cramps at openings in excess of about 300mm either bend the work they are gripping or the cramp bar, or both. The greater distance between the shoes, the greater the arch is likely to be. There comes a point where overtightening can make this excessive and unacceptable, see **figure 28** overleaf.

Tools Section

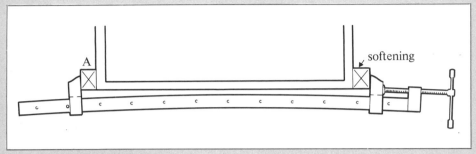

figure 28

A small amount of arching is unavoidable. Cramps with 'T' section bars arch less than those with rectangular ones, and arching is a factor of the number of cramps used. If a single cramp is overloaded it will arch excessively and in all probability will not close the joint. On wide joints a number of cramps have to be used to ensure a tight joint. Even with a number of cramps pulling evenly, arching does happen to both cramps and carcase, and allowances have to be made.

As the forces exerted by the shoe of the cramp rise, the bar and perhaps the piece being joined bend upwards. This has the effect of moving the centre of the cramping force downwards as the shoe rocks on the softening. See point A on **figure 28.**

To reduce this effect, move the softening block up and away from the corner of the piece being joined (but not so far up that it is only pressing on the side) and slide the cramp down before it is tightened. Then, as the cramp is tightened and the bar arches, the contact point of the shoe picks up on the lower part of the softening and the force is applied along the centre of the piece being held. The cramp bar is also low enough not to mark the job as it arches.

Where a rectangular carcase is being cramped together, it is possible that slight arching of the sides will prevent accurate use of a try square to check that the corners are each at 90°. Adopt the diagonal measurement check on page 145. (Keeping Square). Ensure that the cramps are in line with the sides of the carcase to avoid pulling the work out of square.

Like 'G' cramps, sash cramps can be used to pull things out of line or back into shape, as shown in **figure 29**.

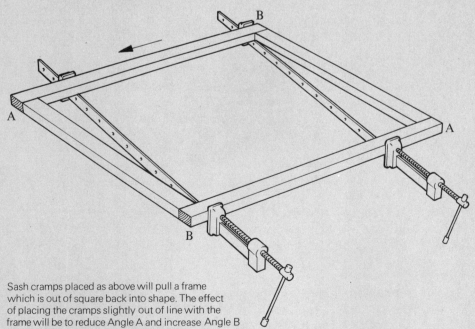

Sash cramps placed as above will pull a frame which is out of square back into shape. The effect of placing the cramps slightly out of line with the frame will be to reduce Angle A and increase Angle B

figure 29

Adhesives

Two main types of adhesive are used for bonding wood to wood in furniture making—PVA and urea formaldehyde.

PVA is a ready-to-use white tacky liquid which is sold in plastic containers with spout-type dispensing caps. It penetrates wood well and should be applied to both bonding surfaces. Excess glue can be removed with a damp cloth before the joint dries. PVA can be thinned with water for special applications, such as sticking paper on to board. It is not suitable for exterior use.

Urea formaldehyde is sold in cans containing a white powder, which has to be mixed with water, preferably in a china, glass or plastic container, to the consistency of a thick cream. Once mixed, it has a limited life before it sets, so only mix enough for immediate use. For the same reason, application should be even and fairly quick. All surfaces should be coated. Brushes can be cleaned with hot water and detergent after use. Remember to close the lid of the powder can after use and to keep it in a dry place.

Urea formaldehyde glues are gap-filling, which means that small pits in the bonded surfaces will remain filled with adhesive after it dries. As always, you should remove surplus glue with a damp rag before it sets, but if, after the joint has dried, you do find some beads of hard glue, they can sometimes be cut away with a chisel. Though more resistant to water than PVA, urea formaldehyde glue is not waterproof and is not suited to outdoor applications.

Hints on Bonding Wood to Wood

Three conditions are necessary for a glued joint to bond properly: the timber must be dry, the joint surface must fit properly and pressure must be applied with cramps during the drying period. The most important of these is that the joint fits properly. A well-made glued joint will be stronger than the surrounding wood, but a poorly cut joint will not gain much strength from adhesive.

Because this initial fitting of the parts is so vital, it is a good idea to assemble your piece of furniture without glue first and to cramp the job together. This trial run will confirm the order of assembly, check that the job will go together properly and give you the opportunity to set all the cramps to the right length for rapid re-assembly. As you take the job apart again, check the internal surfaces of the joints to make sure that they are completely finished.

For successful gluing up, you must have everything ready beforehand. Glue goes off rapidly, as the dry wood sucks the moisture from it. Time is at a premium, and your rehearsal of the assembly will help as far as speed is concerned. On large jobs, have someone with you to help in the assembly and cramping.

If you find that, part way through assembly, everything is going wrong, knock the whole thing apart and wipe all the glue off with a damp rag as rapidly as possible. This is strictly a last resort, but most of us have had to do it at some time.

Other Adhesives

Contact adhesives are used mainly for bonding plastics and foams together and for sticking plastic laminates to worktops. They should not be used for bonding joints in wood, nor are they formulated for it. Their rubbery nature does not allow the permanently rigid bond which is required.

Application is normally done with a shaped spreader which is supplied with the adhesive. Since it is a contact adhesive, both surfaces are coated and allowed to become touch-dry before they are brought together. Pressure is needed at this stage to ensure an effective bond. Excess dried contact adhesive can be removed with a cleaning fluid, which can be bought at most DIY stores.

When using these adhesives on foam materials, be sparing with it. Too much may cause deeper penetration into the cell structure of the foam than is intended. When applying pressure, do so over large areas, not by pressing it hard locally, or a dent may be made which will not release.

Tools Section

After using contact adhesive, replace the cap of the container immediately. Never smoke, nor bring any naked flame into the area where you are using this highly inflammable adhesive or its cleaner. Remember that the fumes are just as likely to catch fire as the adhesive itself.

Scotch (or animal) glue. This old, traditional glue is not easily available nowadays but it has its uses in restoring old furniture. When you are re-gluing old joints or patching veneers, you have to use it because the new glues will not bond satis-factorily over old Scotch glue.

Scotch glue is bought in small solid beads, or pearls. Put them in a pot with cold water and leave them to soak up as much water as they can for two or three hours. The glue must now be heated by placing the pot inside another one with water in it. Boil the whole thing (rather like poaching an egg) until the pearls melt into a heated soup. It is then ready for use. Surplus glue can be removed from joints with a rag dipped in hot water. Brushes can easily be cleaned in hot water too.

Hammers and Chisels

Hammers

The most versatile hammer is the *16oz. claw*, which can be used for driving in nails of all sizes and for withdrawing any which are not driven completely home. See **figure 30**. Buy one with a well-known brand name. The head should have a claw which reduces evenly to a fine point—this will enable you to pull out pins as well as nails. The head should be slightly domed and have a chamfer round it. The handle of the shaft can be made of steel with a rubber hand grip or of timber, which many people find more comfortable.

With careful use, and with the aid of a pin punch, the 16oz. claw is quite satisfactory for driving in panel pins until the purchase of a much lighter *pin hammer* is justified. Pin hammers have a fine round head with a tapered flat head, known as a *cross-pein*, counterbalancing it. This cross-pein is extremely useful for starting to drive small pins in place. Alternatively, small hammers of the same size are made with *ball-pein* heads instead of the cross-pein. They are designed for riveting and may be more useful for those who are engaging in some light metalwork.

Keep the head of the hammer free of dirt, especially grease and oil, or it will slip on nail heads and cause them to bend. Clean the driving face of the head by rubbing it over a sheet of abrasive paper.

Pin punches are driven with a hammer and are made in a number of sizes to suit the various sizes of pin head. The point of each punch is indented to locate over the pin and prevent it from slipping off. The function of a pin punch is to drive pins below the surface of the wood. The hole produced is then filled with stopper to match the timber. One medium-sized punch is all that is required initially.

Pincers and pliers are essentially used for withdrawing nails, pins and tacks. Unlike the claw of the hammer, they can be used very close to the surface of the wood and can therefore grip where the hammer cannot. If a nail head is firmly embedded into the wood and has to come out, a small amount of the surrounding wood can be chiselled out so that the pincers can get a grip. The hole is then filled with stopper or patched with matching timber.

Where a nail or pin projects sufficiently for pincers to get a firm grip without cutting wood away, place a piece of ply or timber between the pincers jaws and the wood to prevent local bruising.

Chisels

The most useful pattern is the bevel-edge type. The strength is more than sufficient to withstand fairly rugged use and its cut away edges allow it to be used in tight corners. However, do not use any chisel of this type as a lever, or it will bend or snap.

An initial set of chisels should include three sizes—18mm ($\frac{3}{4}''$), 12mm ($\frac{1}{2}''$) and 6mm ($\frac{1}{4}''$). When purchased, chisels are ground to an edge ready for sharpening.

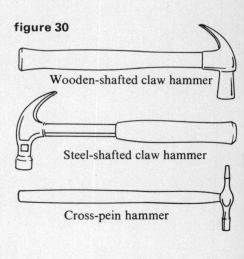

figure 30

Wooden-shafted claw hammer

Steel-shafted claw hammer

Cross-pein hammer

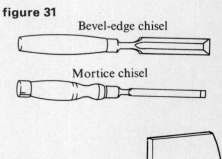

figure 31

Bevel-edge chisel

Mortice chisel

Wooden mallet

They are not ready for use. Refer to page 136 and follow the instructions on sharpening.

Driving chisels with a hammer will split or dent the handles and make them extremely uncomfortable to hand-hold. Avoid this and use a mallet, **figure 31**. A wooden mallet made of beech with a head measuring about 130mm across its widest face is a good, general-purpose weight. Feed it occasionally with raw linseed oil but wipe it thoroughly before use.

Screwdrivers

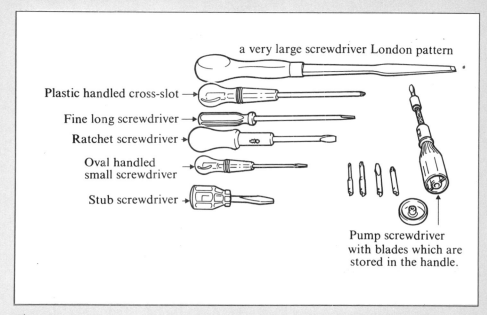

a very large screwdriver London pattern

Plastic handled cross-slot

Fine long screwdriver

Ratchet screwdriver

Oval handled small screwdriver

Stub screwdriver

Pump screwdriver with blades which are stored in the handle.

figure 32

There are two types of screwdriver blade, one for driving straight-slotted screws and the other for those with cross slots. Each is made in a number of sizes to suit the size of slot—the bigger the screw, the larger the driver blade required.

Each blade type is available in a number of patterns. The simplest and cheapest are those with the steel blade running into a fixed handle which may be made from wood or plastic, and is round or oval in shape.

Ratchet screwdrivers have a small mechanism at the base of the handle, controlled by a small button. There are three positions, which give ratchet clockwise, fixed and ratchet anticlockwise actions. The main purpose is to enable the user to tighten or loosen screws without constantly changing the hand grip, as is necessary with a fixed tool. Ratchet screwdrivers are, therefore, much faster in use.

Pump (or 'Yankee') screwdrivers are all fitted with a ratchet and in addition have a spiral fluted shaft which, when the handle is pushed hard downwards, rotates the driving blade. The blade is held in a small chuck and is replaceable with either single or cross slot types. Some makes of pump driver are made with hollow handles in which alternative types and sizes of blade are housed. In addition, small drilling blades are included and these can be used to drill clearance or pilot holes for screws, depending on their size. In use, these pump drivers are very fast, but if they slip from the screw they can do a lot of damage, as the bit drives into the surrounding wood or into you.

Whichever type of screwdriver is used, **figure 32**, it is important to keep the blades square and true. Always use one which is a good fit in the slot, both across and in thickness. A well-fitting blade will reduce the chances of burring the head of the screw.

Files and Rasps

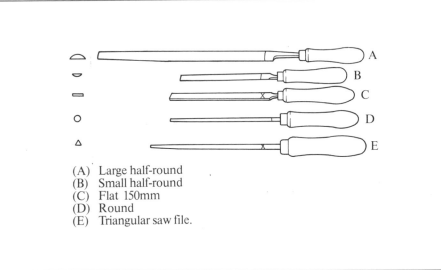

(A) Large half-round
(B) Small half-round
(C) Flat 150mm
(D) Round
(E) Triangular saw file.

figure 33

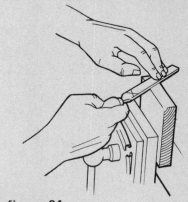

Hold files at both ends, at the front with a handle and at the back with three fingers pressing down on the top.

figure 34

Files are made in a wide range of sizes and shapes as shown in **figure 33**. The tooth pattern varies according to the material they are designed to cut. The tooth size varies to give coarse, medium and fine finish.

The woodworking trades use triangular files for sharpening hand saws, coarse-toothed wood cutting files known as *rasps* and other files of a finer tooth pattern which are normally supplied for cutting metal. These are used to shape details which cannot be cut with the usual bladed tools.

Perhaps surprisingly, wood blunts files quickly, and they need constant brushing with a file brush to keep them free of wood dust, which clogs them rapidly.

A 150mm long, medium-cut file of the sort used by engineers is an asset in any woodworking tool kit. If bought from a tool supplier, it may not be supplied with a handle unless you ask for one. Don't use files without handles. Handles give you something to grip the file with and will also prevent the tang (that is, the spur at the back end of the file) running into your hand if the file slips. (See **figure 34**).

If you have some shaping to do in tightly curved areas, you will find that round files will clean them up easily and quickly. For major re-shaping, rasps are needed. Their cut is coarse and fast and will have to be followed with files and abrasive paper to give a really clean finish.

figure 35

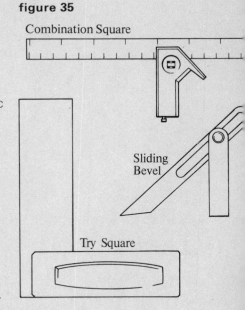

Combination Square

Sliding Bevel

Try Square

Try Square and Sliding Bevel

Try Square See **figure 35**

Buy a try square with a blade length of about 200–250mm, preferably with a plastic stock rather than a wooden one. The wooden stock expands and contracts according to the humidity and is thus less accurate. A smaller, all-steel try square, as used by metal workers, can be useful on small sections but is not vital.

To test a try square, select a piece of timber with a really straight edge. Place the square on it with the stock pressed firmly against the edge as in **figure 36** and draw a line along the top edge of the blade with a very sharp pencil or knife. Then reverse the square stock and compare the line of the blade with the previous line. If they do not match, the square is out of true by half the resulting gap.

When using a square to test the squareness of one edge relative to another, place the stock firmly against the face side and sight the adjacent edge beneath the blade of the square. No light should pass beneath it. A wedge-shaped line of light indicates that the edge is not square and the highest part has to be planed off.

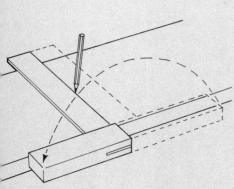

figure 36

Use the square for marking out, checking for square as you plane and afterwards. Use it also for checking work during and after assembly. Always use a square in conjunction with a sharp marking knife or a fine-pointed pencil.

Sliding Bevel

This tool is a partner to the try square. The blade is adjustable to any angle and length through a fixing screw at one end of the stock. The blade is tightened by either a screw or a wing nut. If a choice is available, buy the screw-tightened type, as the wing nut often gets in the way.

Sliding bevels are used in much the same way as try squares, but for marking out or testing a wider range of angles. These tools are not graduated so that if a stipulated angle has to be set it is necessary to use a protractor when adjusting the blade before use.

Combination squares are also available, which as their name implies, combine the functions of both try square and sliding bevel.

Marking, Cutting and Mortice Gauges

All these gauges comprise a stem, fence and one or two spurs, depending on their function. In all cases, the fence slides along the stem and can be tightened with a built-in screw in any position. To reduce wear, the better-made gauges have brass strips let into the face of the fence.

Marking gauges have a single spur or point which is fixed. *Mortice gauges* have two spurs, a forward one which is fixed, and a second which is capable of being moved along the length of the stem on either a simple slide action or on a long screw which is mounted within the stem—these are simpler to adjust finely. See **figure 37**. The spurs of both the marking and mortice gauges are round and pointed. With this profile they are suited to marking lines with or against the grain, and over end grain.

The cutting gauge has a cutter in place of a rounded spur. This is held in place with a wedge which can be tapped out when the cutter needs sharpening. The purpose of this tool is to mark across the grain. It actually cuts the fibres as it marks, where a rounder spur would tear its way across.

Combination gauges are combined marking and mortice gauges. These tools have a single spur on one side of the stem (marking gauge) and two spurs on the other (mortice gauge). This is an ideal tool to start with because of its dual function.

For gauges in use, see Measuring and Marking out, page 142, and Mortice and Tenon Joints, page 153.

figure 37

Marking gauge   Cutting gauge   Mortice gauge

Tools Section

figure 38

Keeping Tools Sharp

The degree of sharpness required for woodworking tools is not always understood, but there is a simple test. A sharp blade should be comparable with a razor blade, and many craftsmen used to test the sharpness of their blades by shaving the hair off their arms. This is not recommended. A far safer alternative is to run the freshly-sharpened blade lightly over the surface of a piece of hanging newspaper. It should cut it without pressure.

The necessary tools for sharpening (or honing) flat blades are a *combination oil stone* with one side medium grit and the other fine grit, a can of fine *machine oil* and a rag. Although it is not essential, the use of a *honing guide* will ensure that the blades are held at the correct angle to the stone and will therefore keep square. Sharpening without a guide results in a curved rather than flat angle in all but the most experienced hands, and this leads to the necessity for re-grinding at unnecessarily frequent intervals.

Most woodworking cutters, excepting plough and combination plane blades, have two angles at their cutting edges; a *grinding angle* and a *honing angle*. The latter is slightly steeper, giving a little more metal immediately supporting the actual cutting edge than a continued grinding angle would produce if it were extended right the way through. Plough and combination blades are sharpened at one angle only. See **figure 38**.

All new woodworking tools with the exception of saws and blades for knives are supplied ground to the correct angle for honing; they are not ready for use.

If you have purchased a new oil stone it will be flat and ready for use. If it is an old one, check to see that it is not hollow. If it is, get some fine carborundum powder from a tool merchant. Sprinkle some on a flat sheet of glass with water, making a sloppy paste, and rub the stone round and round in it. This will cut the surface quite quickly. You will see on inspection which high spots are being removed, because those areas will be lighter in colour. Add water to keep the powder running freely and stop grinding when all high spots have been removed.

If you are unable to get carborundum powder, use the finest silver sand you can get. This is usually supplied by pet shops. Do not use builders sand.

Make a box to keep the oil stone in. Make the top and bottom of the box each half the depth of the stone, with a tight fit in the bottom half and a loose fitting top.

In **figure 40** you will note that the oil stone box has been made longer than the length of the stone and that a piece of end-grain hardwood has been wedged between the box ends and each end of the stone. The tops of those hardwood blocks finish flush with the top surface of the stone so that if the blade being sharpened overruns the end of the stone, it hits wood and is not damaged by striking the end of the stone.

The first task in sharpening all flat cutters is to get the backs truly flat. Although in the making process they will have been mechanically ground flat, this is not good enough. Under magnification, they would appear to be rather like a ploughed field and no amount of honing of the opposite cutting angle would produce anything better than a saw-like edge. Therefore the initial flattening of the back is essential. It takes some time, but only has to be done once. Thereafter very little has to be done to the back during re-sharpening.

Place the blade, back side on to the fine side of the stone, using plenty of fine oil as a lubricant and rub it forwards and backwards, keeping the whole blade surface on the stone in close contact with it—do not rock it whatever happens.

If you are using a new stone, repeated applications of oil are necessary to replace that which has become absorbed. Loose oil on the stone is essential to lubricate it and to prevent it from becoming clogged with metal particles.

Lift the blade from the stone occasionally, wipe it clean and you will see that a much finer and brighter surface appears, where it is being cut by the stone. Continue honing until that shiny area covers the entire width of the cutting edge and back from it by about 3—4mm as in **figure 39**. There is no need to keep honing until

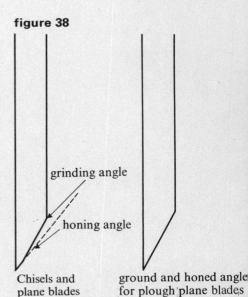

grinding angle

honing angle

Chisels and
plane blades

ground and honed angle
for plough plane blades

figure 39

A

B

more than this is flat across the whole width—the really important part which must be absolutely flat is the tip.

With the back flat, the angled side of the blade can be sharpened. Slide the blade into the honing guide, back uppermost, so that it projects the correct amount to sustain the cutting angle of the blade. The instruction leaflet accompanying the guide sets out the length of the projection. Move the guide to and fro along the whole length of the stone as shown in **figure 40**. Keep the wheel and stone well oiled. If the blade is narrower than the stone, move it to the left, then centre, then right to equalise the wear on the stone. If the blade is wider, it will have to be run at an angle so that the whole of the cutting edge contacts the stone on each stroke.

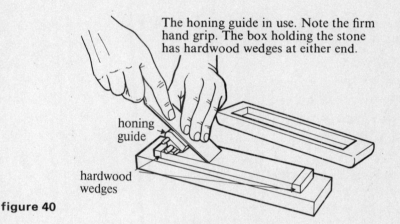

The honing guide in use. Note the firm hand grip. The box holding the stone has hardwood wedges at either end.

honing guide

hardwood wedges

figure 40

After a few passes a small burr will have built up at the edge of the blade and can be felt by running your thumb over the cutter back. Stop honing when that burr can be felt across the whole of the width of the blade but do not remove it from the guide. The sharpening process now involves the removal of that burr, which looks like a very thin wire.

Place the back of the blade flat on to the stone and hone it gently for one or two strokes. This will reverse the burr which can now be felt from the angled face. Repeat that light honing on the angled face, following the honing guide angle until the burr reverses on to the back. Continue honing back and front until the burr breaks off. The blade should be sharp enough to cut paper, and is ready for use.

If you are sharpening without the use of a honing guide, you will have to hold the blade angle by hand. Remember that the honing angle is a little steeper than the ground one on all but plough and combination plane blades. See **figure 38**.

It is important to maintain both the ground and honed angles on cutting edges. As repeated honing makes inroads into the ground angle, it is necessary to recover the situation by honing the grinding angle on the medium grit side of the oil stone. Do not hone the back of the iron on those occasions, as this is not necessary. After honing the grinding angle, turn the stone to the fine side and hone the cutting edge in the same way. Plough and combination blades are ground and honed at one and the same angle.

Chisels and blades (also called cutting irons in planes) need re-grinding to their original profile when they become rounded through repeated honing or badly indented (gapped) through hitting metal or being dropped. If you have a *grindstone* and wish to undertake re-grinding yourself, be sure to do so to the correct angle, maintaining the cutting edge at 90° to the blade side. It is essential that you do not overheat the blade whilst grinding. If the temperature of the steel gets too high, it will lose its properties and never be the same again. Keep the blade in contact with the grindwheel for very short periods and dip the blade into cold water every few seconds throughout the operation.

A safer alternative is to have a tool specialist re-grind your tools for you. Do not accept blades which are returned with blue patches in the steel close to the edge— these have been over-heated.

Tools Section

Sharpening other Woodworking Tools

Saws All handsaws and tenon saws can be re-sharpened. Where a substantial number of teeth have broken off, the saw can be recut. In either case a tool specialist will be able to do the work for you. They also replace broken handles.

Twist Drills can be re-ground and only lose a fraction of their original length. Masonry drills can also be resharpened. Refer to a tool specialist.

Centre and Jennings pattern bits can be re-sharpened with small files. There are two upstanding wings on a Jennings pattern bit and only one on the centre bit. Each should be filed to a sharp edge throughout their arched profile. Do not file off more than is essential, and only file on the inside edges. Remove any burr which may occur on the outside with minimal contact on a fine oilstone. The flat cutting edges of both bits should be filed from the flute side towards the centre screw. Use needle files in all cases.

Ironmongery and Fittings

The range of fastenings and fittings is so vast that no DIY Centre can stock them all. Most shops will have the stock sizes of screws and nails, but special hinges, locks, wire trays, drawer slides and knobs are difficult to find. However, you can usually obtain these items from the small number of specialist suppliers who advertise in DIY magazines and who sell by mail order through a catalogue.

In this section, we confine ourselves to the fittings needed for the projects in the book. You will get to know many others as time goes by, and time spent browsing around ironmongers and DIY Centres is rarely wasted.

Unlike the timber trade, most fittings manufacturers have not metricated and do not plan to do so at the present. Woodscrews are all sold in Imperial sizes, as are most nails. Hinges are another product which remains in inch sizes. Although this may sound impossible to cope with, it is not. Again it is a matter of experience.

Screws see **figure 41**

These are the three types of woodscrew head:
Round Head: All the head stands proud of the surface of the timber.
Countersunk: Set in flush with the surface of wood with the aid of a countersink bit (page 126).
Raised Head: Half countersunk, half roundhead. Set into wood to the depth of the countersunk head portion; the dome of the raised part stands proud.

Each of the different head types is available with either a cross-slot or a single slot. See **figure 42**. The different screwdriver patterns are made to suit them. They are also available in a number of sizes to suit the size of the slot.

Woodscrews are made from a variety of metals and with some different finishes. Steel is the most common, whilst other metals include brass and aluminium. Rust-resistant and decorative finishes on steel screws include zinc, chrome, bronze, black japanned paint and galvanised. Brass screws may be finished in chrome and bronze. Aluminium screws are most often left natural, but they are available with anodised or chrome plated finishes.

So far not metricated, *screw lengths* begin at $\frac{1}{4}$", rising by increments of $\frac{1}{8}$" up to $1\frac{1}{4}$", then by $\frac{1}{4}$" increments up to 4". In furniture making, the most common screw lengths are from $\frac{1}{2}$" to 2". *Screw thickness* is measured by *gauge sizes*, the most common being from 5 to 12, with a No. 12 gauge being the thickest. Gauge sizes rise in single numbers but because demand is greatest for even-number gauges, few stores bother to stock 7s and 9s.

Table 1 shows the pilot hole sizes required for the various screw gauges in both hard and soft woods. You will need this information when counter sinking and counter boring.

figure 41

Types of Screw:

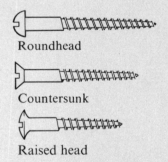

Roundhead

Countersunk

Raised head

figure 42

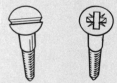

The two types of slots in screwheads
Left: Straight slot   Right: Cross slot

Screw gauge	Pilot hole diameter in mms	
	Hardwood	Softwood
3	1·5	Not necessary use a fine bradawl
4	2	
5	2	
6	2	1·5
7	2·5	1·5
8	2·5	1·5
9	3·5	2
10	3·5	2
12	3·5	2·5
14	4	3

Table 1   Pilot Hole Sizes

igure 43

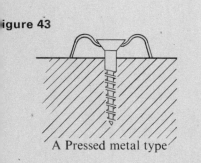

A Pressed metal type

Countersunk type

igure 44

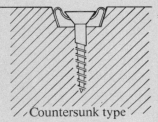

Snap on plastic screw cap

igure 45

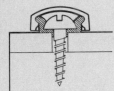

rom left to right: panel pin, veneer pin, ng and short hardboard pins, oval and ire nails

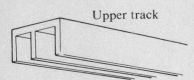

Upper track

Sliding door track.

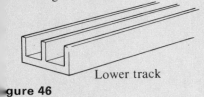

Lower track

gure 46

Screw Caps and Cups

Cups. Two types are available, a surface mounted pressed steel type, which spreads the load on thin materials, and a countersunk type, either pressed steel or solid brass, which is let in to the surrounding timber by drilling a countersunk or counterbored hole to receive it. See **figure 43**.

Caps Made from plastic, these caps comprise a washer and a clip-over cap. The washer is held under the screw head. When in position with the screw driven in, the cap is pressed over the washer and snaps shut. See **figure 44**.

Panel and Veneer Pins see **figure 45**

These fine steel wire pins are commonly used for attaching small pieces of wood and in pinning some joints to reinforce adhesives.

The finer *veneer pin* is very useful for fixing small section beading and moulding. It is so thin that it seldom causes a crack. The heads of both panel and veneer pins are usually punched below the surface with a pin punch of matching diameter. The resulting hole is then filled.

Nails see **figure 45**

Hardboard Pins: these copper-plated square section pins $\frac{3}{4}''$ long have deep drive heads which are designed to finish flush with the surface without the use of a punch. The plating is rust resistant. Some specialists stock hardboard pins which are round in section, have a similar head pattern and are made up to 2″ in length.

Oval Nails: oval in section with small flattish heads for driving into or below the surface with a nail punch. Thickness is proportional to length. Commonly available from 1″ upwards by $\frac{1}{2}''$ increments, they should be driven into timber with their wider dimension in line with the grain.

Wire Nails: round in section with flat, round heads which lie on the surface after driving. Commonly available from $\frac{3}{4}''$ upwards by $\frac{1}{4}''$ and then $\frac{1}{2}''$ increments. Thickness is proportional to length.

Sliding Door Track

Sliding door track for lightweight doors is made in wood and in plastic. In both cases, the upper track has deeper grooves than the bottom one. This is to allow the doors to be lifted up into the top track and then dropped down into the bottom one. The difference in depth of groove prevents the door from coming out until it is lifted again. See **figure 46**.

Tools Section

The track is usually glued to a cabinet, the wooden variety with PVA, the plastic with contact adhesive. Single track is also available and can be used to hold removable shelves, as in Alf Martensson's storage boxes in Chapter 1.

figure 47

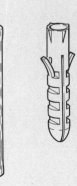

Wallplugs
There are a number of makes in plastic or fibre materials. See **figure 47**. Plug sizes are related to those of screws and in every case it is necessary to use a masonry drill of the same size as the plug. Fibre plugs are made in a number of lengths for a given diameter screw but this is not generally the case with most of the plastic ones. When fixing, be sure that the screw and plug have a firm hold on the block or brickwork. You must go right through the plaster as it will not hold any weight.

Flushmount Fitting
This fitting comprises two interlocking parts which can be used as a linking device for wood panels or upholstered sections. It is fitted with eight screws, four to each component and is only 3mm thick. **Figure 48** shows the mode of action. We used flushmount fittings on Peter Cornish's pine and denim two-seater chair, Chapter 6.

figure 48

Flushmount fitting.

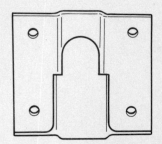

The two halves joined together.

Butt Hinge See **figure 49**
This, the most common of all hinges, requires recessing into both door and carcase edge. A tight-fitting recess adds to the screw-hold by preventing the hinge from dropping. Butt hinges offer an opening capability of 180°, allowing doors to be opened flat. This is especially useful on wall units, where a door left half-open can be easily walked into.

Card Table Hinge See **figure 50**
The hinge is mounted flush with the top of the two surfaces of a folding table or between a table top and a flap. It is also used inside desk flaps. A recess equal in depth, width and the tapering thickness of each hinge leaf is cut away from either flap with a fine saw and chisel. The hinge knuckle is also let into the flap edge so that the gap between the table halves is minimal. Note that a good screw fixing is essential. In the games table in Chapter 2, a length of dowel was let into the edge of the chipboard to ensure a good hold for the screws.

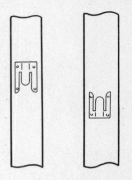

Mode of action.

Flush Hinge See **figure 51**
This pressed steel hinge offers all the advantages of full opening, but screws directly on to the edge of both the door and the carcase or frame. Its combined thickness of about 1·5mm enables the gap required to fit it to be relatively tight. Flush hinges are used in the wardrobe range in Chapter 4.

Glass Door Hinge See **figure 52**.
This special hinge is used to hang the glass doors in the tall cabinet in Chapter 10. This fitting does not require any holes or cut-outs to be made in the 6—8mm thick glass it is designed for.

The metal base sections are let into the cabinet top and bottom by positioning them and scribing round their curved line with a knife. That area is then cut out with a chisel and gouge to the shallow depth required. Two screws secure each to the cabinet. The glass is firmly clamped in place with a plate and screw.

figure 49

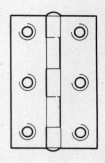

Magic Wires See **figure 53**.
Available in three standard lengths, magic wires are not seen when in use. Holes drilled in the cabinet sides take the wire ends and a single groove of about 4mm in width, stopped short of the shelf front in each end allows the wire to slide in and be hidden from view.

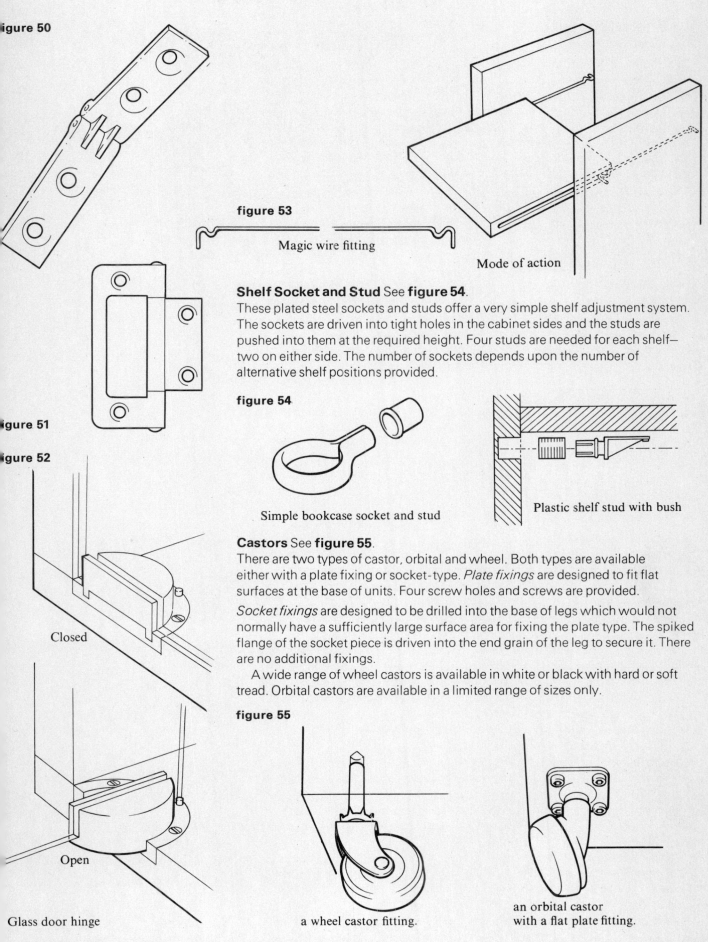

figure 50

figure 53

Magic wire fitting

Mode of action

figure 51

figure 52

Closed

Open

Glass door hinge

Shelf Socket and Stud See **figure 54**.

These plated steel sockets and studs offer a very simple shelf adjustment system. The sockets are driven into tight holes in the cabinet sides and the studs are pushed into them at the required height. Four studs are needed for each shelf—two on either side. The number of sockets depends upon the number of alternative shelf positions provided.

figure 54

Simple bookcase socket and stud

Plastic shelf stud with bush

Castors See **figure 55**.

There are two types of castor, orbital and wheel. Both types are available either with a plate fixing or socket-type. *Plate fixings* are designed to fit flat surfaces at the base of units. Four screw holes and screws are provided.

Socket fixings are designed to be drilled into the base of legs which would not normally have a sufficiently large surface area for fixing the plate type. The spiked flange of the socket piece is driven into the end grain of the leg to secure it. There are no additional fixings.

A wide range of wheel castors is available in white or black with hard or soft tread. Orbital castors are available in a limited range of sizes only.

figure 55

a wheel castor fitting.

an orbital castor with a flat plate fitting.

Measuring and Marking Out

The most important factor in making any piece of furniture is to measure all the parts accurately and to make sure that they are square and true.

Measuring accurately is not difficult. Some of the dimensions in the cutting lists look rather awkward, but in fact there is no more skill required in marking out a length of, say, 999mm than 1000mm. All you require is a clearly-marked measure and a sharp pencil or knife. Do not use a heavy carpenter's pencil—their leads are so thick that accuracy of the sort needed in making furniture is impossible.

The basic tool kit recommends a steel tape measure 2 or 3 metres in length, and a flat steel rule at least 600mm long which will double as a straightedge. Both will be graduated in millimetres and each mark can be clearly seen. The steel tape measure can be used for long dimensions and the flat steel rule can be used for setting tools such as gauges or plough planes, and for marking out joints.

The need for the two types of measure will be quickly appreciated when you begin work. Flexible steel tapes work excellently under tension—where you have the hook over one end of the work—but you really need both hands free to use them properly. The rigid steel rule comes in to its own when you have a tool in one hand and you only have the other hand free to steady the measure. The tab-end on flexible rules also makes measuring from a line on a flat surface difficult and the rigid rule is better in these cases. A 600mm flat steel rule can be unweildy for small measurements. For this purpose, a folding plastic or boxwood rule is a useful addition to your tool kit.

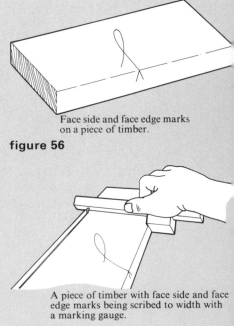

Face side and face edge marks on a piece of timber.

figure 56

A piece of timber with face side and face edge marks being scribed to width with a marking gauge.

figure 57

Preparing Timber

Each piece of timber required in the cutting list should be cut 10–20mm overlength to start with. This allows for marking out the exact length and trueing up the ends later. The first and most important job is to prepare two surfaces of the board so that they are perfectly flat and exactly at right angles to each other. These surfaces are known as the *face side* and *face edge*. Once established, they act as a reference point for all subsequent measurements of thickness and width and help you to keep the work square.

Start by choosing that one of the wider surfaces of the board which has the most attractive grain pattern and plane it flat, both along and across its length. Check that it is flat with a try square, then pencil on to it a *face side mark* as shown in **figure 56**. Now plane the best of the two edges exactly at right angles to the face side, again checking with a try square, and make a *face edge mark* on it. Note how the two marks are joined together in **figure 56**.

You are now ready to bring the board to its correct width and thickness. Start with the width. Set the width required on to a marking gauge and scribe a cutting line on both the face and back sides of the timber, keeping the stock of the gauge firmly opposed to the face edge as in **figure 57**. Now place the board in a vice and plane down the back edge till you reach the marked line. This line is a V-shaped indentation in the wood and you will see it appear as you plane. Plane down to the bottom of the V and no farther. If there is a lot of waste to start with—say more than 5mm—you may find it easier to take off most of it with a saw, then to finish with a plane as above.

Now repeat the whole procedure to bring the board to its correct thickness.

When the timber is square and of the correct cross-section, it is next marked to length. Place a try square with its stock along the face edge and its blade on the face side and make a straight line along the blade with a marking knife. This severs the surface fibres of the board and prevents splitting out when you saw it to length.

Square this line all round the piece of timber, always keeping the stock of the try square on the face side or face edge. Now measure the exact dimension along the board with a steel tape or rule and square round again. The board is now marked to length.

Cutting to length may take place immediately after marking if the piece of timber is being made to fit into an assembly at this stage, or where the ends themselves are being jointed, but wherever possible, the trueing of the ends is left till last. In some furniture projects, cutting to length only occurs after assembly with other parts, for example in Brian Davey's dining chair in Chapter 5. The waste acts as a reinforcement while the glue is setting in an adjacent joint. The instructions for our projects usually state when cutting to length should take place. For most furniture components, cutting to length is done with a tenon saw on a *bench hook* as in **figure 58**, and **59**.

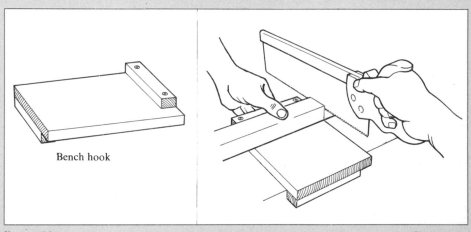

Bench hook

figure 58   **figure 59**

Machine-planed timber is usually fairly square and thicknesses and widths are parallel, but do not take this for granted. Some movement does occur as drying out takes place, and edges may need trueing up before they are accurate enough to proceed with. As a matter of routine, always check timber, first to see that it is flat, second, that its face edges are square to one another, and finally that the width and thicknesses are even.

Sharp, crisp edges and flat even surfaces give things a professional appearance. Having achieved them initially, do not lose them when finally cleaning up with abrasive paper.

Angled Edges
The squareness referred to so far has been that of one face meeting another at 90°. However, the term 'square' in timber also applies to how true something is to its intended angle. It can apply to 30° or any angle. Angles other than 90° are checked with a sliding bevel (see page 135).

figure 60

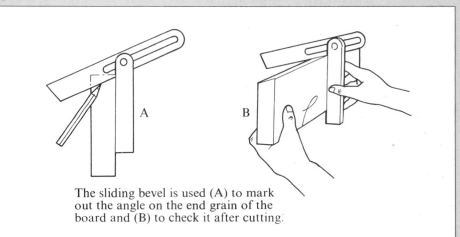

The sliding bevel is used (A) to mark out the angle on the end grain of the board and (B) to check it after cutting.

Techniques Section

To cut an angled edge, first prepare a board with face side and face edge and a rectangular cross section, as described above. Set the sliding bevel to the required angle with a protractor, then mark the end grain of the board as shown in **figure 60**. Remove the waste with a plane or saw, then check the angle of the edge throughout its length with the bevel. Use of rectangular cross section timber to start with ensures that, as far as possible, the angled section will be parallel throughout its length.

Marking Knife

The use of a marking knife is essential whenever a cut line is being set out across the grain. The resulting cut severs the fibres and prevents them from lifting or tearing away during subsequent sawing or planing operations. It is not advisable to use knife lines along the grain because they often close up and cannot be seen properly. There is also the likelihood of the knife being diverted from its intended path by the grain of the wood. Wherever possible, the knife should be run against a steel blade or straightedge. Wooden straightedges are not satisfactory, as the knife blade often bites into the grain.

When marking timber-veneered panels, ensure that the knife cuts right through the face veneer and take particular care near the edge of a board to avoid splintering the edge of the veneer. In some cases it pays to reverse the job and cut from edge to centre on one edge and then on the other. Always mark cut lines on melamine coated boards with a knife, both on the edges and on the faces. This precaution will prevent the edge of the melamine from chipping when sawn or planed.

There are several types of marking knife, including the traditional tool, which has a cutting edge flat on one face and honed on the other. The advantage of this is that the flat side can be used hard against a straightedge or try square without the necessity for tipping it sideways to allow for an angled cutting edge. Among the more recent tools is the tough Stanley knife, which takes a variety of shapes of replaceable blades, and the lighter weight knives, which are supplied with lengths of snap-off blades.

Marking and Cutting Gauges

The marking of lines parallel to the edges of boards or to another line is almost exclusively undertaken by the gauge family (see page 135). Marking gauges work with the grain or over end-grain, and cutting gauges mark across the grain.

Whether cutting or marking, gauges always work from a prepared or planed face side or face edge. In use the gauge is held firmly with the right hand wrapped over the fence which is tipped forward slightly away from the user. The thumb presses the spur or point down on the work, the fence is pressed into the edge of the timber and the whole tool is pushed forward to make its mark. See **figure 57**.

Marking Parts Together

Whenever you have two or more parts which are identical, such as a series of chair legs, or rails, or cabinets sides, mark them all together if possible. This is the way to make sure that you get them all the same length and that any joints in them occur at the same distance from the top.

Opposite cabinet sides can, after initial cutting out, be held together while their edges are finally trued up with a plane. If fixing holes are required, these can be drilled through both pieces while they are together. It all helps to make sure that things which are meant to be the same size do in fact end up that way.

Where eight or so identical parts are required of the same length, it is often possible to grip the rough cut lengths edge to edge in cramps while a square is run across them all to mark the tops and bottoms. When the cramps are released, those marks can be transferred to the individual face sides or all round with further use of the try square.

Labelling Parts

Most pieces of furniture comprise a number of parts which are either identical, or are so similar that there is a chance of mixing them up at some point. To avoid confusion, make a point of labelling each piece, so that you know whether it is a left or right leg, for example. To save difficulty in removing the mark when you no longer need it, pencil it on an edge or back where it will eventually be covered, or use chalk which is easily wiped off. Do not be tempted into writing something on a piece of tape and sticking it on. If you leave that in place for only a short time, the toning down of colour due to natural light affecting the wood could be enough to leave the area you have masked by the tape as a pale patch which is exceedingly difficult to remove. This occurs on natural timber surfaces only.

When selecting pieces for jointing together, set all the parts out in the order in which they will be ultimately jointed or connected together and mark each mating piece with common letters or numbers. You will see that this practice has been followed throughout the book, for example in drawer-making in Chapter 4 and in the cutting of joints (see page 147). Remember when setting out that in almost all cases the face side and face edge marks tell you which are the outward facing sides of each piece.

Keeping Square

As each component of a piece of furniture is prepared ready for final assembly, it is absolutely vital to check that all the faces are square to each other at all times. Use the try square continually. Once inaccurate angles creep in and the piece becomes distorted, it will not stand level, doors will not hang properly, drawers will jam and all manner of other horrors will make their appearance.

A common time when distortion occurs is in final gluing up and cramping. A fixed procedure is used at this time, the stages of which are shown in **figure 61**.

Figure 61

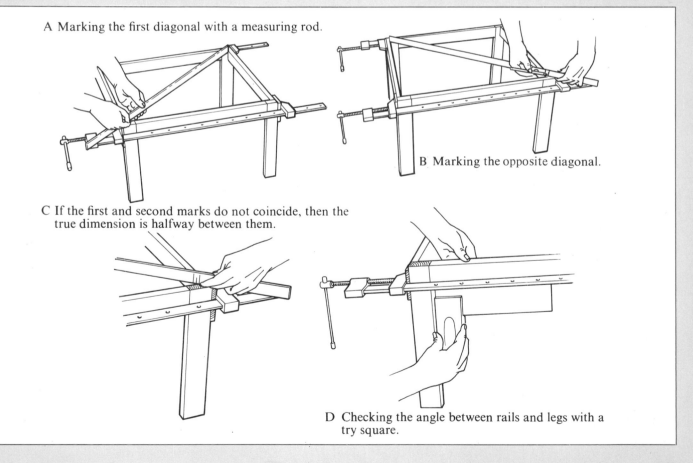

A Marking the first diagonal with a measuring rod.

B Marking the opposite diagonal.

C If the first and second marks do not coincide, then the true dimension is halfway between them.

D Checking the angle between rails and legs with a try square.

Techniques Section

For this purpose you will need a measuring rod, which is simply a straight piece of timber about 20mm × 8mm in section and longer than the longest diagonal of the frame to be assembled. One end should be sharpened to a point.

The illustration refers to the table underframe from Chapter 2, but it applies to all frames and most cabinets too. Should the work you are checking involve angles other than 90°, a sliding bevel set at the true angle will also be needed.

As described in the section on Cramps and Cramping (page 127), it is wise to assemble the whole piece and check for square without any glue, take it apart and then assemble it the second time with glue, ironing out any last problems between the two operations. Once the piece has been assembled with glue, check for square as soon as possible, as the glue begins to stiffen rapidly once it comes in contact with the wood. Any movement of the frame has to be done speedily.

Once the cramps are on, the checking procedure is as follows:

1 Check one diagonal with the rod. Place the point in one corner and make a pencil mark on the edge of the rod exactly in line with the diagonally opposite one. **Figure 61**A. Square that line around the bottom and up the other side of the rod.
2 Change diagonals and check the other way in the same fashion. The pencil line on the rod should be exactly at the corner diagonally opposite to the point. If it is not, and it seldom is in the first instance, place a second mark on the rod. **Figure 61**B.
3 If the initial marks line up, the frame is square. If they do not and you have two lines, mark a third line half way between the two, **figure 61**C. That is the true diagonal measure and the frame must be manipulated until the diagonals in both directions measure up to that line. You may have to over-distort the frame so that it releases back and stays where intended. If you cannot shift the frame by hand, then move the cramps holding the top edges out of a true line with the frame sides. You will then see that as you re-tighten them, the frame will pull diagonally in one direction or the other. If it is the wrong way, then reverse the shift of the cramps to succeed. See Cramps and Cramping page 127.
4 With the diagonals square, use a try square to check legs to rails at each corner, **figure 61**D.
5 The final check is to sight across the top of the opposite side rails. They must be parallel to one another throughout this length. If they are not, adjust the low corner by placing a small wedge beneath the leg to raise it to the required height. Give everything a final quick check to make sure that a late adjustment has not affected other angles, and leave the work to dry.

Lipping Edges

Lippings are thin strips of material used to cover the unsightly edges of chipboard and blockboard. The commonest type of lipping is applied with a hot iron, but solid timber lippings are also used, for example in the dining table in chapter 5, where they have a protective as well as a decorative function.

Iron-On Lipping, properly called iron-on self adhesive edge veneer, is readily available to match all the standard varieties of timber veneered and melamine covered sheets. It is sold in rolls about 2m in length and is wide enough to cover the edge of 16mm thick boards with enough overlap to allow for trimming and cleaning up after bonding.

Before applying the lipping, it is essential that the edges of the sheets are planed square and are free of dust. The technique of application is simple and immediate. Begin by cutting off a length of lipping about 5–10mm longer than the edge being covered. Then with a hot domestic iron, simply press the veneer in place, as shown in **figure 62**, starting at one end and gradually moving along the length. The iron can be used in either a forward or backward direction, whichever you find most convenient. Keep the lipping central in the width of the edge, to allow the

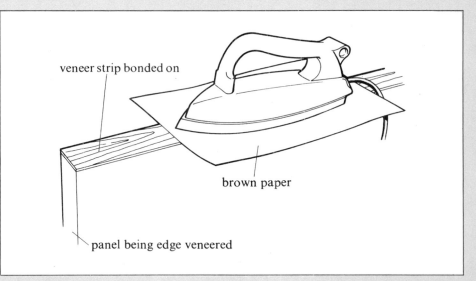

veneer strip bonded on

brown paper

panel being edge veneered

figure 62

surplus to hang equally over the sides for cleaning off later. To avoid marking the sole of the iron, a piece of brown wrapping paper can be placed between the iron and the lipping.

After ironing, and whilst the veneer is still warm, run over the lipping with a flat smooth block of wood to press it home firmly. Allow the veneer to cool completely, then trim it to the exact profile of the board edge with a fine cut 150mm file held at an angle of about 45°. Repeat the whole process on all the edges required, lipping only one at a time. Thicker boards can be covered with two or more strips of lipping running parallel.

For greater durability, or where the lipping is to receive a decorative moulded detail, as in the wall-hung cabinets in chapter 10, the lippings are made of solid timber. The thickness of solid lippings varies according to the job, but it is usually between 4 and 6mm. The width of the lipping should be about 1mm greater than the thickness of the edge to be lipped, to allow for cleaning up.

As before, the edges to be lipped must be square and free of dust. Plane the lippings to the exact cross-section required and apply them with one of the adhesives mentioned on page 131. In most cases, there is no need for pins or nails. Leave to dry in cramps, using pieces of softening a little longer and wider than the lippings, to spread the cramp pressure evenly. Wipe off all surplus adhesive with a damp rag.

When the work is dry, remove the cramps and trim the lippings down to the exact thickness of the board to which they are bonded with a very sharp block plane or a file. For mitred corner lippings, see page 148.

figure 63

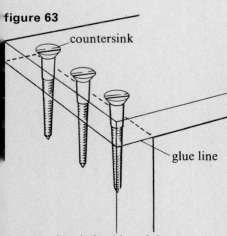

countersink

glue line

A screwed and glued butt joint.

Woodworking Joints

Right-Angled Butt Joint

The simplest of all joints, in which one piece of wood butts up against another at 90° as in **figure 63**. The two pieces of wood are bonded together with wood-working adhesive and the joint is strengthened by pins or screws. The end grain of the butting piece must be planed absolutely flat and square for the joint to work.

Right-angled butt joints are used for the shelves in the wall-mounted storage system in Chapter 1. In most cases the butting piece is clamped in a vice with the edge to be glued upwards. The other piece of wood is laid on top of it and fixed in the correct position with cramps. Clearance holes are drilled through the top piece of wood and into the end grain of the butting piece, using a twist drill in a wheelbrace, then the tops of the holes are countersunk. Glue is applied, the joint is checked for square and the woodscrews are driven in.

Techniques Section

reassembled and checked again for square. Surplus glue is rubbed off with a damp cloth and the joint is left in G cramps to dry.

Sometimes a right-angled butt joint is made simply with adhesive, and screws or pins are not used. Generally this is between two flat long grain surfaces, such as in the L-shaped leg of the coffee table in Chapter 2. After the adhesive has been applied, the two surfaces are usually rubbed together to key the adhesive, so the joint is often called a *rub joint*.

Mitred Butt Joints

Butt joints are said to be mitred when the joint line runs at 45° rather than 90°. See **figure 64a**. Mitred joints are familiar to most people from the corners of picture frames. In woodwork they are often used in the application of lipping to the fronts of cabinets, as in the wall mounted units in Chapter 10.

The best way to cut a mitre is to use a *mitre box*, **figure 64b**. This tool is easily available and is usually made of beech. In it are two pre-cut mitre saw cuts, left- and right-handed, into which a tenon saw can be slipped. The slots direct the cut at the correct angle. To protect the base of a mitre box, slip a piece of waste material beneath the timber being mitred. By moving the waste after each cut, so that the job is standing on flat material, the mitres will not split away on the back.

When fitting mitred lipping to four edges of a cabinet, glue and cramp the longest ones on first. Then cut those which fit between them. By following that method you will be able to adjust the fit of each mitre with a block plane as the second halves of the joint are fitted.

Lap Joint

A lap joint is simply a right-angled butt joint in which the flat member overlaps the end grain of the side. See **figure 65**. It is often used in frames and in drawer making.

Start the joint by cutting the front and side members to length and squaring up their ends with a plane. Mark the thickness of the side member on to the back face of the front member using a marking knife or cutting gauge. Square the lines down across both edges. Set a marking gauge to the thickness of the lap required and mark the end grain and the top and bottom edges of the front member. Remember to work with the stock of the gauge against the face side.

Hold the front, end up, in a vice and saw down the end grain until you reach the squared lines on the edges. Keep to the waste side of the line. Transfer the front to a bench hook, place it back face up, and saw to the waste side of the knife cut line until it reaches the cut made previously. Be sure to keep the cut square by following the lines running across the edges.

The joint is now ready for assembly. Glue the internal faces of the lap and the end grain of the side member. Pin them together. Check for square and leave to dry in cramps.

Housing Joint

The housing joint is commonly used for shelves or dividing panels in cabinets. There are two variations, the *through housing* and the *stopped housing*. See **figure 66**. In either case, the groove in the upright is equal in width to the thickness of the cross member.

The through housing is the simpler joint. It comprises a groove which runs across the grain of the upright and through about one third of its thickness. The cross member is cut square and simply slots in position to make a T joint.

In stopped housings the groove does not go completely across the upright; it stops a short distance from the front edge. The purpose behind this is decorative rather than functional—it merely means that the outline of the groove cannot be seen on the front edge of the upright.

Making the through housing: Before marking out or cutting, ensure that all the timber being used is planed flat, is parallel and is cut to exact thickness.

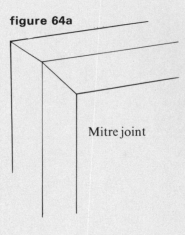

figure 64a

Mitre joint

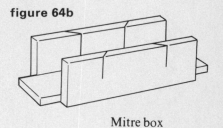

figure 64b

Mitre box

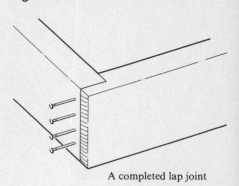

figure 65

A completed lap joint

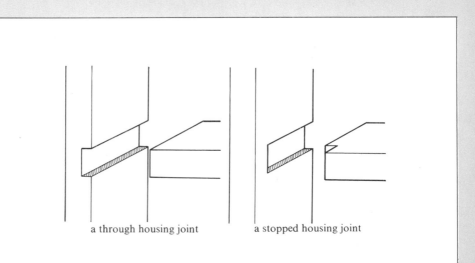

a through housing joint   a stopped housing joint

figure 66

figure 67

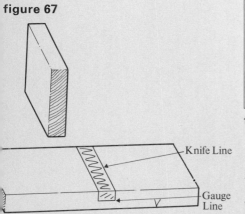

Knife Line

Gauge Line

The housing joint marked out, with two knife-cut lines running across the back face and down the edges. The gauge line runs between the two lines on the edge.

figure 68

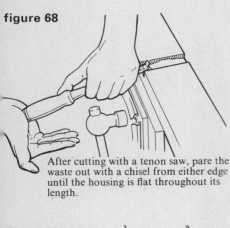

After cutting with a tenon saw, pare the waste out with a chisel from either edge until the housing is flat throughout its length.

figure 69

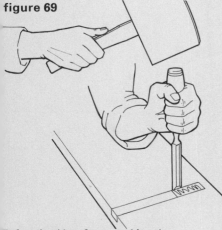

Before the sides of a stopped housing can be sawn, about 50mm of the groove has to be removed with a chisel.

Place the upright flat on the worktop and mark the bottom line of the housing joint. If you are cutting a housing joint at either end of a shelf, mark both uprights together so that they are at exactly the same place relative to one another. Note that in most cases the joint will occur on the inside of a job and will therefore be marked and cut on the back face—the face side will be facing down. Square the line across the width of the timber with a knife cut. Position the cross-member beside and touching the line, and mark the other side of the shelf to establish the width of the groove. Remove the cross-member and square the second mark right across with a knife cut. Square both lines down both edges. Set a marking gauge to the depth of the housing and mark a line along both edges between them. See **figure 67**.

Use a tenon saw on a bench hook to cut the waste side of both lines across the grain and down to the gauge line. Pare away the waste between the two saw cuts by working a chisel at an angle from the edge up towards the centre as in **figure 68**. A number of cuts should be made to reach the full depth. When one half has been cut, reverse the side and cut from the other edge. Then change the angle of the chisel with each successive cut until the whole length of the housing is flat. The joint is now ready for assembly. It may be glued, or pinned and glued, depending on the rigidity of the surrounding parts.

Making the stopped housing: Mark out in the same way as for a through housing but do not carry the knife or gauge lines on to the face edge. Mark a line between the two knife lines running across the side about 10–15mm in from the face edge. This is where the housing will stop.

In a stopped housing, you cannot saw down the sides of the groove immediately because there is no room for the end of the saw to move forward and back. For this reason, chop out about 50mm of the groove to full depth, using a chisel and wooden mallet. You can then cut the remaining edges of the housing with a tenon saw and chop out as for the through housing. See **figure 69**.

Cut away the front edge of the shelf to match the stopped housing end and the joint is ready for assembly.

Halving Joint

In the halving joint, half the thickness of each member is cut away, so that when the two parts are joined together, the original thickness of the wood is restored. See **figure 70**.

The first job, as usual, is to ensure that all the timber is cut to the correct length and cross section. Measure the distance from the end of each member where the joint should go, mark with a pencil and square round, using a try square. Mark a

Techniques Section

second line parallel to the first, exactly the width of the other piece of wood, and square round again. (The easiest way to make sure the width is correct is to offer up one piece of wood to the other). Now set a marking gauge to half the thickness of the parts and scribe between the width lines already marked.

If you are making a cross-halving, the waste will be cut from the face side on one member and the back side of the other member, so that the face sides come together on the finished joint. Choose which is which and shade the area to be cut away with a pencil. If you are making the halvings for the bunk bed in Chapter 3, make sure both face sides are directed outwards. Finally go over the lines which cross the grain with a knife, working in the shaded waste areas only. A marked out joint is shown in **figure 71**.

To cut the joint, place each piece in turn on a bench hook and saw on the waste side of the knifed lines down to the scribed line of the gauge. Make a number of parallel additional cuts in the waste, to make chiselling easier at the next stage.

Pare away the waste wood with a wide chisel, working at an angle from each edge in turn towards the centre. This will avoid opposite edges splitting out. Gradually lower the angle of the chisel in the final stages, until it cuts a flat plane between the gauge lines on opposite sides.

The joint is now ready for assembly. Only glue is needed to hold it together. Great care should be taken with the halvings for the bunk beds at this stage, as they may snap across the short grain. The text of Chapter 3 suggests ways of preventing this by using short lengths of dowel let into the timber.

Dowel Joint

The dowel joint is essentially a right-angled butt joint which has been strengthened by (usually) three dowels glued into holes in the opposing joint faces. See **figure 72**. It is frequently used in the projects in this book, for example the elm dining set, Chapter 5.

Dowels are small cylindrical pegs of wood. They can be bought ready cut in 6, 8 and 10mm diameters. The 6mm dowels are about 30mm in length and the 8 and 10mm are about 40mm. This varies between one maker and another. Ready-made dowels have chamferred ends and flutes for glue along their length. They fit holes drilled with 6, 8 and 10mm dowel bits. See Drills and Drilling page 123.

Dowels can be made more cheaply from uncut lengths of hardwood dowel rod but they are only effective if the dowel rod you buy fits the dowel bit exactly. It is therefore advisable to drill a sample hole with the bit and to try this on the rod before you buy it.

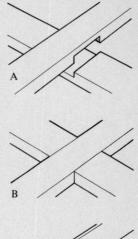

Halving joints in different sections of timber. A, B a simple cross-halving; C halving joint across the width, as in beds, Chapter 3.

figure 70

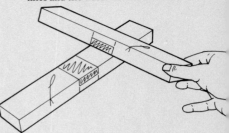

A halving joint ready for cutting. It has been marked out with knife cut and gauge lines and the waste has been shaded

figure 71

figure 72

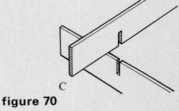

gap left for glue

side rail

dowel

upright

figure 73

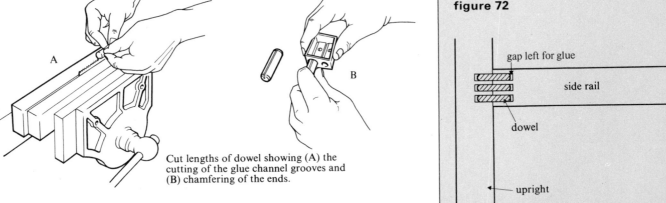

Cut lengths of dowel showing (A) the cutting of the glue channel grooves and (B) chamfering of the ends.

To make your own dowels, cut the well-fitting dowel rod into the lengths you require. Then with a tenon saw held upside down in a vice, run each dowel lengthwise over the saw teeth to form two or more shallow grooves. See **figure 73**A. These are glue channels and allow excess glue to flow out of the hole as the dowel is driven in. If the groove is not there, there can be sufficient pressure to split the joint or to force the glue out through the side of the timber.

Next, chamfer each end of the dowel pieces. This can be done in a number of ways but the quickest is to do it with a pencil sharpener, **figure 73**B. The reason for chamfering is to allow the dowels easy entry into the holes. Minor misalignments are then taken up without too much trouble.

Although in terms of diameter there is not a great deal of difference between the 6 and 8mm dowels, the 8mm has almost twice the amount of timber, and therefore strength, in it. By comparison the strength difference between 8mm and 10mm dowels is 50%. You will see that the right choice of dowel size is as important as is the number you use.

Use dowels in combinations of two for narrow rails and three or more for wide rails in frame making. In jointing cabinet sides, use three on narrow units and up to six on those of 600mm width.

No dowel is stronger than the wood surrounding it. Too large a dowel will leave insufficient wood to support it, so that a compromise has to be reached. A rough rule of thumb is to use dowels of not less than one third and not more than one half the thickness of the wood they are being fixed into. If two thicknesses are being joined, calculate on the smallest.

Marking out for Dowel Joints and Drilling

As with all joints, it is essential that all the component parts are planed square and to their final size before setting out begins. All parts should be marked with face side and edge and should be identified by name or number, so that you know which piece is being jointed to which. All ends of members which butt on to others must be to length and trued up and square before marking out begins.

In all cases a dowel joint creates either an L or T shape when complete. In these instructions the piece of timber which butts up to the other is referred to as the side rail, and the one which passes over the end of the side rail is referred to as the upright as in **figure 72**, but this is merely a convention to aid clarity. There are three methods of marking out and drilling a dowel joint. They are given below:

Method 1. Mark the top and bottom position of the side rail on to the mating edge of the upright with a pencil line.

Set a marking gauge to half the thickness of the side rail and scribe a line (from the face side) down the length of its end grain. Use the same gauge setting to mark a matching line (again from the face side) on to the mating edge of the upright between the pencilled lines.

Place the two pieces of timber in a vice, with the face sides in contact and with the end of the side rail lined up with the pencil lines on the edge of the upright.

Square a line across both pieces to mark the centre point of the dowel holes as in **figure 74**. Space them evenly and make sure that when drilled, the top and bottom dowels will not be too near the edges of the side rail.

If you are confident that you can drill holes of the required depth centred on those marks and square in both directions to the face, do so, but it is better, if possible, to use a drill stand, at least for the upright. The holes should be drilled with a dowel bit to a depth equal to half the length of the dowel plus 1mm for clearance. Insert the dowels dry, to try the fit of the joint; if the joint lines up perfectly, remove the dowels, glue, re-assemble and cramp together until dry.

Method 2 makes use of *centre points*, which are little studs with a point at one end, available from most tool shops. The stud end fits into a dowel hole and the point faces outwards.

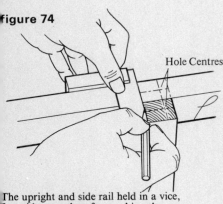

Figure 74

Hole Centres

The upright and side rail held in a vice, face sides together, for marking the centre points for the dowels.

Techniques Section

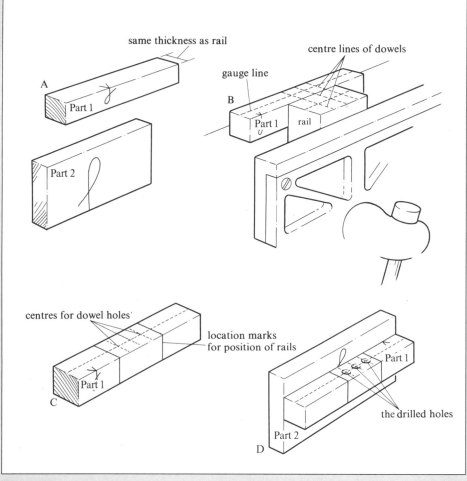

figure 75

Mark out the end grain of the side rail only and drill two or three holes in it (depending on the width of the rail) using a 6mm dowel bit. These holes need only be roughly positioned. No marking out is necessary. Insert a centre point into each hole.

Place the upright and the side rail on a flat surface, face side down. Line up the side rail with the pencilled position for it on the upright and push the two together. The sharp ends of the centre points will mark the centres for the dowel holes in the upright.

Method 3 makes use of a simple wooden dowelling jig. This is especially useful when a number of identical parts have to be drilled in the same way. Very accurate steel dowelling jigs are available from tool shops, but they need an experienced user and are outside the scope of this book.

Start by marking the position of the side rail on the upright, as in method 1. Set a marking gauge to half the thickness of the side rail and scribe a line across its end grain.

Now set about making the jig. Plane up two pieces of hardwood as in **figure 75**A. Part 1 is the same width as the thickness of the side rail and is 21 mm thick × 150 mm long. Part 2 is 150 × 70 × 21 mm. Take the gauge already set for the side rail and mark a line along the face edge of Part 1.

Place the side rail end upwards in a vice with Part 1 next to it, as in **figure 75**B, their face sides in contact. Mark the centre points for the dowels on the end of the side rail and on the face edge of Part 1 as in method 1. Also mark on Part 1 the positions of the edges of the side rails. Remove pieces from the vice.

The marks showing the positions of the edges of the side rail on Part 1 should now be squared all round it with a try square. See **figure 75**C. Drill holes of the appropriate diameter through the centres on Part 1, using a drill stand to be sure the holes are vertical.

Screw Part 1 to Part 2, face sides together, as shown in **figure 75**D to form a T-shape. The jig is now ready for use.

Place all the uprights together side by side so that the edges which are to receive the side rails are uppermost. Mark lines across them all where the side rail must be placed.

To use the jig, grip it and either type of rail in a vice with the T piece against the face side and top lines matching as in **figure 21** on page 124. Drill the holes through the jig into the rails to the required depth. The pre-drilled holes of the jig will help to keep them square.

Mortice and Tenon Joint

A mortice and tenon joint consists of a slot, or mortice, in the upright and a tongue, or tenon, in the side rail which fits into the mortice. See **figure 76**.

As a rule, the mortice and tenon each occupy about one third of the thickness of the wood in which they are cut. For example, if a table rail and leg each of 28mm thickness are to be joined, the width of the mortice will be about 9mm. The length of a tenon must depend upon the timber it is going into and whether it is going right through or only part way. There is no rule about the length of tenons, but wherever possible make the length not less than three times their thickness.

Before marking and cutting out, have all the timber planed to width and thickness and marked with a face side and face edge. Set out the pieces in the order in which they are to be jointed. Mark the shoulder line of the tenon with a knife cut across the grain. Mark right around the wood with a try square, taking care to keep the stock of the square on either the face side or face edge when doing so.

Mark the position of the tenon rail on the mortice piece. Set the spurs of the mortice gauge to the width of the chisel you intend using to chop out the mortice. If you have a mortice chisel, use that in preference to any other. Set the gauge fence away from the nearest spur by the amount you wish to have the mortice set in from the face side of the timber. (On the 28mm example with a 9mm mortice, the fence would be set in 9mm also).

Tighten the gauge so that the setting will not slip and scribe the gauge lines for the mortice on the upright and right around the end and sides of the tenon. To avoid any confusion when cutting, shade with a pencil the areas to be cut away. See **figure 77**.

Use a tenon saw to cut away the waste at either side of the tenon. Each cut is approached from three angles as in **figure 78**. This helps to ensure a true cut, following the gauge lines. Make the first cut down one side and across half the end grain, the second at the same angle from the other side, and the third from the end down the length of the tenon until the shoulder line is reached. Each of these cuts should be made so that the thickness of it brushes the centre of the gauge line on the tenon side with the rest occurring in the area of waste.

The final stage is to cut the shoulder and remove the pieces of waste. Take care and keep the tenon saw exactly in line with the shoulder mark and square to the line at the edges. The job is best done on a bench hook. See **figure 59**, page 143.

The mortice is most accurately cut out by drilling a series of holes, close in diameter to the width of the slot, on a drill stand. This will ensure squareness, which is all-important, and leaves less to be chopped out with a chisel. If you do not have a drill stand, get someone to sight the drill for square as it enters the wood for each cut. It may help to position a try-square next to the drill with its blade pointing upwards. Drill as many holes as you can side by side along the length of the mortice. Avoid drilling right up to the end lines, leaving a little for the chisel to take out and square off. See **figure 79**. Chop the remaining waste out with a chisel. Be careful not to cut beyond the gauge lines.

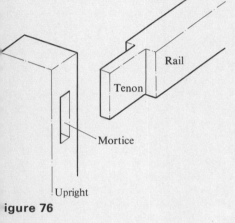

igure 76

igure 77

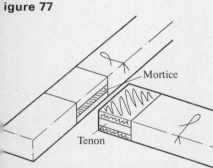

A mortice and tenon joint marked out. The parts to be cut away have been shaded with a pencil as a reminder.

igure 79

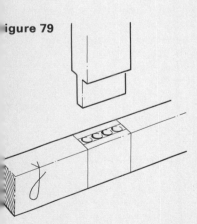

Drill the bulk of the waste out between the gauge lines on the mortice. This makes chiselling far easier.

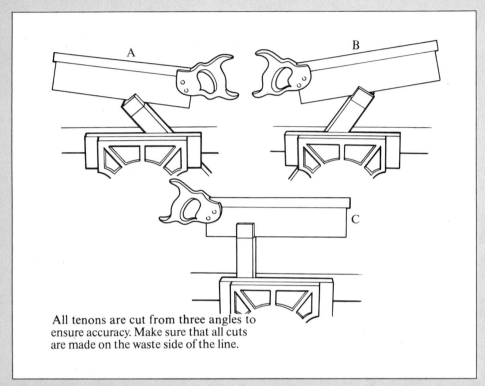

All tenons are cut from three angles to ensure accuracy. Make sure that all cuts are made on the waste side of the line.

figure 78

With all the waste removed to the correct depth, fit the tenon into the mortice. Some easing may have to be done. As you do it, test the assembled joint to ensure that it is flat when it is together.

The traditional way of cutting a mortice is to chop the whole thing out with a chisel. Start chopping out at the centre and work backwards towards the end lines, checking to see that you are cutting square to the edge at all times. Make a series of cuts in the depth, and do not attempt to cut out the waste in one pass. Leave about 2mm waste at each end of the mortice until the job is nearly complete, then chop the ends out square with the chisel.

Cutting Grooves and Rebates

A rebate is a right-angled ledge cut in the side of a piece of wood, see **figure 79**. It is rather like a groove with only one wall and it is not surprising that grooves and rebates are cut with the same tool—the *plough plane* shown in **figure 80**. The plough is one of a family of specialised planes such as the *rebate plane* and the *combination plane*. The rebate plane will not cut grooves and the combination plane is expensive and cuts several mouldings that only experts are likely to need, so the plough is the best choice for beginners.

The plough plane consists of a steel body holding a narrow blade. Two rods projecting from the body hold the *side fence*. This device controls how far in from the edge of the timber the groove will be made. There is also a *depth fence*, which as its name implies, controls the depth of the groove or rebate.

There is a risk that the side fence will mark the side of the timber during planing, so fit it with a small rectangular hardwood batten. You will find two screw holes in the side fence for just this purpose. The batten should extend approximately 25mm beyond the side fence at each end.

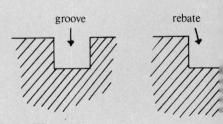

figure 79

figure 81

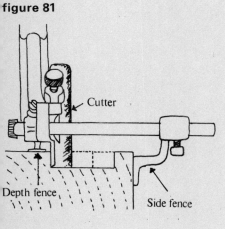

Cutter

Depth fence   Side fence

figure 80

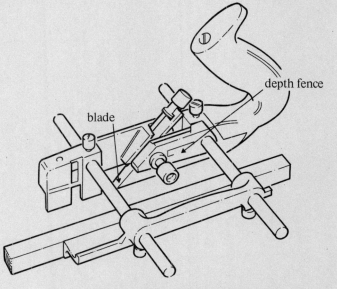

blade   depth fence

The plough plane. Note that the side fence has been fitted with a protective hardwood batten.

Using the Plough Plane

The plough plane is supplied with a number of blades of different widths from 3·5mm up to 12mm. Some include Imperial width cutters in addition. All are finely ground ready for sharpening on an oil stone, see page 136.

The blade should be adjusted to give a fine cut and should just project below the level of the body casting. If grooves of a width greater than the largest blade supplied are required, this can be achieved by making two or more cuts side by side. The one nearest the edge of the work has to be cut first.

It is most important that the work should be held firmly so that it will not move during the cutting operation. Timber of small cross section, below say 50mm square, presents a particular problem in that it is too small to be gripped in a vice and still to allow the side fence of the plough plane to pass freely. One solution to this problem is given in **figure 5** page 98 (wall mounted cabinets) and this simple jig can be adapted to take a range of sections.

An alternative method of holding the work is shown in **figure 82**. The bar of a sash cramp and a piece of timber about 18mm thick (labelled A in **figure 82**) are held in the jaws of a vice, the timber lying behind the cramp bar. The section to be

figure 82

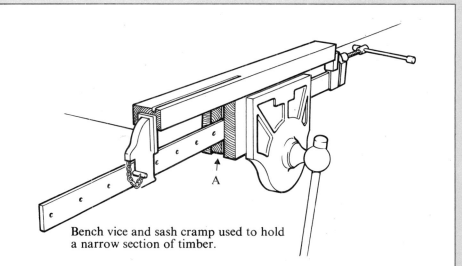

Bench vice and sash cramp used to hold a narrow section of timber.

Techniques Section

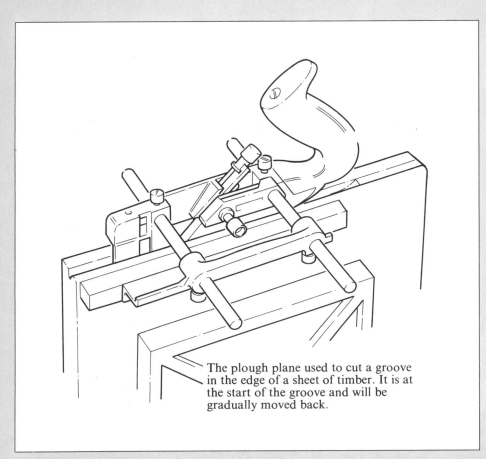

The plough plane used to cut a groove in the edge of a sheet of timber. It is at the start of the groove and will be gradually moved back.

figure 83

grooved lies on top of a piece A and is held steady at its ends by the jaws of the sash cramp, which are set down so that they do not get in the way of the groove.

If a grooved solid section has to be added to a panel of blockboard, as in the case for the sliding door track on the wall-mounted cabinets in Chapter 10, then glue the section to the panel first and then cut the grooves. This simplifies holding, since a large panel is more easily held to the bench during the grooving operation.

A plough plane will not cut across the grain, so when setting out your timber, make sure the grooves or rebates run along the grain. Unlike a smoothing plane, the plough should not be used in long strokes from end to end of the work. It must be used in a series of short movements of about 100–150mm in length. Start cutting the groove at the end farthest from you and with a series of cuts work the groove down to its full depth, at which point the depth stop will be riding on the top face of the work as in **figure 83**. Then gradually retreat, maintaining the short stroke action and not moving farther back until the full depth of the groove is obtained. Keep the plough plane level across its width at all times and do not use dull blades or they will tear the work.

The plough plane cannot be used by itself to cut grooves in the end grain of timber, as it will split out the grain at the corners. To avoid this, it is necessary to cut away the far end to full depth by hand, using a tenon saw and chisel. Mark the position and depth of the groove to be cut. Then saw down the waste side of the groove sides and remove the waste with a chisel. The resulting cut should be wedge-shaped, removing the groove profile to full depth for about 10mm.

Grooves may either run through from one end of a piece of timber to the other, or they may stop within the substance of the timber. Stopped grooves can be cut with a plough plane, but this involves a considerable amount of hard work with a chisel. Cut the groove in the normal way, stopping the cut at the required place. The resulting wedge left by the necessary angle of the plane's cut must be chopped

figure 84

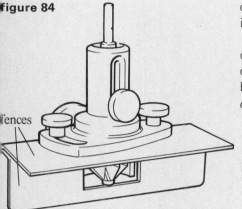

The shaper craft tool.
A variety of cutters can be fitted to it for
different jobs. The cutter shown is for
chamfering edges.

fences

out by hand with a broad chisel cut along each side of the groove. A narrow chisel is used to chop out the end and to pare the wedge out to the depth of the groove.

The plough plane will only cut grooves in solid timber and in chipboard. It will cut the core material of blockboard, but not its face veneer. It cannot be used to cut across the grain of solid timber, nor will it cut melamine coated nor veneered board. For all these purposes, you need a power drill attachment called a *shaper craft tool*. See **figure 84**.

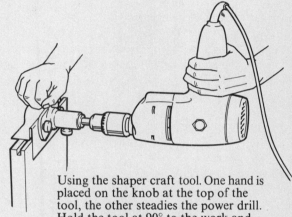

Using the shaper craft tool. One hand is
placed on the knob at the top of the
tool, the other steadies the power drill.
Hold the tool at 90° to the work and
keep the fences pressed into the timber.

figure 85

Using a Shaper Craft Tool

This attachment to an electric drill is cheaper than the plough plane but its cutters have a limited life and cannot be re-sharpened. New ones have to be purchased from a tool shop.

The cutters produce a reasonably fine cut, which can be cleaned up with abrasive paper. They will cut with or across the grain and will penetrate through plywood and blockboard without tearing. The tool does need to be held firmly and is inclined to wander unless particular care is taken to guide it and the attached portable electric drill together. A range of standard cutters is manufactured, some of them shaped to give moulded profiles.

Before fitting the attachment to the drill, or when changing settings or cutters, always disconnect the drill from the power supply. Never leave the trigger switch lock on when the drill is not in use.

Mount the attachment into the chuck of the drill and tighten it well. Ensure that the cutter-retaining bolt is tight. Adjust the depth of cut and its distance in from the edge of the material with the knurled knobs set in the moulded body of the attachment. Test the setting on a spare piece of timber before you begin on the actual workpiece. The cutting action is a single movement forward from start to finish. See **figure 85**. Feed the cutter forward slowly. On end grain or cross gain cuts, slow the rate of cut right down in the final stages to prevent splitting. If the cutter should begin to smoke or jump, you are feeding it too fast, or the cutter is blunt and should be replaced. Deep, wide cuts often require cutting in two stages. Always use high drill speeds.

To start cutting, place the attachment in position but not in contact with the timber. Switch the drill on and gradually lower or advance it on to the work. On completion of a stopped end cut, switch the drill off and allow the cutter to stop before removing it. For straight through cuts, allow the cutter to clear the work completely before switching off.

Techniques Section

Stopped grooves are particularly easy with this attachment. The cutter can be 'dropped' into the work or lifted from it as required. Because the cutters are circular, they will leave a radiused end, which has to be cut away with a chisel.

When cutting large numbers of stopped grooves, all of the same length, as in the drawer sides for the wardrobe range in Chapter 4, the jig shown in **figure 86** can be a time-saver. It consists of a chipboard base which is screwed to a bench cramp casting. This holds the electric drill. The rotary cutter, used in the shaper craft tool above, is clamped directly into the chuck. The other layers of chipboard form a table, whose height is adjustable so that just enough of the rotary cutter projects above it to cut the correct depth groove. The wooden fence is positioned so that the groove is at the correct place in the wood.

The pieces to be grooved are laid on the table with the groove surface downwards and are slid across the cutter. A line is marked on the table and when the wood reaches this point, it is lifted off the cutter, so that the groove stops at the correct point. Never hold the back end of the wood being grooved, without being fully aware of the position of the cutter.

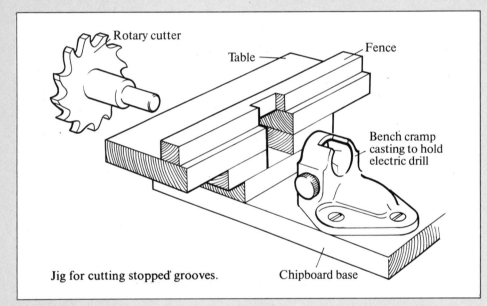

Rotary cutter

Table

Fence

Bench cramp casting to hold electric drill

Jig for cutting 'stopped' grooves.

Chipboard base

figure 86

Finishing Techniques

It is an unfortunate fact of life in woodworking that all the stains, polishes and varnishes which are used to finish a piece of furniture will show up with merciless clarity every little dent, scratch and irregularity in the surface. The difference between an indifferent and a professional looking piece of work is nearly always a function of how long you have spent cleaning up the surface with progressively finer grades of abrasive paper.

Types of Abrasive Paper

The most readily available is glass paper. It has a sandy colour, which probably accounts for it being commonly and incorrectly known as sandpaper. Like all papers, it is made in a wide range of grit sizes from very coarse to extra fine.

Garnet paper is often preferred by furniture makers because it cuts longer and faster than glass paper. The range of grit sizes is large. This particular paper is manufactured in sheets and rolls. The narrow ones 115mm wide and 25m long, are made to fit orbital sanding machines of the type shown in **figure 87**.

Coarseness of cut is a factor of grit size: a 60 grit is as coarse as you are likely to need. Then there are 80, 100, 120 and 150 which is reasonably fine. Open coat papers with identical grit sizes are available and preferred by many users. This expression means that the grains of grit are wider spread and less likely to clog than in the standard material. Other types of abrasive paper include those with grits of flint and aluminium oxide. Some of these materials are mounted on cloth rather than on paper. At the very fine end are the 300 and 400 grits. These are commonly known as flour papers and are used for superfine finishing, including rubbing down between coats of polish and cellulose paints.

Wet-or-dry paper is one which, as the name implies, can be used with or without water—the paper backing is waterproof. This material is not suited to rubbing down wood, but it is ideal—especially in a wet state—for rubbing down painted surfaces between coats or prior to re-painting. Wet-or-dry papers cut very rapidly indeed as the water floods out the cut-away paint particles.

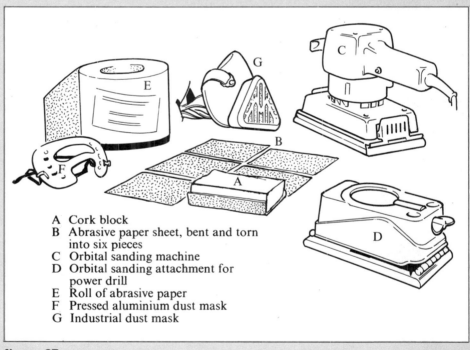

A Cork block
B Abrasive paper sheet, bent and torn into six pieces
C Orbital sanding machine
D Orbital sanding attachment for power drill
E Roll of abrasive paper
F Pressed aluminium dust mask
G Industrial dust mask

figure 87

Using Abrasive Papers

The paper can either be used by hand on a sanding block or on an orbital sander. The latter may be a machine in its own right or an attachment to a power drill, see **figure 87**.

The number of tons of middle grade (M2) glass paper sold in this country every year is a sad reflection on DIY enthusiasts. The author of this piece was once heard to suggest, perhaps cryptically, that he wouldn't use M2 to rub down his garden path! If the tools you have used are sharp, then fine grade (F2) glass paper or 100 grit garnet paper is as coarse as you will need. To use harsher papers would mean roughening up the already smoother surface left by a hand plane.

Techniques Section

There are a number of rules about the use of abrasive paper which, if followed, will make it last longer and will give superior results.

1 For hand use, fold, then tear, sheets of abrasive paper over the sharp edge of a board or bench. One sheet should be divided into six pieces, which will fit a cork sanding block economically.

2 Don't use folded sheets of abrasive paper. It just wastes it.

3 Use abrasive papers in conjunction with a cork sanding block. This helps to maintain surface flatness and squareness at edges—essential details in giving anything a professional look.

4 Always follow the direction of the grain. Cutting across it will scratch so deeply that hours of work will be required to remove the marks.

5 Turn the paper in use from time to time to prolong its life.

6 Keep all abrasive papers dry. If they are damp when used they will shed their grit in seconds.

7 When sanding a moulding or curved surface, make a block to support the paper as near as possible to its profile. Abrasive paper wrapped around a dowel or a piece of broom handle is often very useful.

8 Do not use a rotary or disc type sanding machine on anything which is likely to be stained or polished. The fast rotary action is too harsh and cannot be controlled sufficiently to avoid scouring. The use of these machines near edges of veneers often results in their cutting right through them without warning.

9 If you wish to machine sand, use a belt or preferably an orbital machine or attachment. Use these in the direction of the grain, in conjunction with an open coat grit.

10 Always complete sanding jobs in strong light so that you can see any areas which have been missed.

11 Brush away sanding dust as you work and clean the work off completely before staining and polishing.

12 For all major sanding jobs, wear a dust mask. Two types are illustrated in **figure 87**. Of the dust masks, the pressed aluminium is about one quarter the price of the industrial model. It is readily available through large chemists or most DIY centres. It comes in a pack complete with a few replaceable cotton filters. The industrial version is sold with an individual pack of 100 filters.

13 If you are using machine planed timber it will probably have a rippled surface which is caused by the fast feed of the machine against the rotating cutters. Wherever possible, use a finely set smoothing plane to flatten the surface. This is most easily done before assembly. Getting rid of the ripples with abrasive paper is a long hard slog which is often unsuccessful.

Staining

Staining means altering the colour of the wood by applying a darkening or colouring liquid which soaks into the grain. The liquid evaporates leaving the colour deposited permanently within the top surface of the wood.

Most stains are now spirit based and sold mixed and ready for use. They are best applied liberally with a rag or fine brush. Being based in spirit, the colour takes rapidly, and over-brushing an area which has already been stained can lead to further local darkening if it has been applied too thinly in the first instance. It is essential that staining is done carefully, systematically and fast in order to achieve even results.

In the preparation stage prior to staining, the surface will have been rubbed down to a fine finish with various grades of abrasive paper. Particular attention is needed to make sure that all traces of excess glue have been removed. If any is left on the surface the stain is unlikely to take over it.

The method to adopt for staining is to do one complete surface at a time without stopping. Do not start in the middle of an area and work towards one end and then the other. The time lag in returning to the centre will mean that the stain has already penetrated there and starting off again may cause an uneven line.

Once you have stained something you are committed. It is therefore advisable to stain and varnish or polish some sample pieces, so that you know what the end result is likely to be. To avoid waiting about for sample pieces to dry, do your sampling in an odd moment while you are making the piece of furniture. Be systematic about it and make notes of the stain, whether applied with brush or rag, how it was rubbed down before polishing and so on. Then when the time comes to begin on the actual piece of furniture, you will have a complete record of the process you have already proved. Remember when sampling that different woods take the same stain differently. Sample all the woods you have used, to ensure compatibility.

Stain is terrible stuff to get off clothing, hands and the floor, so prepare beforehand. If you have to use it indoors, warm, dry conditions with plenty of ventilation are essential. Cover the floor with polythene sheet and newspaper, wear old clothes and rubber gloves and have plenty of spare rags about for rapid mopping-up in case of accidents. Remember that most stains and varnishes are highly inflammable, so do not smoke nor have a naked flame in the room. Wherever possible, stand whatever you are to stain off the floor and at a convenient height, so that you can reach and see all the surfaces. There is no substitute for good, strong daylight, so work near a window.

Work methodically and stain complete surfaces at a time, starting at one end and finishing at the other. Do not use so much stain that the excess runs over the edges on to other surfaces. This can easily lead to stripes which are very difficult to remove.

When all the surfaces have been stained, allow time for the stain to dry. Some rising of the grain may have taken place. If this is so, rub the surface with flour paper in the direction of the grain until the surplus is removed. A further very light application of the stain may be necessary to re-colour the spot where pips have been rubbed off. A second application of stain may be required if the job ends up lighter than intended. If this is the case, use the same care as for the first coat. Wipe off excess stain when surfaces are completed and after they have absorbed all that they will take in.

Varnishes

There are two types commonly available, polyurethane and epoxy. The former is ready for use and is sold in a range of colour tints, clear matt and clear gloss. Epoxy finishes are mixed from two components just before use. In both cases pay particular attention to the maker's instructions. Either type is applied with a brush.

The initial coat of either finish acts as a seal. When it has dried, it will be necessary to rub it over to remove pips and any runs which may have occurred. Flour paper or fine wire wool will do this quickly.

If you are using one of the coloured polyurethanes, use a first coat of clear polyurethane as the seal. This will give the tinted coats an even surface to build upon and will avoid uneven depth of colour, where some parts of the timber have been more absorbent than others.

Epoxy finishes comprise two chemicals which have to be mixed thoroughly together before use. The proportions of one part to the other must be followed carefully. Once mixed, the resin and catalyst combined have a limited pot life. This means that they will harden in a short time and go solid in the pot if not used. Mix no more than you require for immediate use.

In both cases, speed of drying is in direct proportion to the temperature in the room and to the degree of ventilation. The chemicals react with one another and need plenty of air changes to allow drying to take place quickly. Do not apply a further coat before the previous one is hard. Rub down slightly between each coat. Following the final coat of epoxy varnishes, it is advisable to rub the surface over with burnishing cream. This is available from the DIY shop either separately or in the same pack as the epoxy lacquer.

Techniques Section

Teak Oil

This oil is applied liberally with a pad of rag so that it 'floods' the surface. After a few minutes all excess is wiped off and the surface is allowed to dry. Rub over the surface with fine wire wool to remove pips between coats. Four or five coats will be required to give a deep lustre. 'Danish' oil is a variety of teak oil which contains particles of melamine. It gives a rather more matt finish than teak oil.

Cellulose

Cellulose paint is sold in a vast range of colours and tints in all garages and motor accessory shops. It is also stocked in most departmental and DIY stores. Pure cellulose is available in a range of can sizes, both clear and in a limited range of colours. The aerosol range is wide and offers the easiest method of handling and application, but it is expensive. You will also need to buy cellulose thinners, which is used to remove the substance from your hands and to clean brushes and spray guns.

Use aerosols 300 to 400mm from the surface, keeping the fan of paint spray moving forward all the time to prevent pools or runs. Several thin coats are better than one or two heavy ones. Rub over the surface with flour paper or wet and dry between coats to keep it free of pips. Allow each coat to harden before applying the next.

Always use cellulose in a very well ventilated area which is warm and dust-free. Remember that it is highly inflammable.

To achieve a really satisfactory finish, cellulose does need to be sprayed. Brush application is too slow because of the rate at which this material begins to set. There are several makes of spray gun which are sold for the DIY user. Few of the types which atomise the paint are effective. To achieve a professional finish, air driven guns with pressures in excess of 70 lbs per square inch are required.

When spraying cellulose, a mix of paint and thinners is necessary. The proportion can be as high as 50% of each. This has to be established with test runs. If you are spraying only part of a surface, mask the remaining area with paper and masking tape to protect it. The spray carries for a surprising distance.

Introduction to Upholstery

The complexities of traditional upholstery techniques have almost exclusively given way to the far simpler foam systems. Only a few remaining workshops in the country now deal with the hair and fibre stuffings which were extensively used until well into the '60s.

Foam upholstery is far cleaner to handle and is much easier to cope with. With care, a few hand tools, and somebody who is handy with a sewing machine, many upholstery jobs can be successfully undertaken at home. There are a few basic principles which it is as well to understand before you start.

Foam Upholstery

Foam can be bought in a wide range of firmnesses, in sheet or chip. Thicknesses vary from as little as 5mm up to 100mm or more. Those of 25mm, 35mm, 50mm, 75mm and 100mm are more or less standard. Sheet lengths and widths vary a little from supplier to supplier but are often about 2m and 1·25m.

Like most materials, it is advisable to buy foam from a specialist shop or department. They will be able to advise you on the quality and hardness required for the job you are planning.

Foam is deceptive in its feel. Testing it by pressing it with your hand is very unreliable unless you are handling it daily. If you want foam of a given thickness for a seat, sit on some of it before you buy it. What may feel fine at 100m thick is usually far too soft at say 25mm.

The firmest upholstery foams are for dining or office chair seating, where they are thin and the base beneath is hard. As thickness of seat increases, so the firmness reduces. Back and arm foams are generally softer, but even these have to be sufficiently firm to prevent the sitter feeling frame members through it.

Chip or crumb foam is usually sold in ready made-up bags. The hardness of this also varies from one supplier to another.

Cutting Foam

All sheet material can be cut with a saw-tooth edge bread knife. The blade works better if it is wet, but the cut will not always be true. Cuts made by suppliers are usually done on either a band knife machine or a special portable foamsaw which resembles an extra long double-bladed jig saw. The two blades work reciprocally in opposite directions, and for home upholstery an electric carving knife does a similar job.

Before you get your supplier to cut the foam to size for you, get some impression of the accuracy of his cutting. If his stock looks as if it has been hacked about, you had better order oversize and true it up yourself. Remember squareness is all important when it comes to the fit of cushions.

Mark foam with a felt-tipped pen against a template of the shape you require, or against a straightedge. Wherever possible, use a straightedge to cut against. Better still, if you can line up a straight-edged board beneath the foam as well, you will be sure of cutting straight in length and square in thickness at the same time. See **figure 88**.

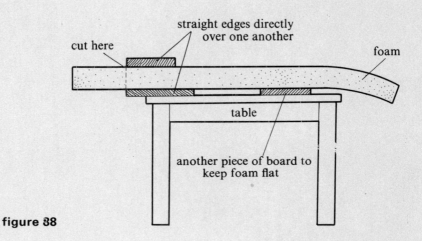

figure 88

Well-shaped cushions and covers depend upon well-cut interior foam. The final cover will follow whatever is inside it, so take extra care when marking out and cutting.

If covers are limp, they look dreadful and are constantly creased. A good-looking cover is always under slight tension and any creases, which are pressed in when the covers are sat on, are pulled out when the chair is empty. This tension is built in by making the foam slightly larger than the cushion cover. If you measure a chair and find that the distance between the arms is say 550mm, cut the cover to fit, but make the foam interior about 560mm. Very firm foams will need less of a compression allowance than soft ones.

Remember that the compression of foam in covers also applies to thicknesses. Instead of buying thicker foam, the practice is usually to make the cushion borders slightly smaller to compensate.

Laminating and Bonding Foams

Laminated foam is used in the upholstered suite on page 73 to form shaped arms and back. This technique can also be used to build foam up in thickness. When laminating or bonding, remember that glue lines are eventually harder than surrounding foam. They can be seen through thinner covers and felt if they occur

Techniques Section

in the top layers of foam. If for one reason or another, a joint is to come to the surface, stop gluing about 5mm in from the outside edge. This unglued area will help to disguise the hard edge of the glue line.

Apart from giving a permanent shape to a cushion, laminating is also used to vary the hardnesses of foam within overall thicknesses. On many seat and arms quite hard foams are used as base materials and softer ones are bonded on as a top layer to give a more resilient feel to the upholstery when it is complete. One rule applies in laminating whatever the shape, and that is to make all the parts oversize initially. Trim them after they are bonded. See adhesives page 131.

Cutting and Sewing Covers

In **figure 89**, the sketch of a chair shows the direction which a patterned cover should take when it is completed. This can be ignored when plain fabrics are used, provided that they do not shade, like velvet or velour.
Figure 89 also includes the names of the parts which make up the cover, with their abbreviated letters. It is usual to mark these on the reverse side with tailor's chalk so that, once cut, you know which piece is which and can join them in the required order. You may also add 'right' or 'left' (R or L) if you need to identify arms or borders.

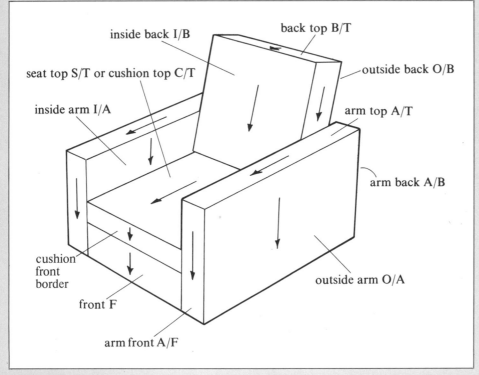

figure 89

If you intend piping the joins, cut the material for the piping on the cross, as in dressmaking. It won't fray as much as material which is cut in line with the weave.

When marking out, do so on the largest flat surface which you can find. The floor is often best. Keep the fabric as flat as possible, with the selvedges pinned out if necessary, to prevent the material from moving as you measure and mark.

For economy, and as an eventual guide to how much fabric you will require, plan the sizes and shapes you will need, to scale, on a piece of paper. Remember to make seam allowances at each edge of about 15mm and keep that as a constant. If you make some at 10mm and others at something else, when it comes to pinning together, the edges won't match. A constant allowance helps to make that part of the job very much simpler. Patterns for covers are given in our upholstery projects.

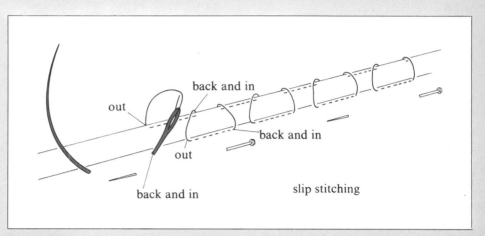

figure 90

When sewing, use heavier threads than you would in dressmaking. You will also need a half-round needle for *slip-stitching*, which is used in upholstery to sew together those parts of a cover which cannot be machined prior to fitting. In our projects, it is used to close cushion covers after the foam has been inserted.

To close a cushion cover, start by knotting one end of the thread, and secure that to the inside of the fabric at one end of the opening. Now close the opening by folding both edges inwards by the correct amount of turning and pin the two sides together. In the television programmes, Peter Cornish sewed up his cushion cover without pinning it, but pins are a wise precaution for the beginner. The pins should run parallel to the seam, as shown in **figure 90**.

Place the needle between the folded edges of the fabric and bring it through the fabric and out on one side. Pass the needle over the seam and stick it into the fabric at a point *behind* where it has just come out, so that the stitch slants diagonally backwards—see **figure 90**. Take in about 5mm and bring the needle out again on the same side at the centre of the fold. Pull the thread after each stitch and the seam will close tightly. Again pass the needle over the seam and stick in into the fabric behind the point of exit on the other side. Continue this stitching of alternate sides along the entire length of the seam. When the end is reached, tie off the thread and tuck the end back into the seam.

When the covers are sewn, press them well before fitting them and pay particular attention to hems and turnings. As you slip the covers on you will find that the hems become rather twisted about by the foam. Straighten these out to lie in one direction only, and that will improve the look of all seams.

OUR RENOVATION PROJECT

David Day and Albert Jackson

In six of the ten television programmes accompanying this book, we renovated an old oval dining table and six chairs which we bought for about £80. This section describes in detail how we bought and renovated the furniture and, whilst it is primarily of interest to people who watched the TV programmes it should be of help to other readers, since the principles of renovation are much the same whatever the piece of furniture. We also showed how to make a garden table out of an old sewing machine. Instructions for this are at the end of the section.

Buying Old Furniture

Renovating an old piece of furniture may at first seem laborious, but it can be both fun and financially rewarding. You will have the satisfaction of personal achievement plus the knowledge that your piece is probably unique.

The first step is to decide on your needs. For example; do you want a dining table to go with chairs you already have, or do you need storage furniture, perhaps a chest or a cupboard? Is the piece to be used as an everyday functional item like a table, or is it to be more of a decorative piece to enrich your interior? Does it need to compliment the room, say a highly decorative cabinet in a modern setting, or is it to create an original period setting in an older house? Of course, whatever your needs may be, your final choice will be limited by what you can find and the price you can afford, but at least you will have some idea of what you are looking for.

There are several ways to find your ideal piece of old furniture. It is possible you may already have furniture that has been in the family for years and has now been relegated to the attic. Tastes change with the passage of time and it could be that an item, long disliked by the family, takes on a new meaning when looked at with an unprejudiced eye. Perhaps the cheapest way of obtaining old furniture is to buy directly from the original owners. These are usually contacted through small ads in local papers or newsagents. This is, after all, the source of all items that come on the market and you are more likely to find a bargain this way. In some cases jumble sales can provide good hunting, but they do not usually cater for large items of furniture.

For the widest choice, whilst still remaining within reasonable price limits, a visit to an auction room is recommended. There are usually a number of auction rooms in most big cities, holding secondhand furniture sales at weekly or fortnightly intervals. Again, check the local papers for addresses. These auctions can provide anything from a fly-blown old mirror to a full size wardrobe, usually with more than one example of each to choose from. The sales themselves take place in a large room or hall, with the items for sale displayed all round and very often stacked to the ceiling. The customers stand in the narrow passages formed by the furniture or sit in the central area, usually on chairs that are for sale. They are very casual occasions with a certain amount of chatter continuing throughout the sale, and usually a fair amount of banter between the regular dealers.

The sale rooms normally have a viewing on the day before the actual sale, when you can browse at your leisure to see if there is anything of interest. A printed catalogue is a worthwhile investment and costs only a few pence. Each lot is numbered and a brief description is given in the catalogue. It is a good idea to set yourself a price limit before going to the actual sales, and to mark your catalogue with your estimate. Stick to this limit or you can find yourself being swept along by the enthusiasm of others. If you are in doubt about the value of an item that interests you, ask one of the staff what he thinks it will sell for. It is also a good idea to attend an auction beforehand, to get a feel for the value of the items. Make a note of the prices paid for various items so that you can spot a real bargain when it comes to your turn.

The sale is conducted by the auctioneer, who suggests an opening bid. If this is taken up he will ask for further bids until only one offer remains. If the auctioneer's opening price is too high, he will ask for a bid from the floor and work up from there. It is his job to get the best price he can for the goods, but if there is no reserve price and the other customers are not interested in your piece, you may find yourself with a fair bargain and a big smile on your face.

Auctions take place once a week or less, and consequently it can take time to find what you are after. An alternative is to go to an area where a number of antique or secondhand furniture shops are grouped together along one or two streets, or to a large warehouse containing various smaller businesses. Your main advantage is a wide choice with the minimum of leg work. You will, however, pay a little more for the furniture. Most dealers buy from auctions in the first place. Some will sell the furniture without improvement. Others make minor repairs or even full restoration before putting them on sale. The prices are fixed to cover expenses plus a profit, but depending on the item and its condition it is often possible to haggle over the price, particularly if you are buying a number of pieces.

Buying furniture is very much a matter of personal choice, but there are certain points which may be of help. First check for condition. Is it sound and free from serious attack by furniture beetle? Can it be repaired by you with your equipment or does it need specialist skills, which could prove expensive? Do not be put off by surface appearance due to a bad finish, be it varnish or layers of paint. If the piece is sound, nicely proportioned and maybe has interesting mouldings, the effort of stripping will be worthwhile. Make sure it is suitable for your needs. No matter how attractive it may be, if it is too large for your house it is a bad buy. Try not to take on too much work at once. Remember renovation is an economical way of furnishing in style, but it does require a fair amount of effort and time. If you get bored halfway through your money will be wasted.

We set out to make up a dining set for six people. We first of all bought an oval table from an auction. Having inspected it beforehand we decided it was sound and only in need of re-finishing. One of the first things to check on a table is the construction of the top. It is essential to know if it is veneered, because this can affect the method used to strip the surface. Ours was quarter veneered in mahogany on a core of plywood or blockboard. The change in grain pattern made it easy to detect that the top was veneered, but if it had been matched in strips it would have been more difficult. If it is not obvious whether it is veneered, look at the underside to see if it matches the top surface. It may not necessarily be the same colour, as the top could well be stained darker. Another check is to look at the edge of the top. If there is a show lipping all round it is likely to be a veneered top. The veneer may lap the lipping, in which case look at the edge of the top to see if there is side grain running all round. A solid top can normally be identified by the appearance of end grain. Table underframes are almost always of solid timber construction.

The chairs were bought from a shop and were originally used as catering chairs, probably in a hotel restaurant. They were once gold in colour, but had suffered the ravages of time and were in poor decorative condition. Some had damaged split cane seats. Before we bought them a simple test was applied to the frame to establish what wood was camouflaged by the paint. A quick rub with a pad of wire wool revealed white beech, a common hardwood used for turned legs. This was encouraging because it cleans up well and looks attractive when finished with a clear lacquer or coloured stains. We found that sets of 4 to 6 chairs are fairly expensive, but if you can find chairs that were made in bulk or for contract use, such as in restaurants, cafes, or church halls, these are usually cheaper.

Identifying the Finish

When it comes to renovating furniture, what we are largely talking about is re-finishing. Firstly determine what finish has been applied. It could be French polish, usually recognised by its hard gloss finish. Wax polish is very often used on solid wood furniture to bring out the natural grain, but does not have such a high gloss as French polish. Paint, of course, is easily identified.

Identification at this stage could affect the choice of the new finish. For example, if a modern plastic coating is applied over a previously waxed surface which may still contain traces of wax in the pores, it will not dry properly. To test

Our Renovation Project

for French polish, take a clean cotton rag dipped in turpentine and gently rub a small area of the surface to remove any wax polish. Next repeat the operation with a clean rag dipped in methylated spirit. This will quickly soften French polish and will show as a stain on the cloth. Small blemishes can be repaired using French polish kits available from DIY shops. For large areas, it is better to strip the whole surface using a non-caustic paint stripper and to build up the finish again.

To remove wax polish entirely, use wire wool and turpentine substitute and when dry, scrub with water and detergent. Finally rinse with water, to which you have added a little acetic acid (white vinegar), and allow to dry.

Paint and varnishes can be removed with a variety of stripping solutions. Several brands are available and can either be a thin jelly or a creamy paste. They attack the solvents in the finish, causing it to soften, so that it can be removed by scraping or brushing. Choose a non-caustic brand, as these are less harmful to use and less likely to affect the new finish if not completely removed. Full instructions for using chemical strippers are given under the renovation of the dining table.

Renovating the Dining Table

The table top was badly marked and appeared to have been re-finished at some-time with insufficient care. The surface lacquer was brittle and flaking around the damaged areas, due to a poor 'key' between the original and present finish. It obviously needed stripping back to the veneer.

We also decided to remove the decorative plates and cheap plastic trim from the underframe. The holes left by the fixing pins would need to be filled and a new finish applied. We decided to use a hardwearing black plastic coating which would hide the filler and also provide a practical but sophisticated finish. To complete the set, the same finish was to be applied to the chairs.

The first job was to remove the decorative plates and fill the holes with wood stopping, applied with a putty knife. When this had dried, the surface was rubbed down to a flush smooth finish. The under frame was cleaned throughout, using steel wool and turpentine substitute (white spirit) to remove any traces of furniture polish and to provide a 'key' for the plastic coating. It was also washed over with water and detergent and then dried.

There is always one stage in a renovation job when you are caught napping and ours was when we came to strip the top. The lacquer, although cracked and brittle, was iron-hard and several millimetres thick. It took very many applications of chemical stripper and hours of careful scraping before it was clean. In addition, we found that the top was not the warm red mahogany we had thought, but an indifferent sandy-coloured veneer. The colour had been achieved by red stain which also had to be removed. When eventually clean, the surface was rubbed with white spirit and Grade 2 steel wool and wiped with a clean cloth. When it was thoroughly dry, the surface was sanded with fine glass paper wrapped around a block, always working with the grain to remove all traces of the original dark stain and to smooth the surface.

The top was dusted off ready for a new coat of mahogany stain. This was applied with a cloth which immediately brought out the rich figure of the veneer. When dry, the surface was wiped over with a clean cloth to remove any surplus dye. For staining techniques, see page 160.

As the mahogany veneer on the table top was close grained, it did not need filling prior to applying the finish. Had it been an open grained wood, the surface could have been treated with a grain filler to fill the pores.

We used Danish oil, page 162, a new type of finish suitable for all types of wood, which was applied with a cloth 'rubber'. A number of coats were applied in the direction of the grain, each being sanded between applications. Finally the top was finished with a wax polish.

While the top was being finished, three coats of black epoxy plastic coating were applied to the underframe, each being rubbed down with fine steel wool and finally burnished to a high gloss with a burnishing cream.

Renovating the Dining Chairs

The first stage of renovation was to remove the split cane seats. This was simply done using a trimming knife to cut through the strands, and pulling the loose ends through the holes in the frame. After the application of chemical stripper, steel wool was used to clean the frame, which was then rinsed and dried. When thoroughly dry, the chairs were rubbed down with steel wool to a smooth finish, ready for the plastic coating.

The chairs were made from white beech, a light-coloured timber that had been discoloured by the previous finish. Had we required a natural finish or a light coloured stain, this would have presented a problem, but it could have been remedied by the application of a proprietary bleach for wood. In our case, however, we were using an opaque paint finish so bleaching was unnecessary.

Four coats of black epoxy plastic coating were applied, rubbed down between each application, and finally burnished.

The chair frames could have been re-caned, but we decided to fit seat pads. First a pattern was made using thick paper. The shape formed by the rebate, which took the original cane-work, was traced out on to the paper and cut out.

The shape was then transferred to 6mm thick plywood, which was cut to shape using a power jigsaw. A coping saw could have been used as an alternative. The seat shape was chamfered all round to thin down the edge. Two fixing battens cut from 19×19mm (PAR) soft wood were glued to the underside of the plywood for attaching the seat to the frame. The position of each batten was marked on the underside of the plywood shape along the seat side rails.

A 12mm plastic foam pad was cut to shape 6mm larger all round. This was bonded to the top face of the base-board with contact adhesive, **figure 1**.

The covering material was cut roughly to shape, and approximately 38mm larger than the seat board. This was stretched over the board and stapled to the underside, as described for the dining chair seat pad in Chapter 5. The complete pad was fixed with four screws through the battens into the chair frame.

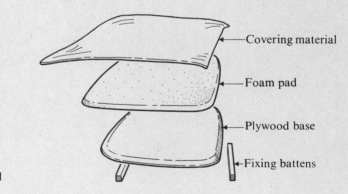

Covering material

Foam pad

Plywood base

Fixing battens

figure 1

Tools and Equipment

Before starting any job it is essential to have the right equipment. Preparation of surfaces is relatively straightforward and does not require expensive materials.

Stripping Knife A stripping knife or wallpaper scraper is used to remove the softened finish. These have flat blades available in various widths and are ideal for large flat areas. Use a shave hook for scraping straight mouldings. See **figure 2**

Paint Brush A paint brush is used to apply the stripper. Use an old brush, preferably 38mm or 50mm wide, to fit the standard jam jar, which makes an ideal container for the solution.

Steel Wool Wire wool is sold in rolls or packs and is made in various grades. It is used like an abrasive pad and is ideal for removing stripper from small crevices,

Our Renovation Project

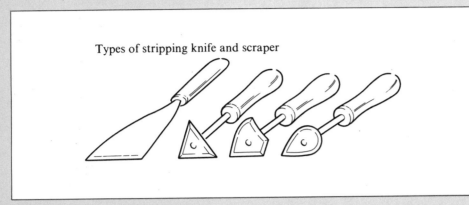

Types of stripping knife and scraper

figure 2

particularly on turned sections where scrapers are unsuited. It can also be used to rub down awkward surfaces prior to finishing or for smoothing lacquered surfaces. Use grade 2 or 3 for cleaning work and the very fine grades 000 or 00 for rubbing down fine finished surfaces.

Cabinet Scraper Use a cabinet scraper to remove fine shavings from hardwoods It is commonly used for smoothing difficult grain. It should not, however, be used in local areas only, as this can cause shallow depressions, which will show when a gloss finish is applied. The whole surface should be scraped working diagonally from both sides and finally working with the grain. Standard scrapers are rectangular steel plates sharpened on two long edges to form a burr which makes the cut.

Shaped scrapers can be made by filing a small scraper to the required shape for finishing mouldings. The scraper is gripped between the fore-fingers and thumb and bent into a shallow curve. It is held at an angle to the work and pushed away from the operator. A cabinet scraper with an angle cut out of one side is used for cutting the scratch mouldings in Chapters 2 and 10. **Figure 9** in Chapter 2 shows the direction of action of the scraper.

Sanding Block A sanding block should be used when working a flat surface or a moulded edge. In the latter case, a shaped block should be used. Sanding blocks maintain the correct shape and prevent edges being mis-shaped due to careless sanding. Manufactured blocks are usually made from cork, but a home-made wooden block can be used.

Sand in the direction of the grain, as any cross grain scratches are difficult to remove and can show badly when the finish is applied. For details of abrasive paper, see page 159.

Stripping

Stripping furniture can be laborious, but it is not strenuous work and revealing the original material, often under layers of grime many years old, can be a real source of delight.

The best method is to use a chemical stripper. Stripping furniture with a blow lamp is not recommended as serious damage can result from scorching. Only a great deal of work with a scraper and sandpaper will restore it.

Stripping with a chemical stripper is messy work. It is a good idea, therefore, to wear old clothes or an overall and rubber gloves. Spread sheets of newspaper around the work area and have a wad of paper handy to wipe the scraper. You will also need a bowl of water or a bottle of white spirit to rinse off the stripper. The manufacturer's instructions will specify which is best suited to their product. White spirit is preferable, as it does not raise the grain of the timber, but it is obviously more expensive than water. A sponge is handy to apply the liquid and wipe off the residue. The stages of stripping are shown in **figure 3**.

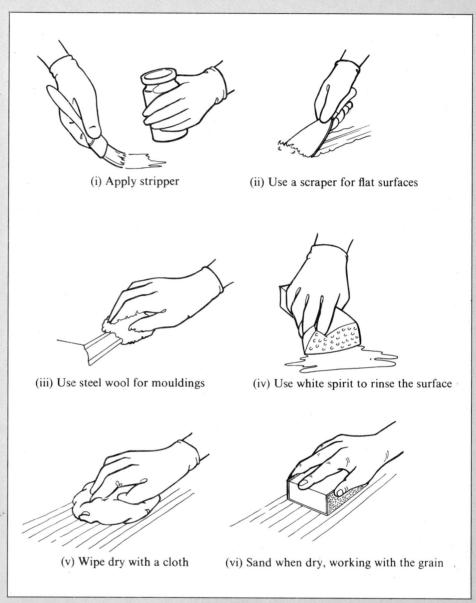

(i) Apply stripper

(ii) Use a scraper for flat surfaces

(iii) Use steel wool for mouldings

(iv) Use white spirit to rinse the surface

(v) Wipe dry with a cloth

(vi) Sand when dry, working with the grain

figure 3

Apply a thin coat of stripper with a brush over a manageable area and leave it for about one or two minutes to soften the surface. Apply a second liberal coat, which is dabbed on and left for the recommended time for the finish to soften completely. Do not allow the stripper to dry. Test with a scraper to see how it has penetrated. When it has softened, scrape off the finish, wiping it from moulded surfaces with steel wool. For stubborn finishes more than one application of stripper may be necessary. Finally rinse and dry with a cloth. Allow to dry thoroughly before sanding.

Industrial Stripping

If stripping your own furniture does not appeal to you, send it to an industrial stripping company. These firms clean and prepare furniture for the antique furniture trade and operate in most big cities.

The process entails immersing the furniture in a bath of heated caustic soda, which dissolves and softens the varnish or paint finish. It is then removed from the bath and washed down with clean water from a hose and scrubbed with a stiff brush. It is a very harsh process for wood, although it is effective and fast. It leaves furniture in poor condition, with rough grain and weakened joints in some cases, where the animal glue has been removed. The process is only suitable for furniture made from solid wood, and is a positive menace for furniture which has been steam-bent, for example hoop-back chairs. If you have any doubts about the suitability of the process for your furniture, the company should be able to advise you.

Repairing Holes

Small holes can be filled with beeswax. The wax is melted in a shallow tin on a cooker ring set at a low heat. The liquid wax can be coloured to match the wood by adding small amounts of powdered dye. The mix should be carefully stirred and regularly tested for shade. Pour the liquid wax into aluminium foil moulds shaped to make short sticks and allow to set. Hold the stick over the hole and melt the wax with a warm soldering iron. Fill the hole until it overflows, to allow for shrinkage. When set, scrape off the excess with a knife. If necessary rub down with fine abrasive paper ready for polishing. Holes or cracks in wood that is to be painted can be filled with wood stopping, which is supplied as a thick paste.

Deep holes in the side grain are best repaired by inserting a patch of matching wood. Matching the patch to the original wood can be a problem, due to the mellowing of the wood which takes place over a period of time. It will probably be necessary to stain the patch to match the surrounding wood. Cut a diamond shape insert slightly larger than the hole, with its long axis running with the grain and a slight taper on the sides. Place it over the hole and draw around the shape. Chop out the recess using a sharp chisel and carefully level the bottom. Try the insert for fit before gluing in place. Wipe away any surplus glue with a damp cloth and allow to set. Plane the insert flush with the surface with a finely set block plane. Sand carefully, ready for polishing. If the colour match is poor, stain should be applied before polishing.

Shallow dents can often be removed by damping or steaming. A damp cloth placed over the dent and left a couple of hours should raise the grain and lift the dent. The application of heat provided by an electric iron can speed up the process.

Stripped screw holes are often a problem with old furniture. In some cases a larger gauge screw can be substituted, but if you intend to fit a hinge, the same sized screw should be used. In this case the hole must be plugged. First remove the fitting. Trim a short length of dowel with a sharp chisel and make a tapered peg slightly larger and longer than the hole. Apply a dab of glue to both peg and hole, and drive in the peg. When the glue has set, cut the dowel flush with the surface. Drill a suitable pilot hole in the plug and re-fit the screw.

Repairing Table Tops

In the course of restoration work it may be necessary to take the furniture apart. Table tops are often in need of repair and have to be removed for ease of handling. A top can be fixed to a frame in various ways according to its construction.

If the top is made from solid wood it will probably be fitted with shrinkage plates or 'buttons'. Shrinkage plates are made from metal and have a slotted hole to take a fixing screw. See **figure 4**.

Buttons are wooden blocks with a tongue on one side which are screwed to the underside of the top. The tongue locates in a groove around the inside of the table frame. Both types allow for the expansion and contraction of the top. A solid top must be refitted with this type of fixing.

Tops made from a complete board, such as plywood or chipboard, are less likely to 'move' and are sometimes pocket screwed or fitted with counterbored screws. See **figure 5**.

Pocketed screws are screwed at an angle through the frame into the top. The head of the screw is concealed in a drilled 'pocket' on the inside of the frame. Counterbored screws are screwed straight up through the frame rail, which is partly drilled out to receive the head. A counterbored hole can be concealed with a wooden plug. These will need to be drilled out to remove the screw. New plugs can be cut with a plug cutting bit when the screws are refitted.

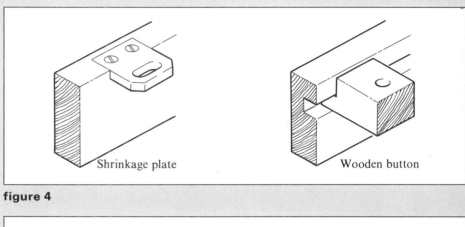

figure 4

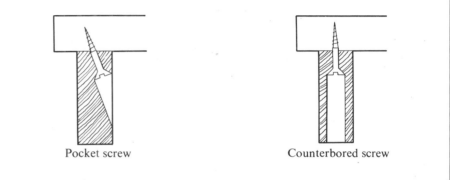

figure 5

Old table tops made from solid wood sometimes have wide gaps where the joints between the boards have opened up. This is usually due to glue failure. If the boards are butt jointed and not warped, the edges can be cleaned with a block plane and re-glued. In some cases the boards are dowelled. In this case, cut through the dowels, plane the edges square and fit new dowels. Occasionally a top which appears to be dowelled will not pull apart even when the joint is loose. This is because countersunk screws have been used as pegs which locate in a keyhole shaped housing on the other edge. The boards can be separated by first knocking alternate boards from opposite ends to align the screw heads with the larger hole in the edge. The boards can then be pulled apart. This technique is used to pull the joint together without need for cramps. To cramp up a solid table top, use sash cramps placed above and below the top to counteract any bowing across the width. If the top was badly bowed to begin with and sash cramping has not corrected it fully, lightly cramp the top to the table frame with 'G' cramps. Damp the top and gradually pull it down in stages until it meets the frame where it can be retained with its screws. The top can then be finished in situ.

Repairing Veneers

Light damage to a veneered surface can be repaired reasonably simply. A common fault with old furniture, usually due to exposure to damp, is blistering or peeling veneers. Small blisters can be pressed back in place using a hot electric iron and a damp cloth, to soften the scotch glue before pressing the veneer back into place with a block of wood. A weight will help keep the veneer flat while the glue sets. Peeling veneers can be replaced in the same way. If the glue line is contaminated with dust and grit, it is better to remove the veneer altogether using a damp cloth and iron. The old glue should be wiped or scraped from both the veneer and the base board. If the veneers are curled, they can be flattened with a hot iron to make re-laying easier. The veneers should be kept damp for easier working. When the veneers are flat they can be re-glued using scotch glue and pressed into place with a veneer hammer.

Our Renovation Project

Patching Damaged Veneer

A small defect can be repaired by applying a patch of matching veneer. The most difficult part of this work is finding a suitable veneer. Veneers can vary in thickness, depending on the method used to cut them from the log. Sawn veneers used on older furniture are thicker than sliced veneers, which are more common today. The high wastage in the production of sawn veneers makes them expensive and difficult to obtain. One source for such veneer is from an old piece of furniture with similar veneer, which may be past restoration. The alternative is to build up the thickness with thinner veneers glued together.

To make and fit the patch, lay a piece of veneer over the damaged area, matching the grain as much as possible. Using a sharp trimming knife, cut the veneer into a leaf shape patch, cutting through the surface below at the same time, **figure 6a**.

Take great care not to let the veneer move while cutting, and cut through in one slice. Remove the damaged veneer within the cut lines with a sharp chisel, **figure 6b**.

Scrape any glue from the exposed surface. Damp the patch, apply scotch glue to both surfaces and press into place with a hot iron. Place a piece of brown paper between the iron and the veneer. Finally use a veneer hammer to squeeze out the glue. Wipe the surface, cover with paper and a flat board. Cramp down or apply a weight and allow to set. When dry, clean down with a cabinet scraper and fine glass paper ready for finishing.

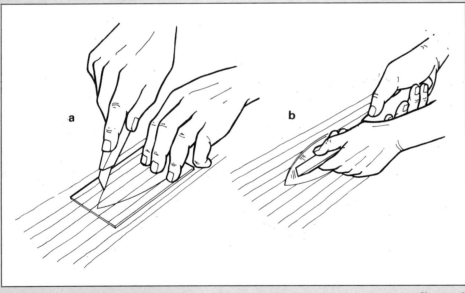

figure 6

The Garden Table

With a little imagination, an old treadle sewing machine can be transformed into an attractive garden or conservatory table.

The first task is to find an old sewing machine with a decorative cast iron underframe. These machines are fairly common and can be bought from an old furniture warehouse at reasonable price. The antique trade is beginning to notice the value of these decorative machines so the prices are beginning to rise. At the moment they are on the fringes of the antique 'circuit', so the best places to find them are used furniture shops.

Once the machine has been located, check that the underframe is sound. Cast iron is not only heavy but also brittle. Should it have been dropped while in transit it could be cracked and this cannot be repaired easily. Do not worry if the sewing machine or table top is damaged, as long as the underframe is in good condition.

Removing the Underframe

To remove the underframe, disconnect the drive belt from the pulleys. With the complete machine placed upside down on the bench, remove the four screws that fix the cast iron underframe to the table top. The frame can then be lifted off and the table top dispensed with. The sewing machine itself is usually an attractive item with coloured and engraved designs on the body and the coverplates. This can make an interesting decorative object for living room shelving.

It is important to remove the treadle mechanism so that a young child cannot accidentally injure itself in the moving parts. The mechanism in the machine we bought was held by screwed pin bearings with a lock nut to secure them. The lock nuts were released with a spanner and the bearings removed with a screwdriver. The treadle and the large flywheel were removed in one piece, with their connecting rod in position. To complete the dis-assembly the guard was removed by taking out the fixing screws.

The frame was rubbed down with steel wool and white spirit and wiped dry to remove the grease, ready for painting. We applied oil based gloss paint with a brush, but you could use cellulose paint in an aerosol spray. This is quicker but more expensive.

Making the Table Top

A top can be made in a number of ways. Perhaps the simplest is one cut from 18mm exterior grade shuttering plywood. A rectangular shape is best suited to the underframe, but the size can vary. It should, however, not overhang the frame by more than 250mm all round.

Shuttering plywood usually has one good face, which should be used for the top surface. Chamfer the edges all round and round off the corners before sanding. Seal all round with clear polyurethane. Apply several coats to build up an impervious layer, rubbing down with abrasive paper between. When dry, fix the top to the frame.

The tiled table top shown in the programme used the same type of plywood, but this time the best face was on the underside. The rougher surface of the second side provided a useful key for the tile adhesive. Tiles are available in a wide range of shapes, sizes and surface finish. The most common sizes, however, are 108×108mm and 152×152mm. The thickness can vary according to the function of the tile. Wall tiles are generally thinner than those used for floors. It is important to buy the correct type of tile according to the use of the table. If it is to be used as an interior plant table, any tile can be used. If it is to be left out in the garden, the tiles should be frost proof. Your supplier will advise you.

Having selected the tiles, calculate the number you will need to cover your table top. If in doubt, consult your supplier. Lay some of the tiles out on the base board side by side in an L shape. If the tiles do not have spacing lugs in their edges, use matchsticks to space them equally. This will give the correct length and width of the top. See **figure 7**.

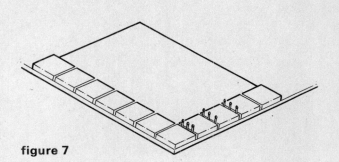

figure 7

Our Renovation Project

Cut the board to size and plane or power saw a 45° degree bevel all round. This will visually thin down the edge. Smooth the edge with glass paper and apply polyurethane varnish to seal all surfaces throroughly and allow to set.

Bond the tiles to the board using synthetic neoprene rubber adhesive sold in tubes. For the first row of tiles, apply two or three equally spaced beads of adhesive along the surface, spaced according to the tile size. Lay a run of equally spaced tiles flush with the edge of the board, and carefully press them into place, again spacing with matchsticks. Check that they are level with a straightedge or batten. Repeat the procedure across one end, **figure 8**.

Continue to lay the remaining tiles in rows, checking for level. Allow the adhesive to set as recommended by the manufacturers. Remove any spacing matchsticks and fill the gaps with a waterproof grouting. Apply the grouting with a filling knife or sponge and work it into the gaps. Wipe over the surface to remove any excess grouting. Compact the grout in the grooves using a blunt stick and allow to dry. Glazed tiles can be polished after the grout has dried, but textured tiles must be cleaned well while still wet using a clean damp sponge. The table is completed by screwing the underframe to the top with four screws.

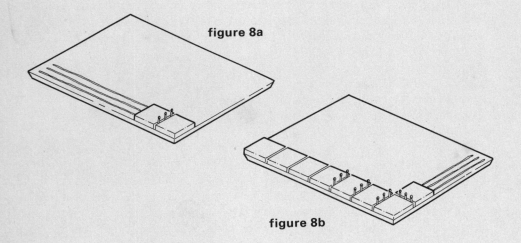

figure 8a

figure 8b